Bruno Serralongue

Table of Contents

Manifestations du collectif des sans-papiers de la Maison des Ensembles, place du Châtelet, Paris

[Demonstrations by the Maisons des Ensembles sans-papiers collective, place du Châtelet, Paris]
2001–2003

Demonstrations by the Maison des Ensembles group of immigrants who have been denied proper legal recognition began in 1999. Since then, every Thursday and Saturday from 17:00 to 19:00, they march around the fountain on the Place du Châtelet, with a banner calling for the regularization of all immigrants in their position. The first photograph is dated September 8, 2001. It is the starting point of a series that I planned to continue over a year, taking one photograph at each demo. Paradoxically, the best thing would have been for this series to be cut short, since the end of the demonstrations could be taken to signify definitive regularization. This did not happen, so I ended the series. As of January 11, 2003, the series comprises 45 photographs.

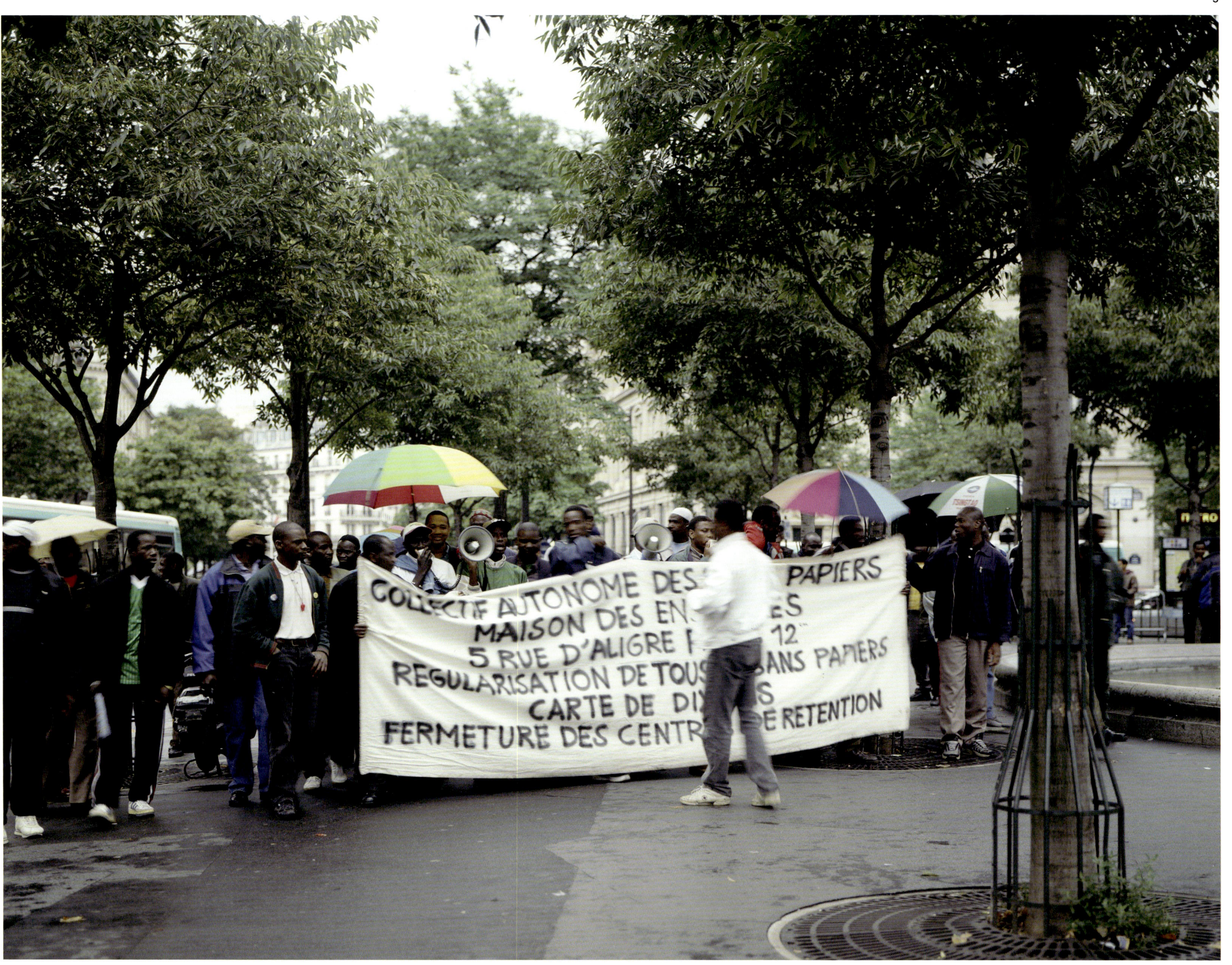
COLLECTIF AUTONOME DES PAPIERS
MAISON DES EN ES
5 RUE D'ALIGRE 12
REGULARISATION DE TOUS SANS PAPIERS
CARTE DE DI S
FERMETURE DES CENTR E RETENTION
METRO

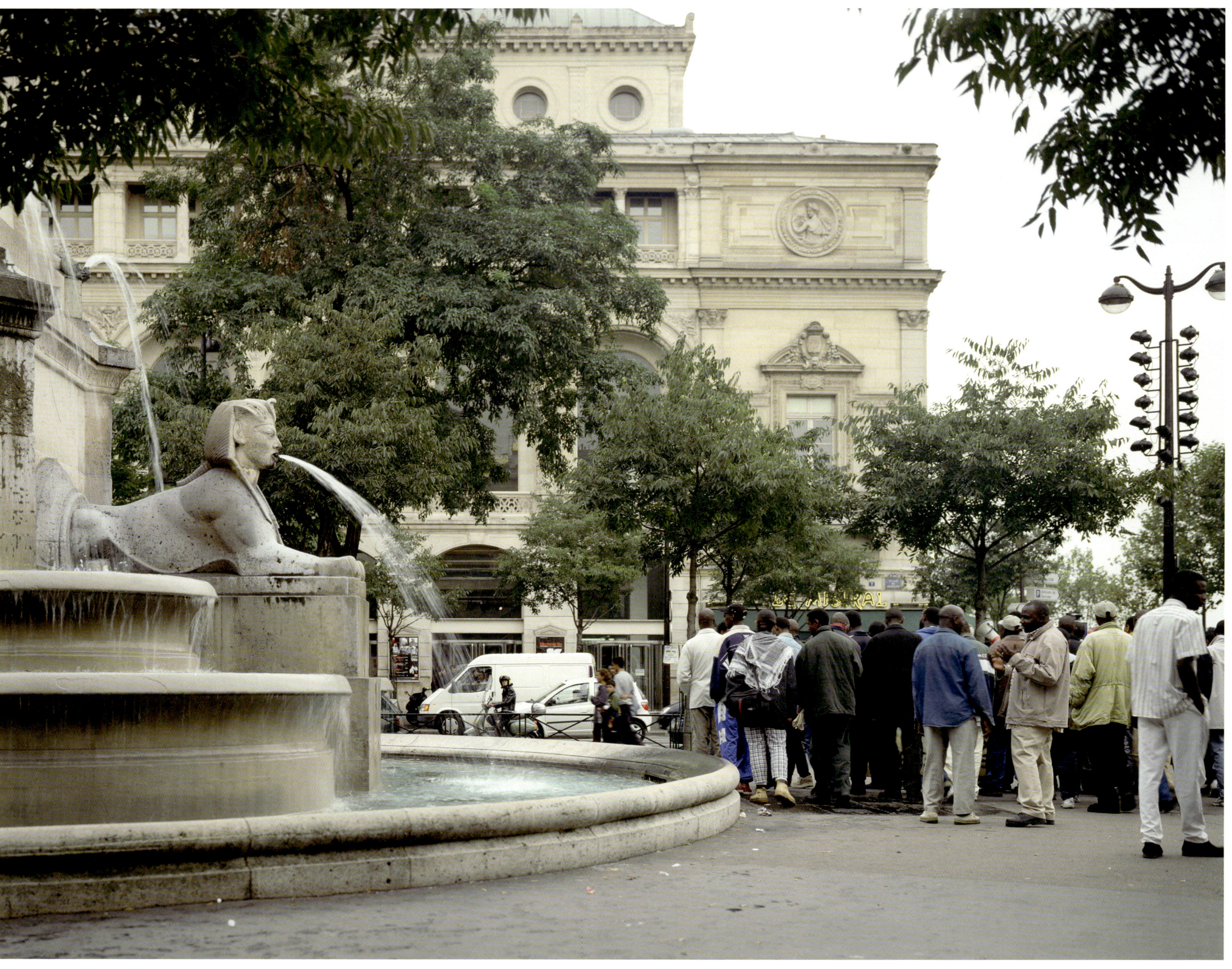

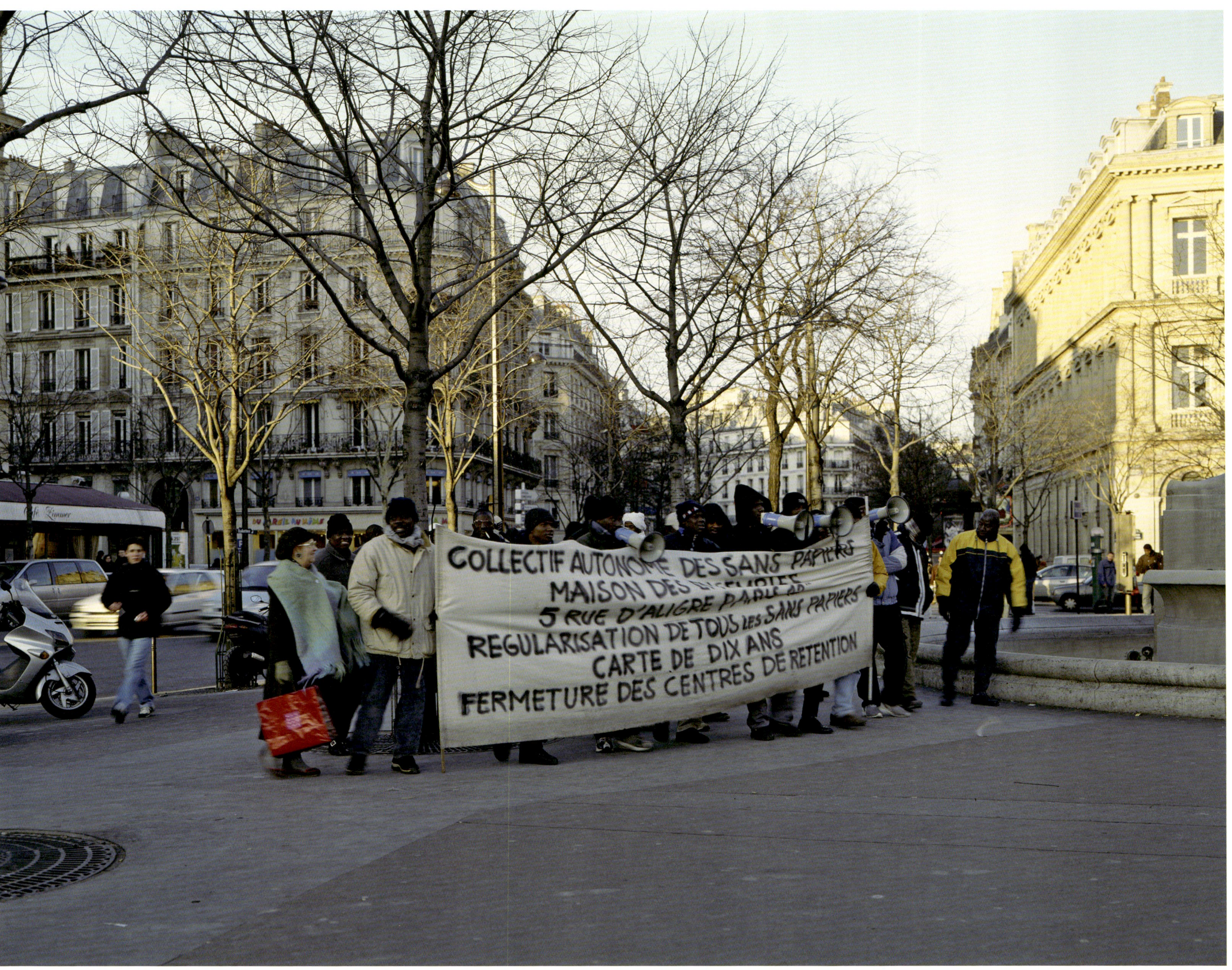
COLLECTIF AUTONOME DES SANS PAPIERS
MAISON DES
5 RUE D'ALIGRE
REGULARISATION DE TOUS LES SANS PAPIERS
CARTE DE DIX ANS
FERMETURE DES CENTRES DE RETENTION

Earth Summit, Johannesburg
2002

The World Summit for Sustainable Development (WSSD) took place in Johannesburg from August 26 to September 4, 2002. This Earth Summit followed the one held in Rio de Janeiro in 1992, at which the conventions on climate change and the protection of biodiversity had been adopted. This was the biggest summit ever organized by the United Nations. 65 000 delegates representing governments and heads of states from more than 100 countries, civilians (who had organized their own summit in the Exhibition Park), non-governmental organizations, and the private sector attempted to adopt concrete measures for world economic growth which would be compatible with the preservation of the Earth's natural resources. Access to clean drinking water (which 1.1 billion human beings are without) and electricity (which 1.6 billion people are without) were the main themes of this summit.

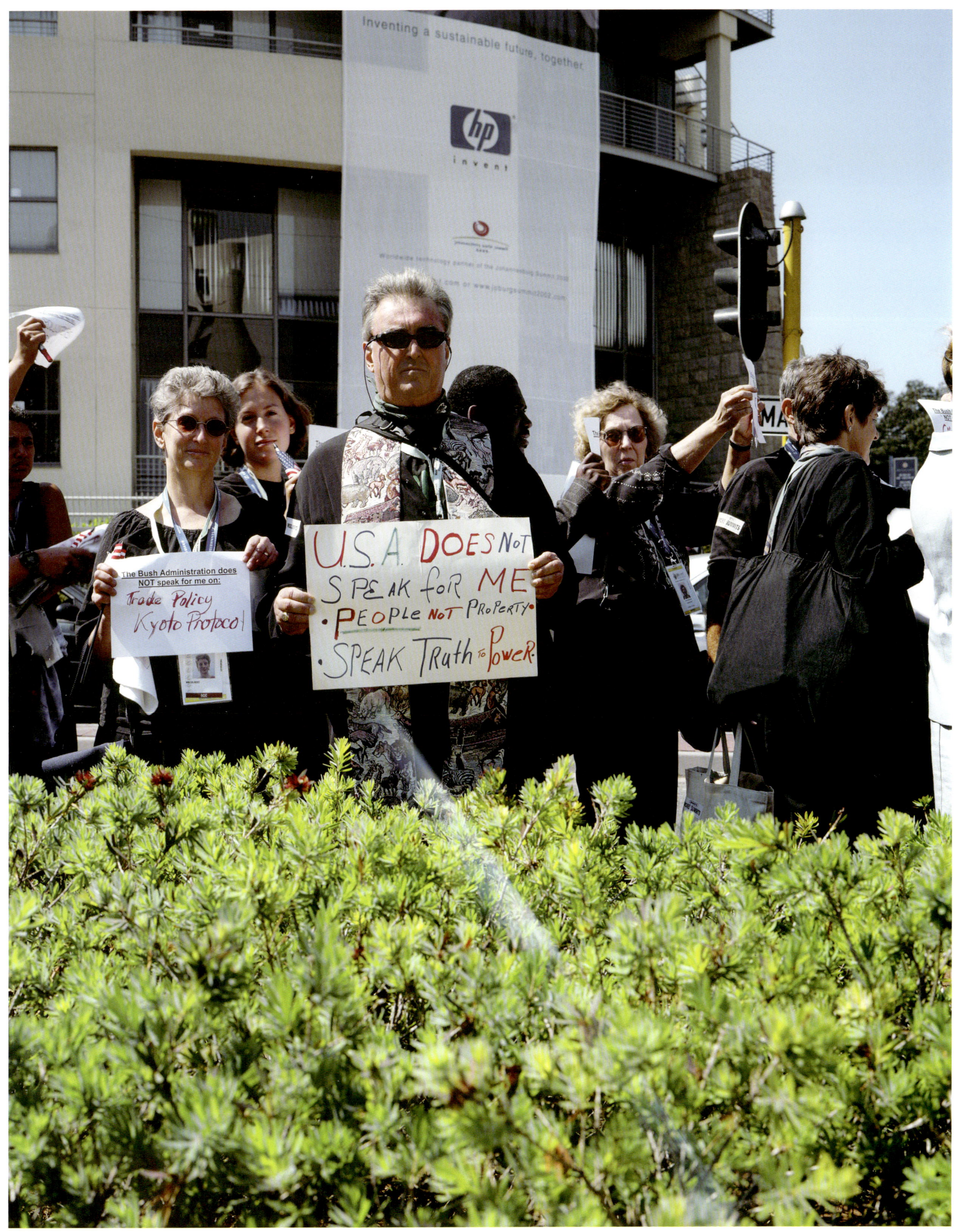
Inventing a sustainable future, together
hp
invent
The Bush Administration does NOT speak for me on:
Trade Policy
Kyoto Protocol
U.S.A. DOES NOT SPEAK for ME
• PEOPLE NOT PROPERTY •
• SPEAK Truth to Power.

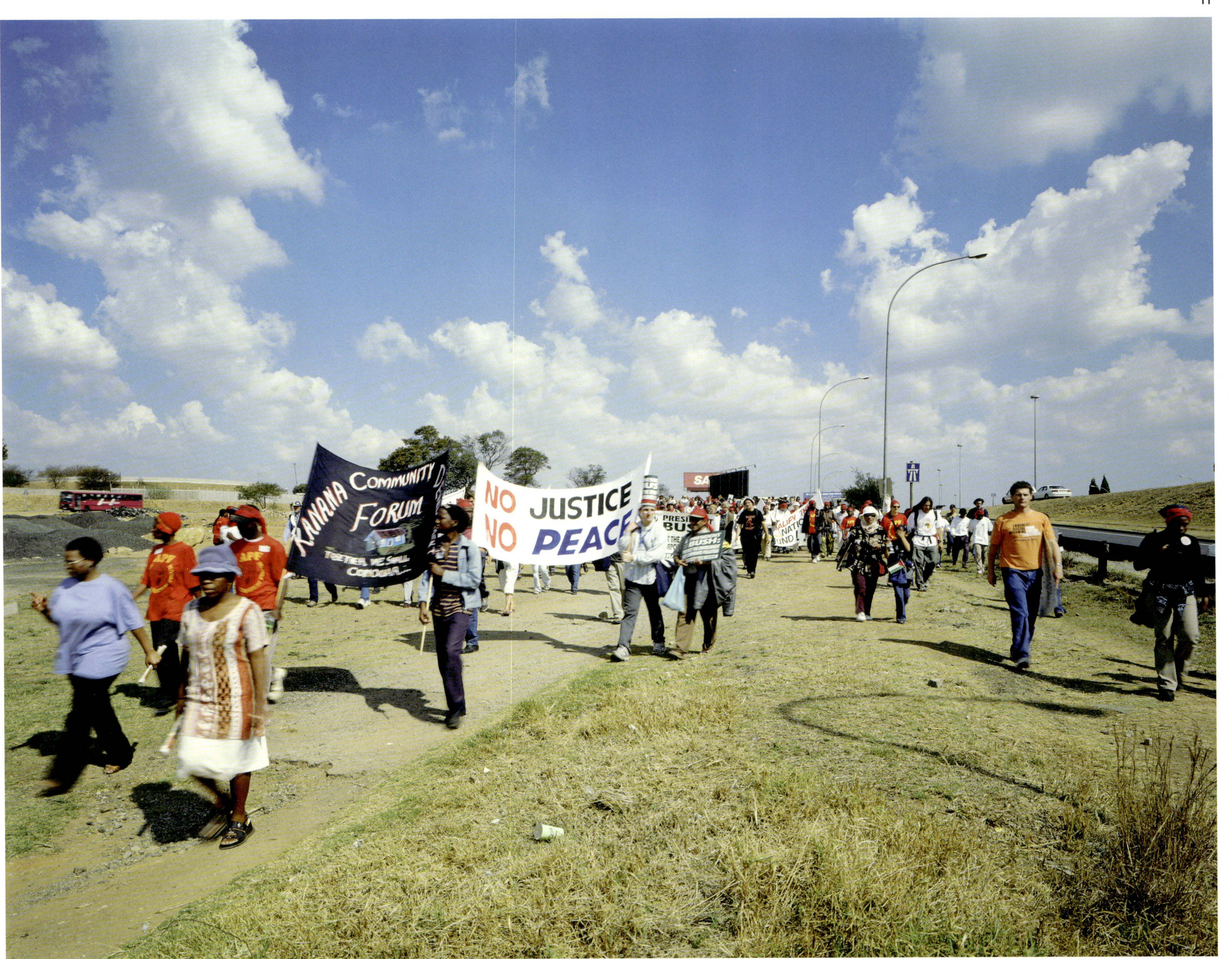
KANANA COMMUNITY FORUM
NO JUSTICE
NO PEACE

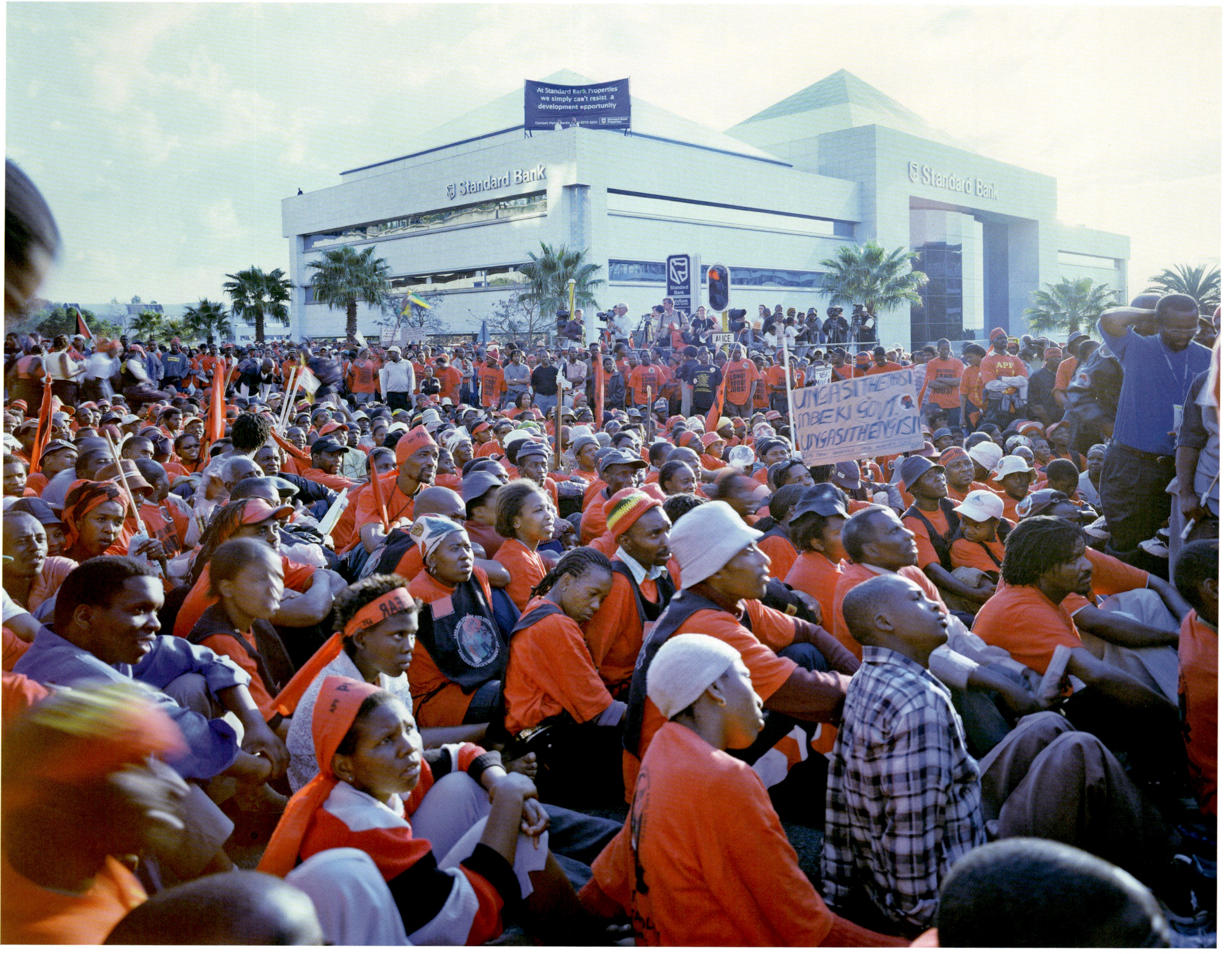
At Standard Bank Properties
we simply can't resist a
development opportunity
Standard Bank
Standard Bank
UNGASITHEMBISI
MBEKI GOVT
UNGASITHENGISI

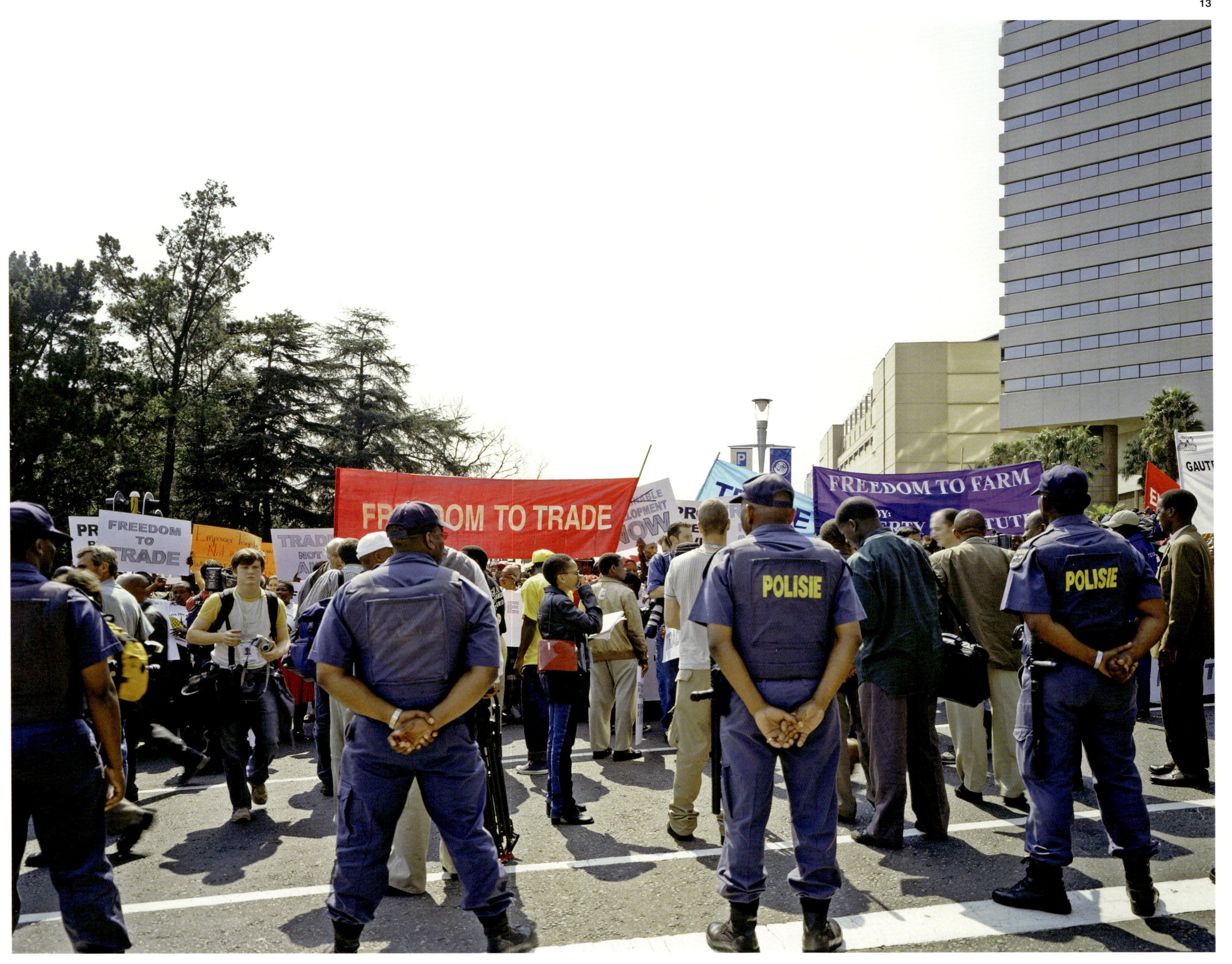
FREEDOM TO TRADE
POLISIE
POLISIE
FREEDOM TO FARM
FREEDOM TO TRADE

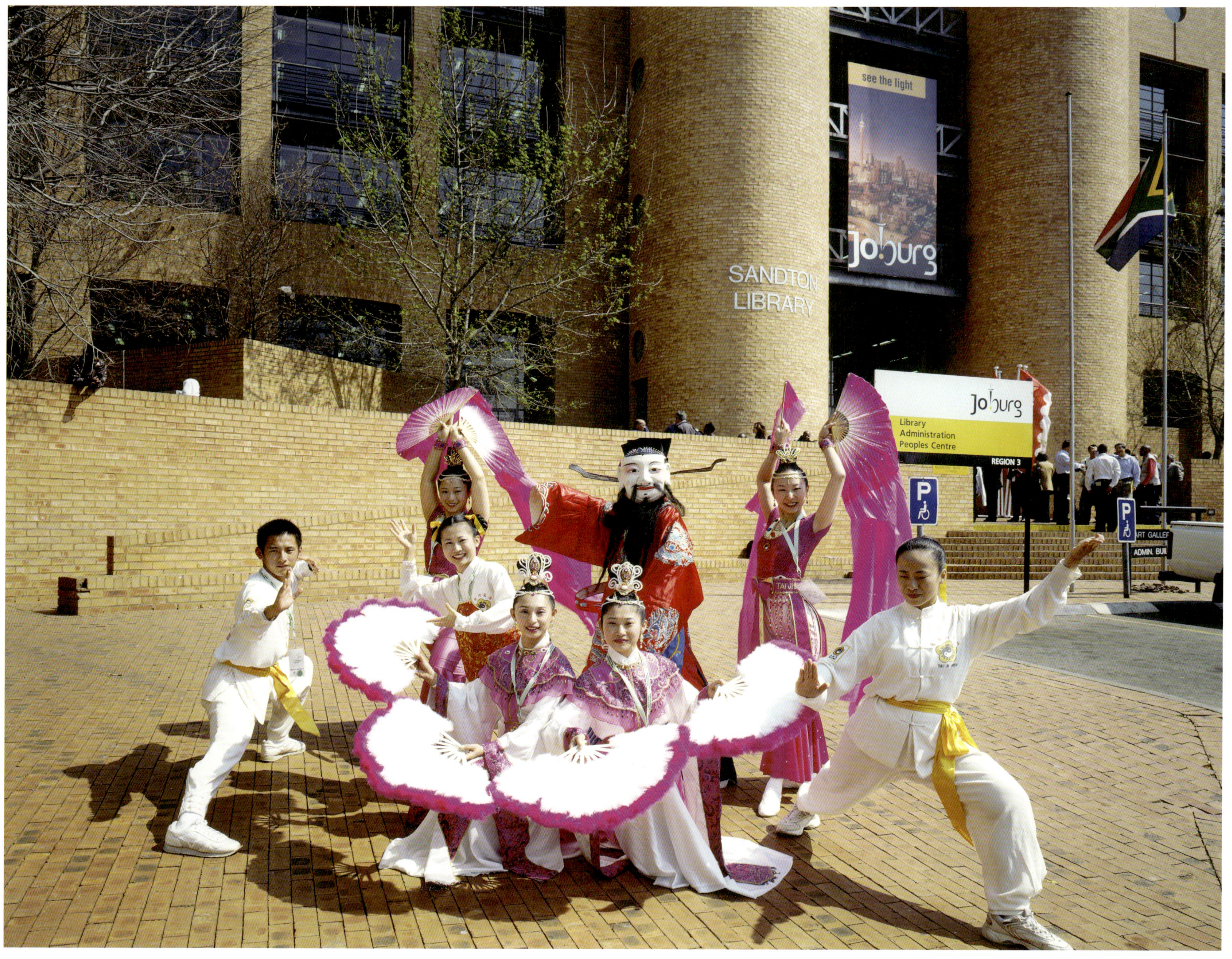
see the light
jo'burg
SANDTON
LIBRARY
Jo'burg
Library
Administration
Peoples Centre
REGION 3
P
ADMIN. BUI

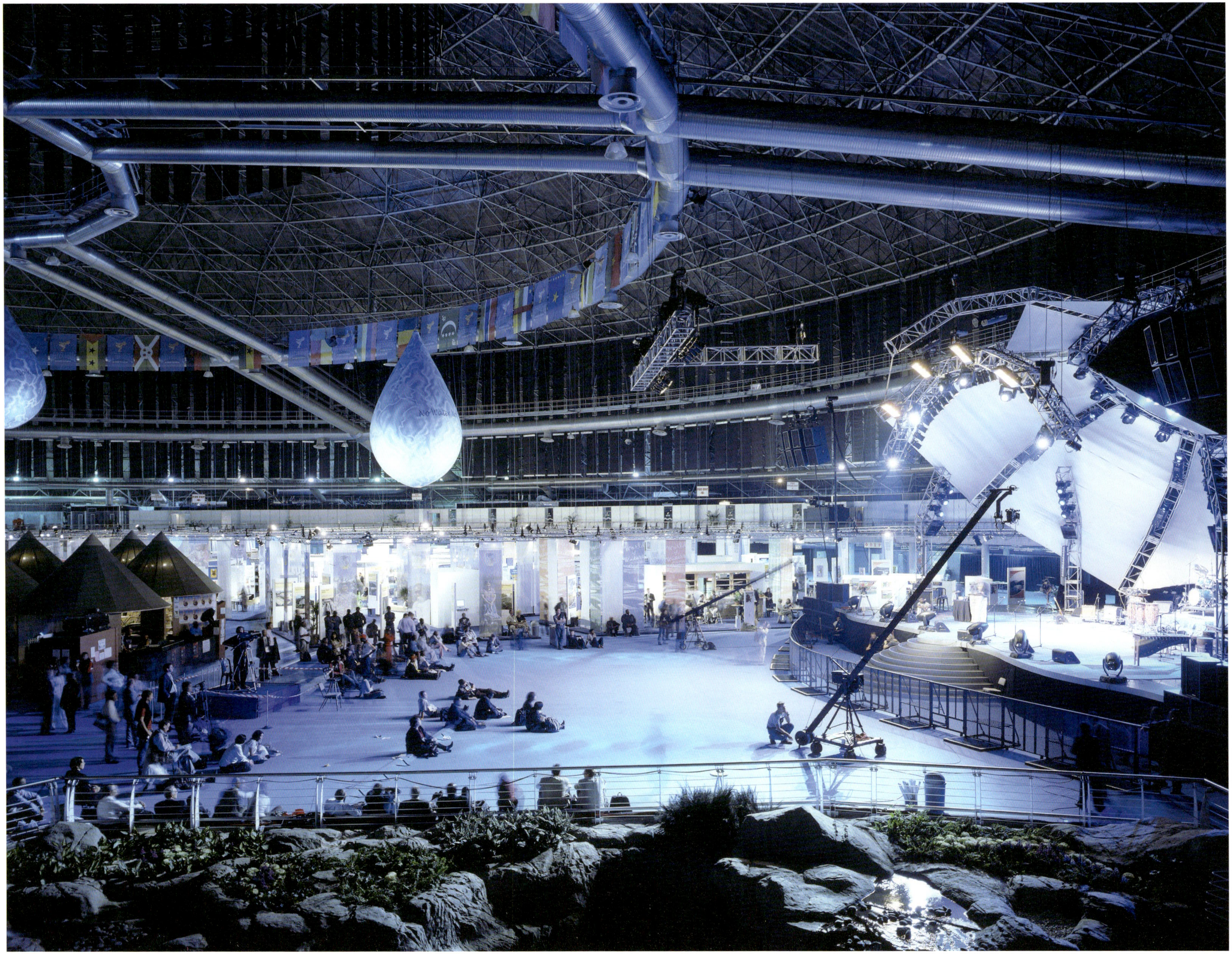

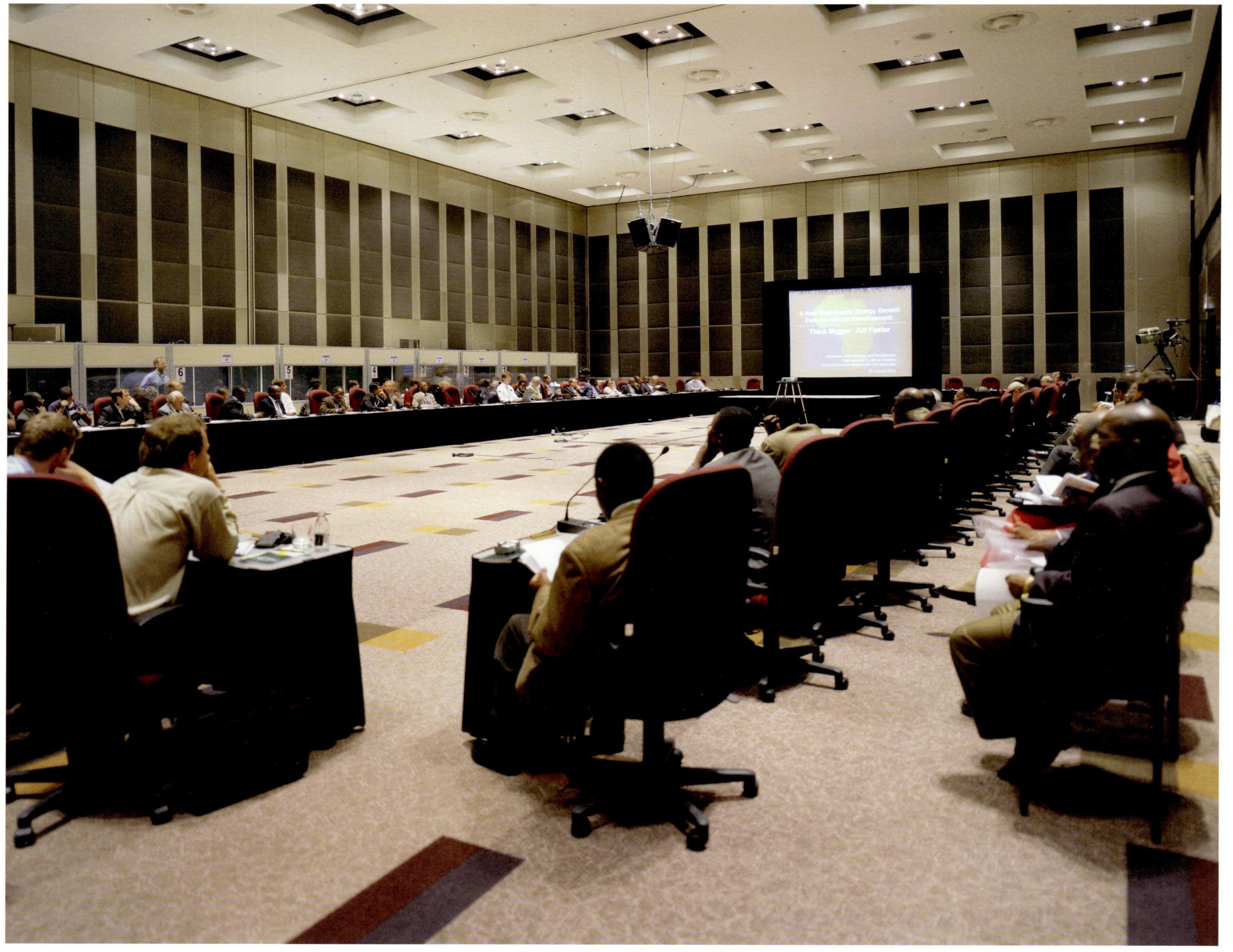
A New Sustainable Energy Growth
Path for African Development:
Think Bigger Act Faster

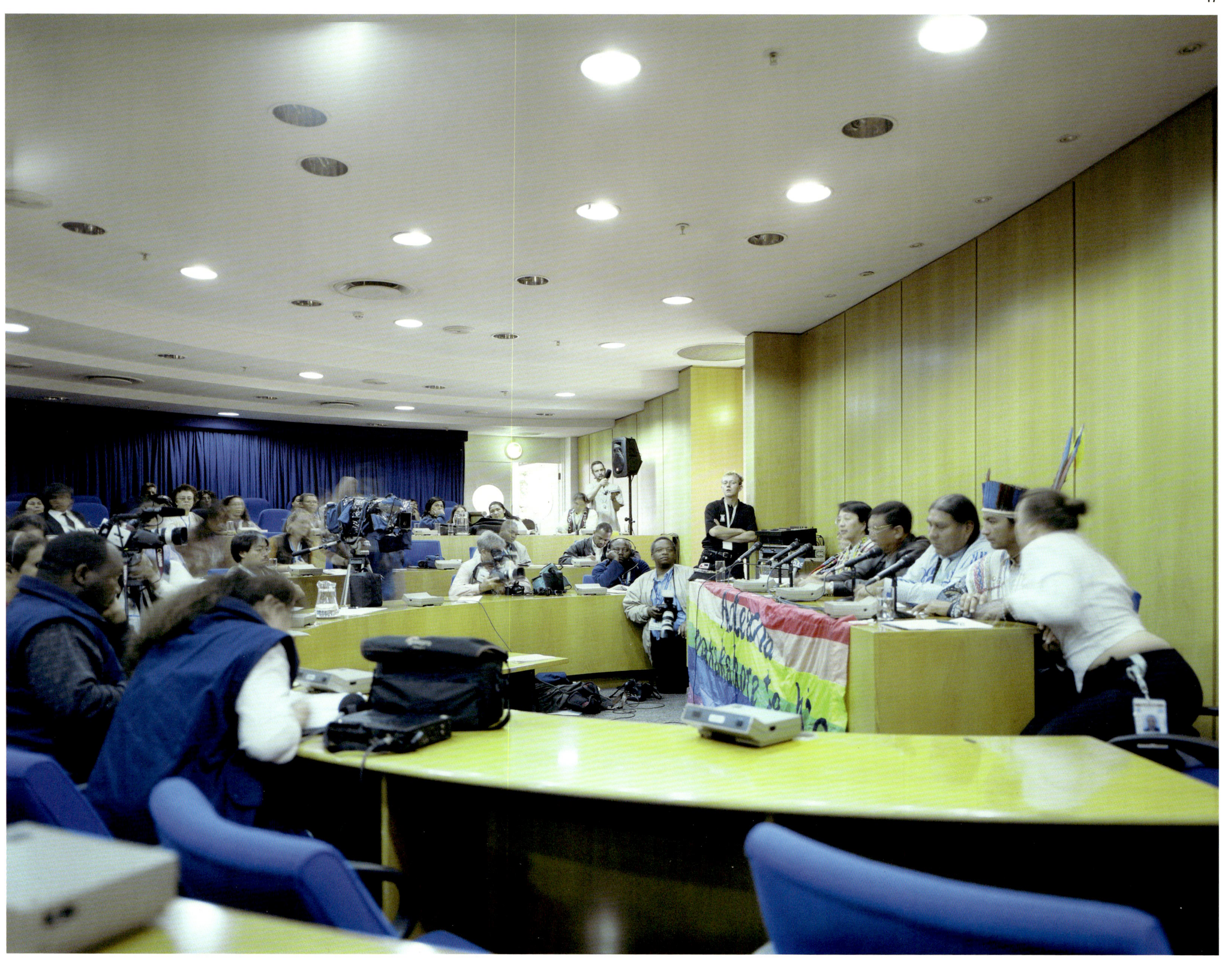

Risk Assessment Strategies
2002

During one week I took a class entitled "Hostile Environment and First Aid," offered by the firm Centurion. Founded in 1993, Centurion's aim is to reduce the risk taken by journalists when they have to work in dangerous zones (zones of armed conflict, or zones devastated by natural disasters). Up to the present time, 7 000 journalists have taken this class.

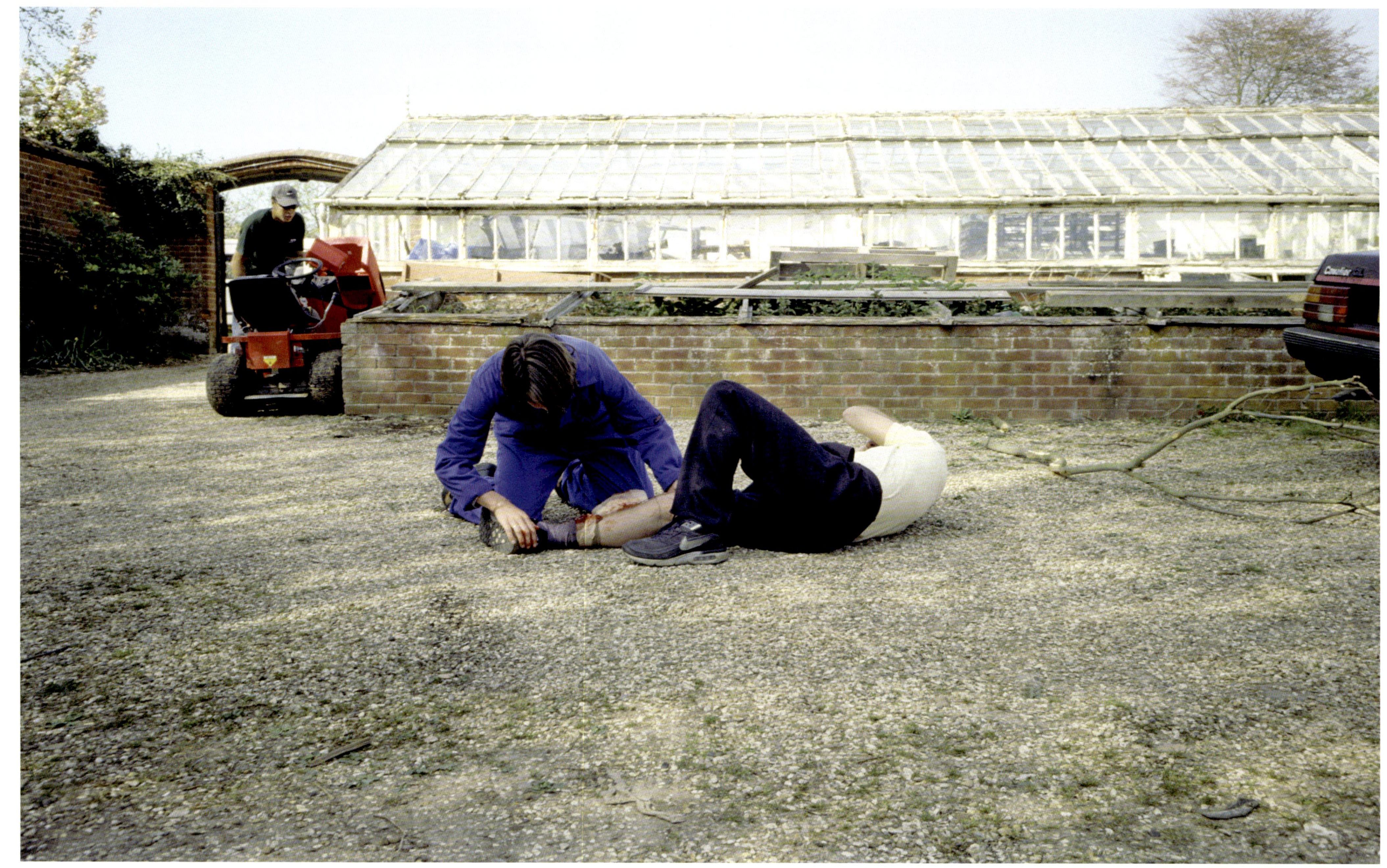

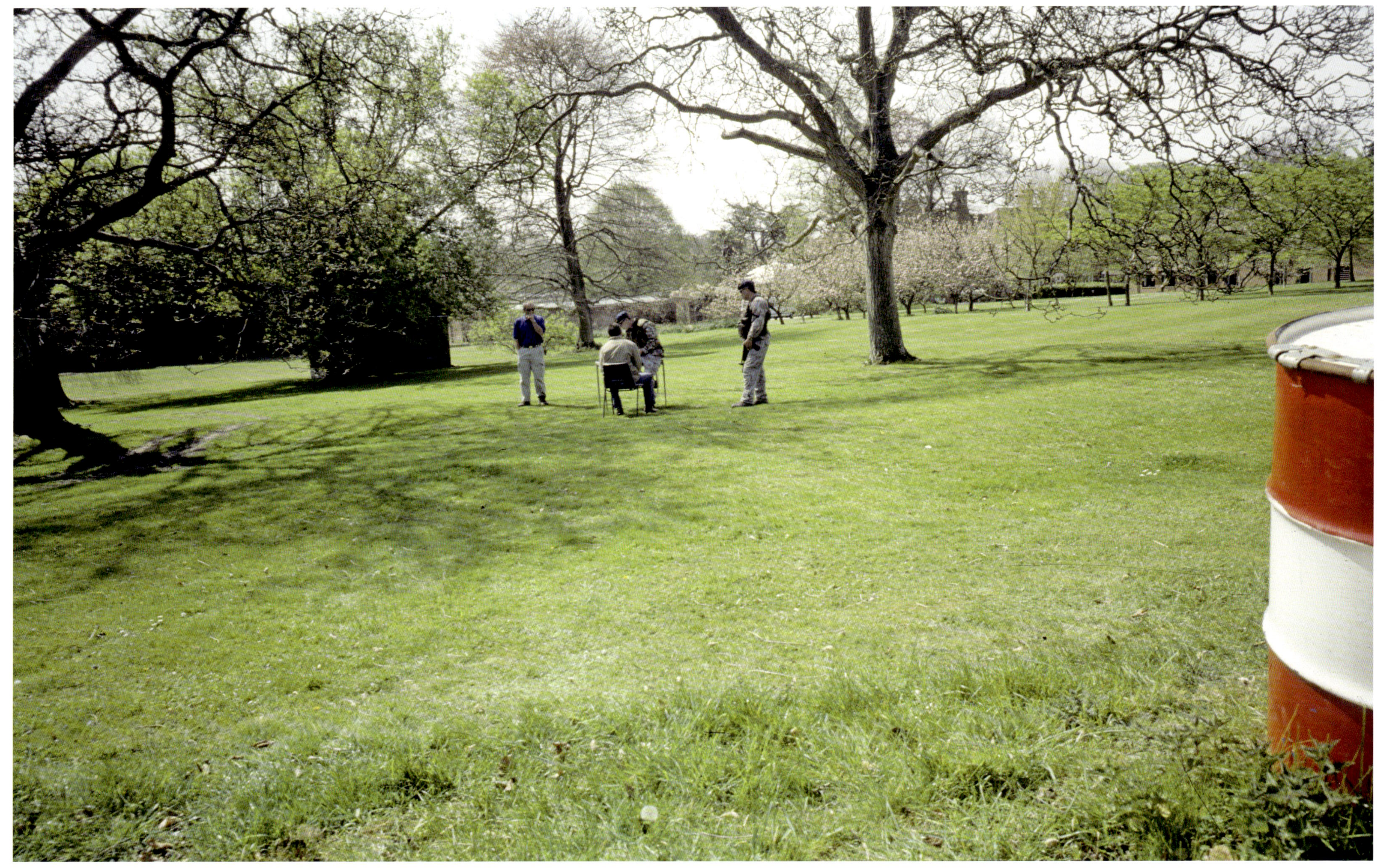

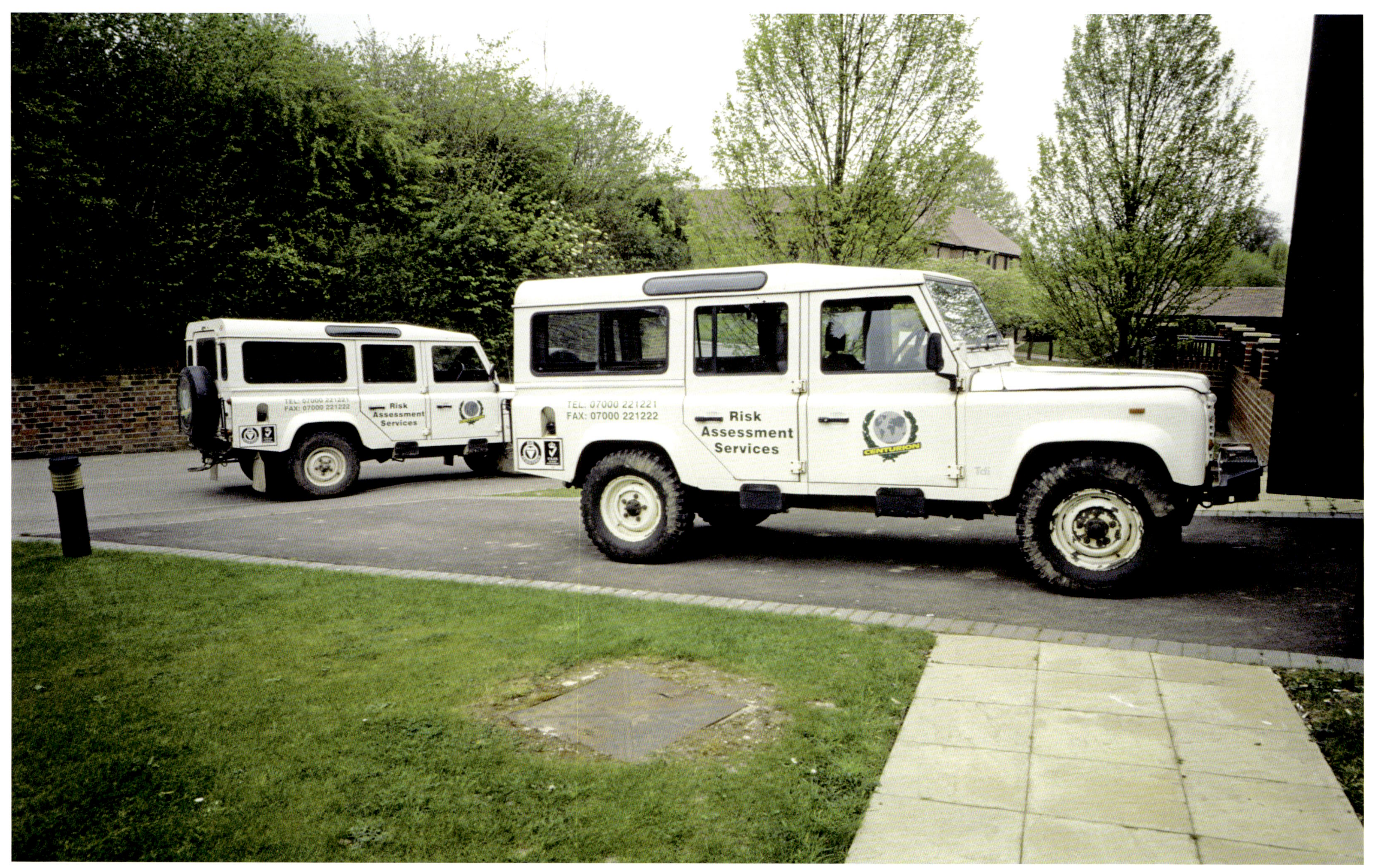
TEL: 07000 221221
FAX: 07000 221222
Risk
Assessment
Services
CENTURION
Tdi
TEL: 07000 221221
FAX: 07000 221222
Risk
Assessment
Services

Sommet mondial sur la Société de l’information, Genève
[World Summit on the Information Society, Geneva]
2003

More than 16 000 government representatives from 176 countries, the private sector, and civilians met in Geneva between December 10 and 12, 2003, for the first phase of the World Summit on the Information Society. The goal of the summit was double. On the one hand, and according to the first and ambitious paragraph of the “Final Report,” the aim was to start building a new kind of society, a “development-oriented Information Society, where everyone can create, access, utilize, and share information and knowledge, enabling individuals, communities, and peoples to achieve their full potential in (…) improving their quality of life, premised on the purposes and principles of the Charter of the United Nations and respecting fully and upholding the Universal Declaration of Human Rights.” On the other hand, the “Plan of Action” strives to evaluate and follow up progress in bridging the digital divide between rich and poor countries, and to ensure that by 2015, “more than half the world’s inhabitants have access to Information and Communication Technologies.”

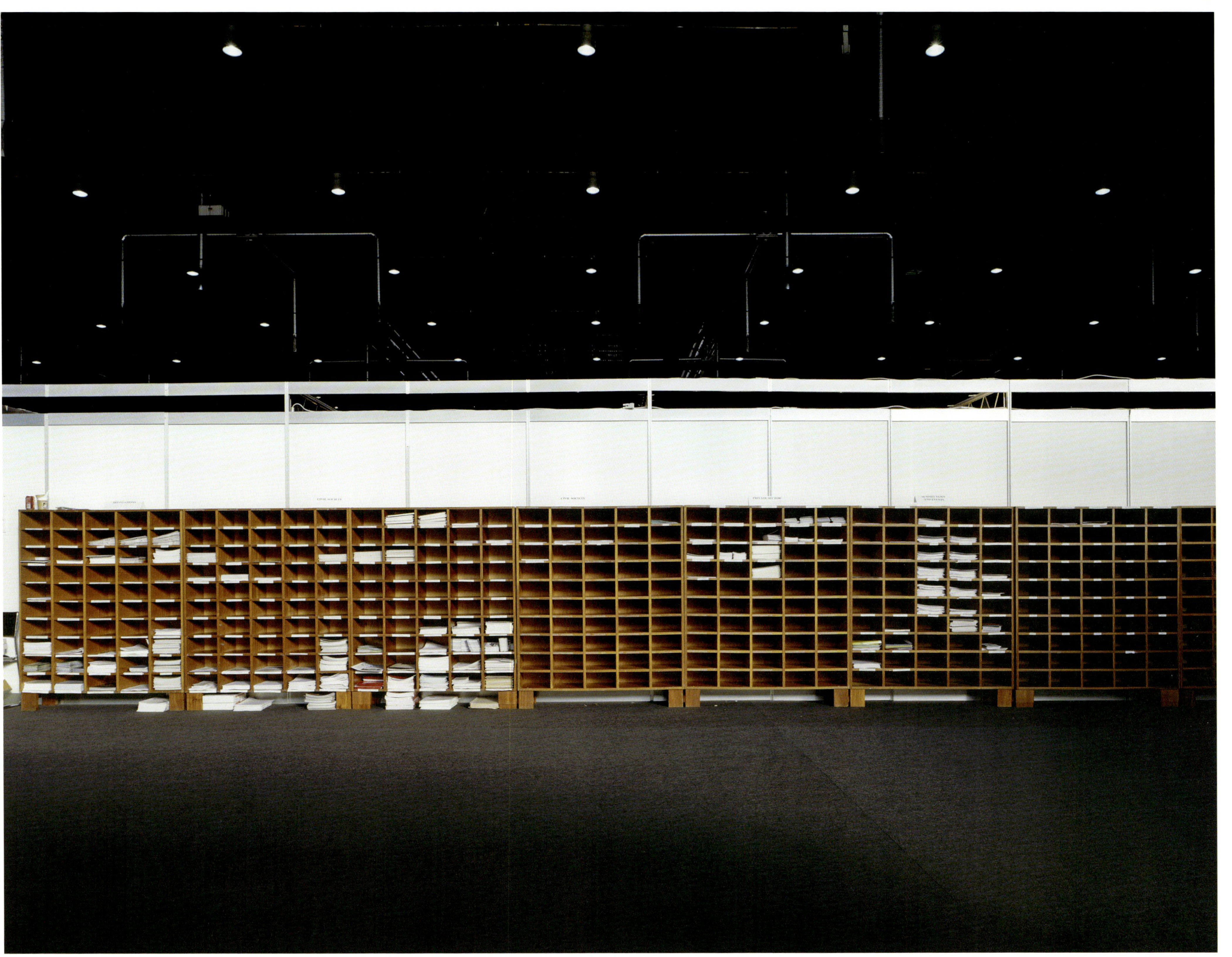

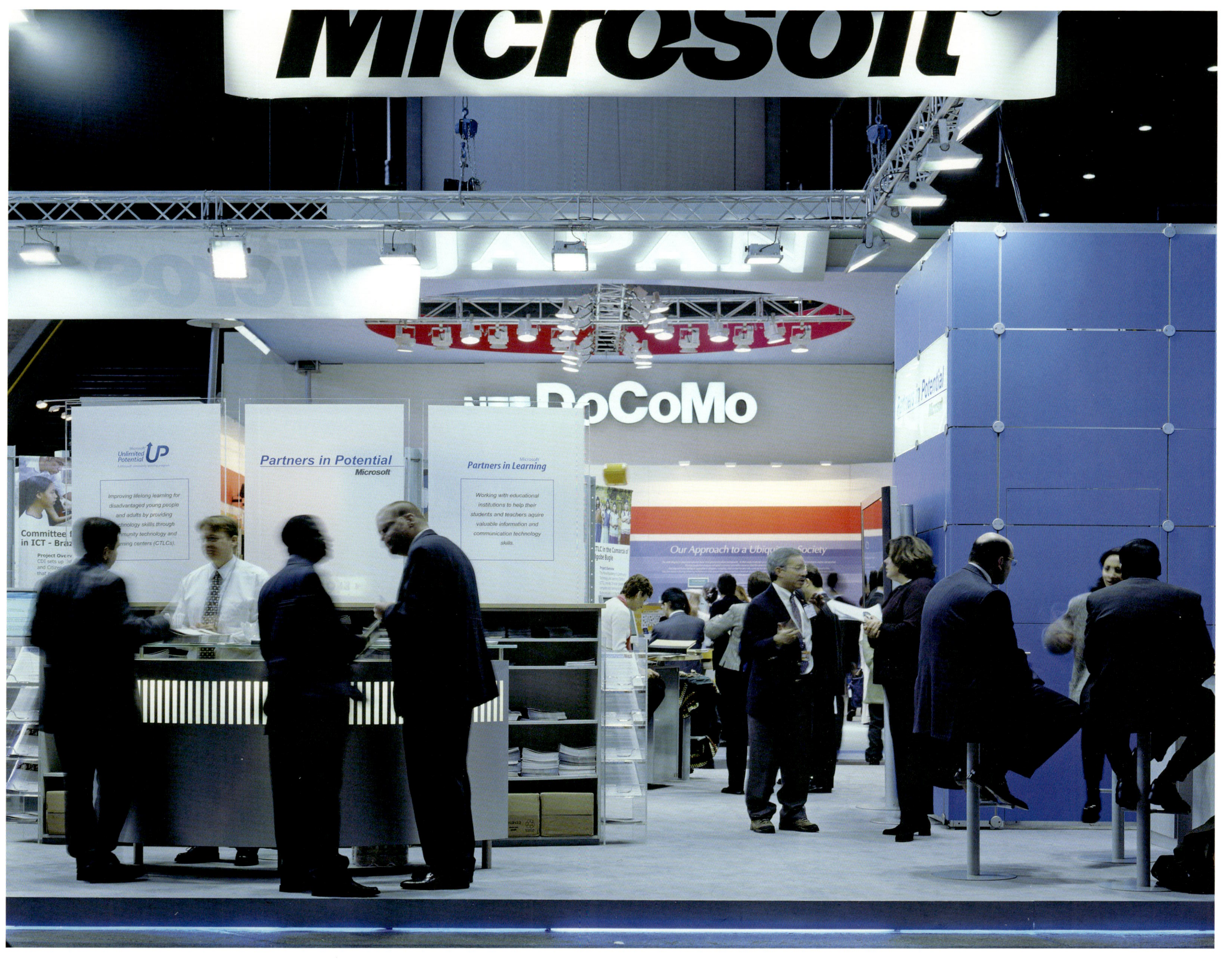
Microsoft
JAPAN
DoCoMo
Unlimited Potential
Partners in Potential
Microsoft
Partners in Learning
Working with educational institutions to help their students and teachers aquire valuable information and communication technology skills.
Our Approach to a Ubiqu Society

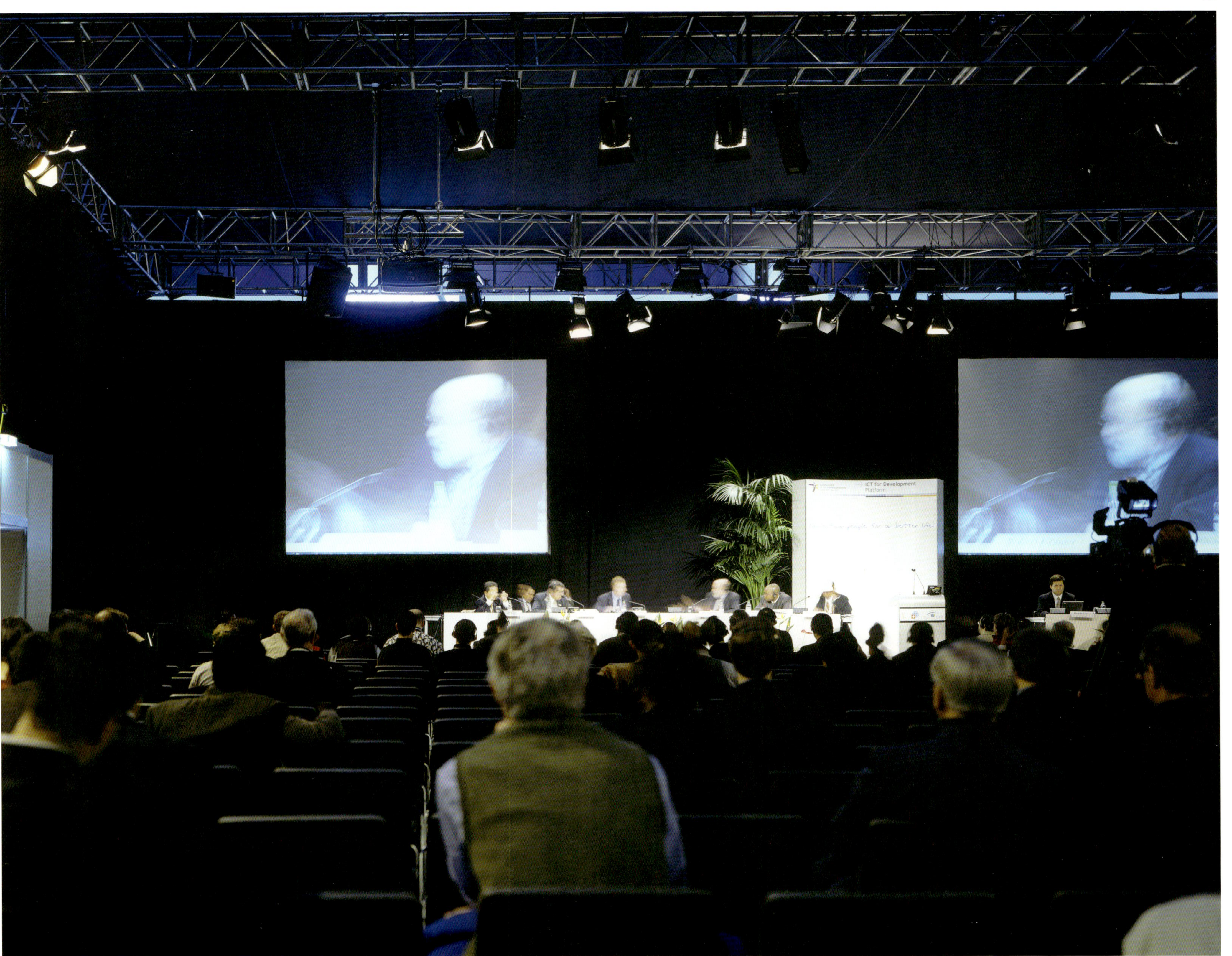
ICT for Development
Platform

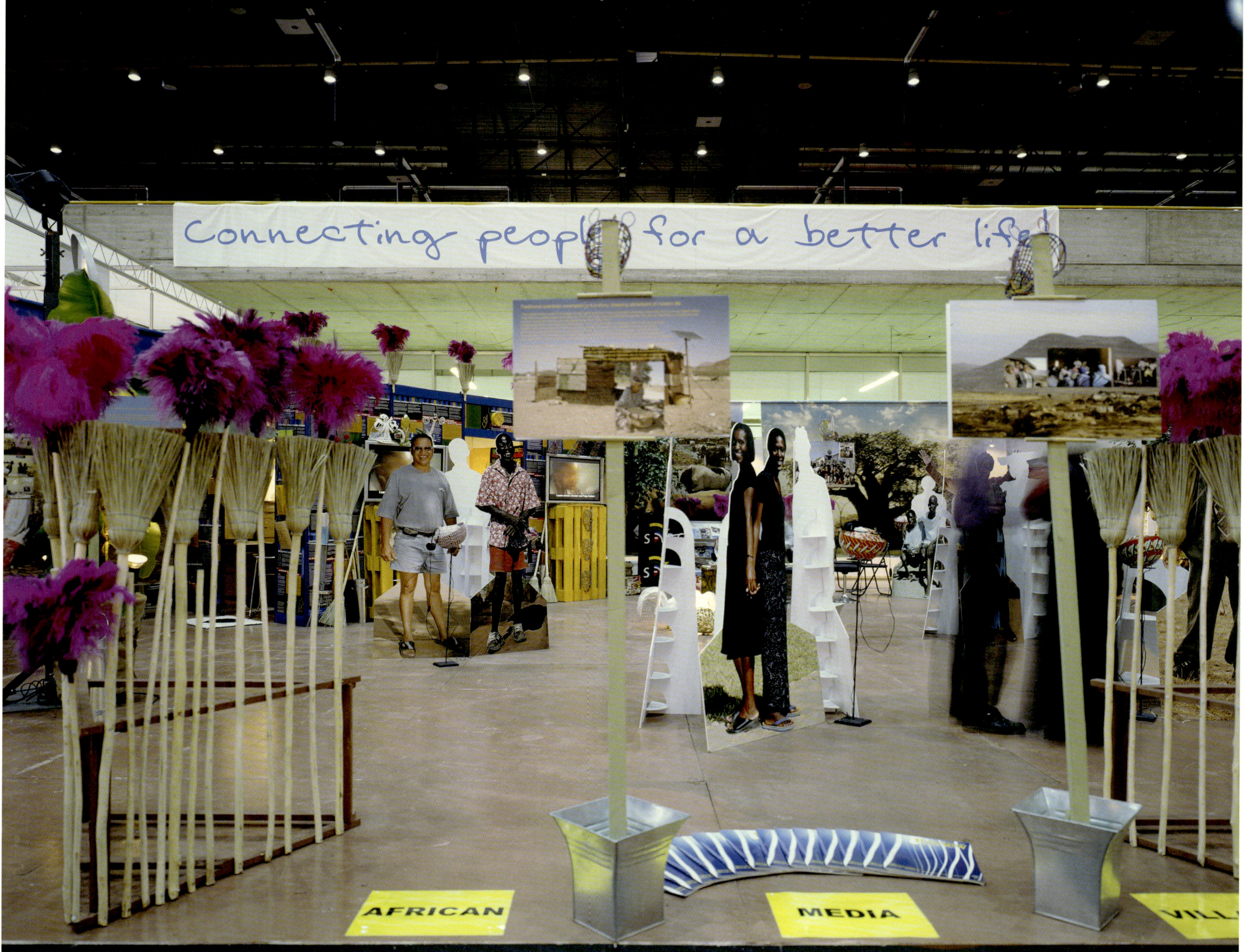
Connecting people for a better life!
AFRICAN
MEDIA

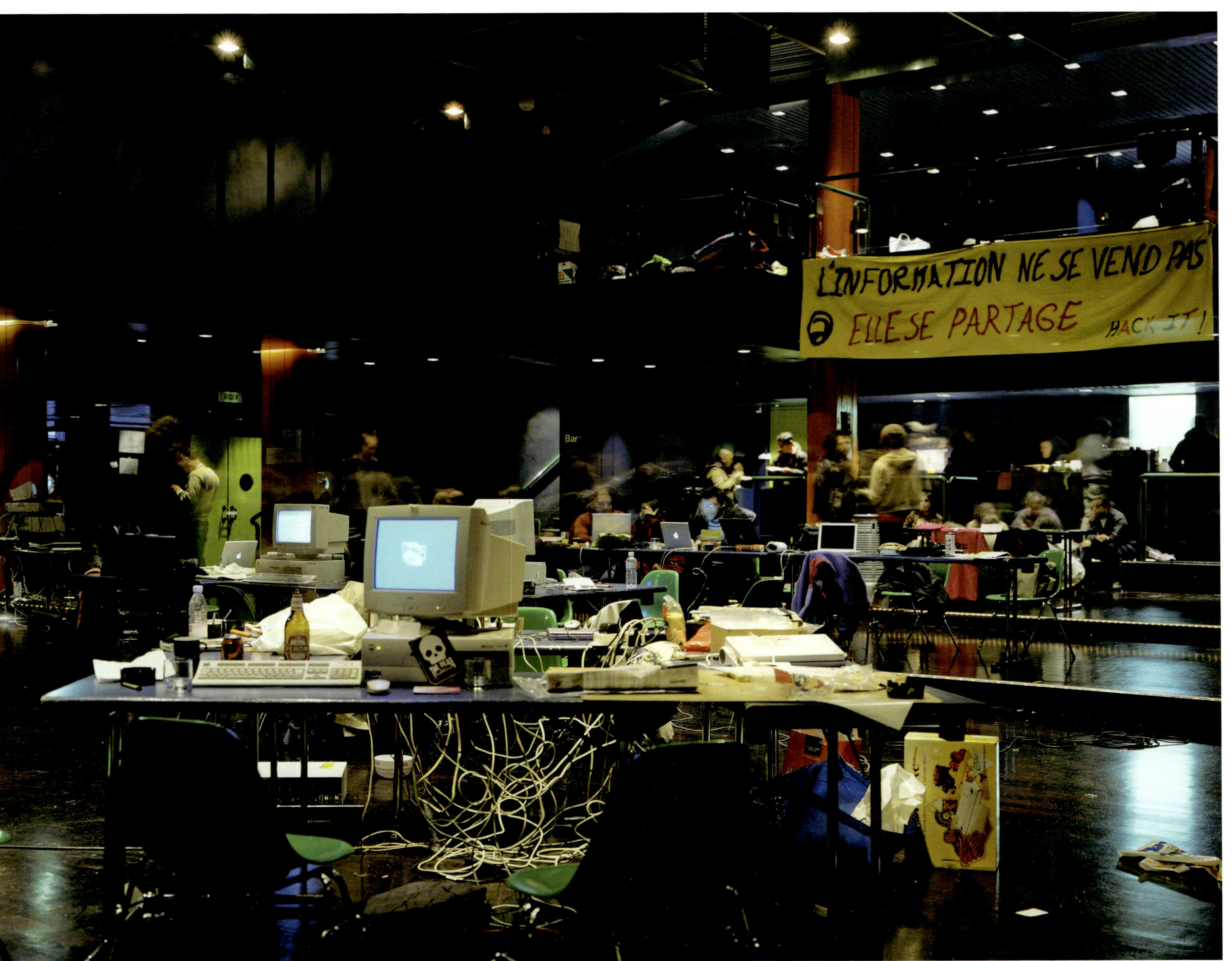
L'INFORMATION NE SE VEND PAS
ELLE SE PARTAGE
HACK IT!
Bar

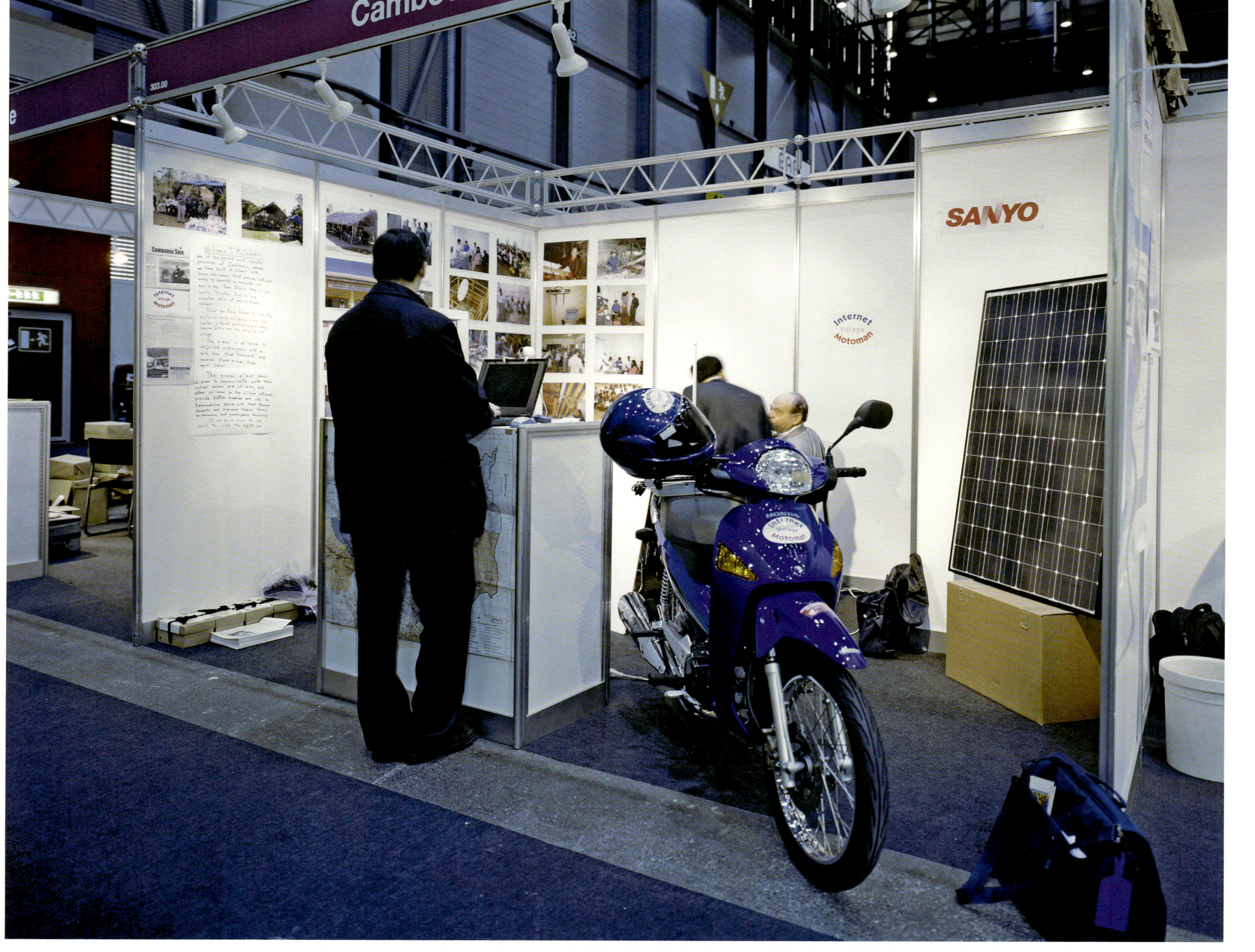
SANYO
Internet Village Motoman
303.00

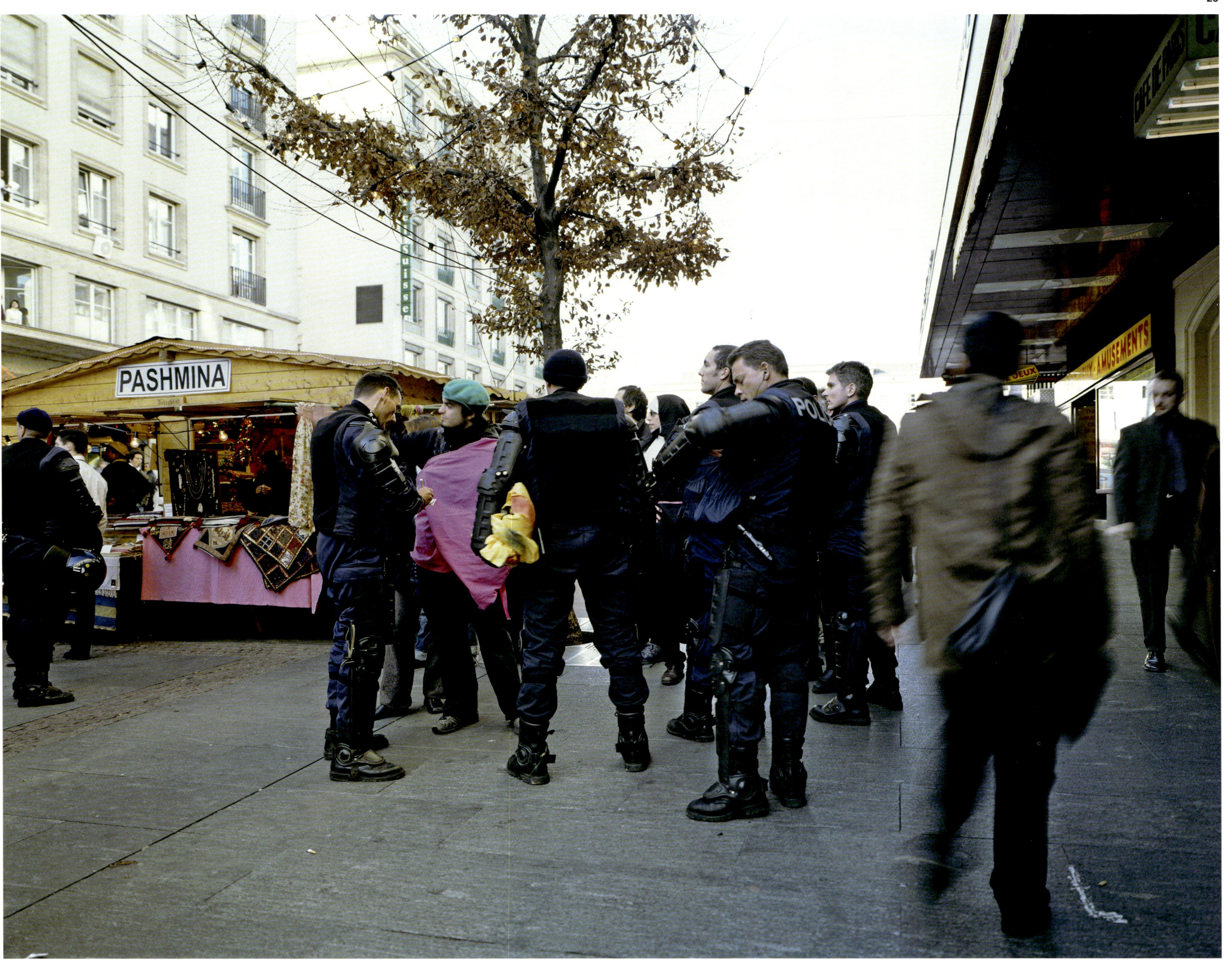
PASHMINA
Suisse
POLICE
JEUX
AMUSEMENTS

World Social Forum, Mumbai 2004

The fourth World Social Forum took place in Mumbai from January 16 to 21, 2004. Slightly more oriented toward Asian countries than previous forums, some 150 000 people came to the financial capital of India to declare that, "another world is possible." Discussions not only highlighted the drifts of global economics and of World Trade Organization; the 2 500 conferences, seminars, and workshops gave also voice to India's social problems: religious intolerance, exclusion due to the caste system, and the position of women in society.

The activist Maude Barlow, president of the Canadian Council and member of the network "Our world is not for sale," declared that, "for the first time the forum touched the poorest strata of the population on earth." Indeed, more than 80% of the participants were Indians, and a majority came from the countryside or underprivileged urban neighborhoods.

In Porto Alegre (Brazil, 2001), the public had mostly been composed of the middle and upper social classes and, among them, many officials and professors. "Unlike previous occasions, this forum is a place for social expression, not for intellectualization. It offers a platform for the people, some of them have never before had the opportunity to express themselves in such a visible way," said the leader of Confédération paysanne, José Bové, of the Mumbai Forum.

This success is worrying to the organizers and founders of WSF, for they think that a limit has been reached, beyond which the "Movement of Movements" might become unintelligible and unable to formulate concrete proposals.

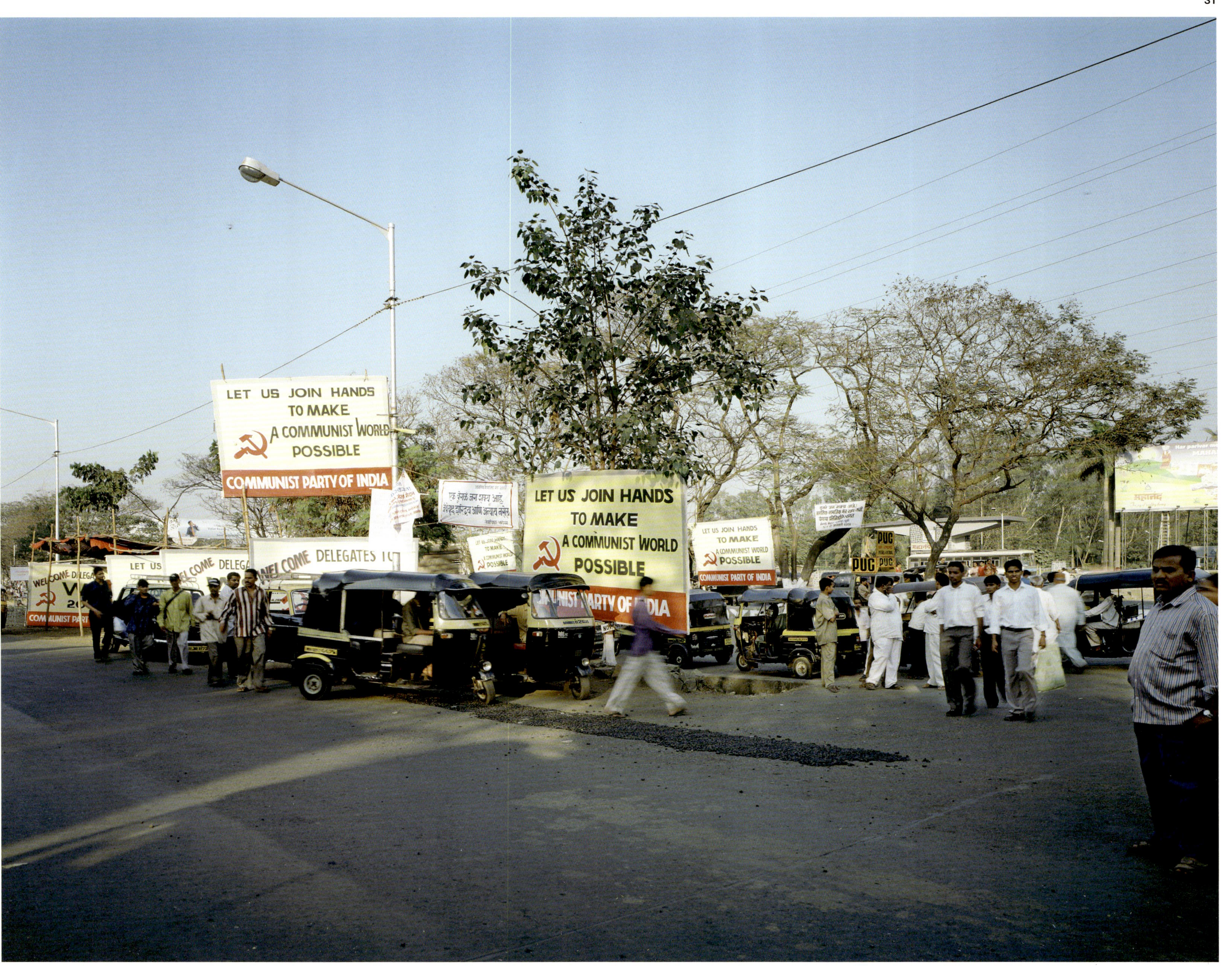
LET US JOIN HANDS
TO MAKE
A COMMUNIST WORLD
POSSIBLE
COMMUNIST PARTY OF INDIA
LET US JOIN HANDS
TO MAKE
A COMMUNIST WORLD
POSSIBLE
LET US JOIN HANDS
TO MAKE
A COMMUNIST WORLD
POSSIBLE
COMMUNIST PARTY OF INDIA
WELCOME DELEGATES TO
PUC

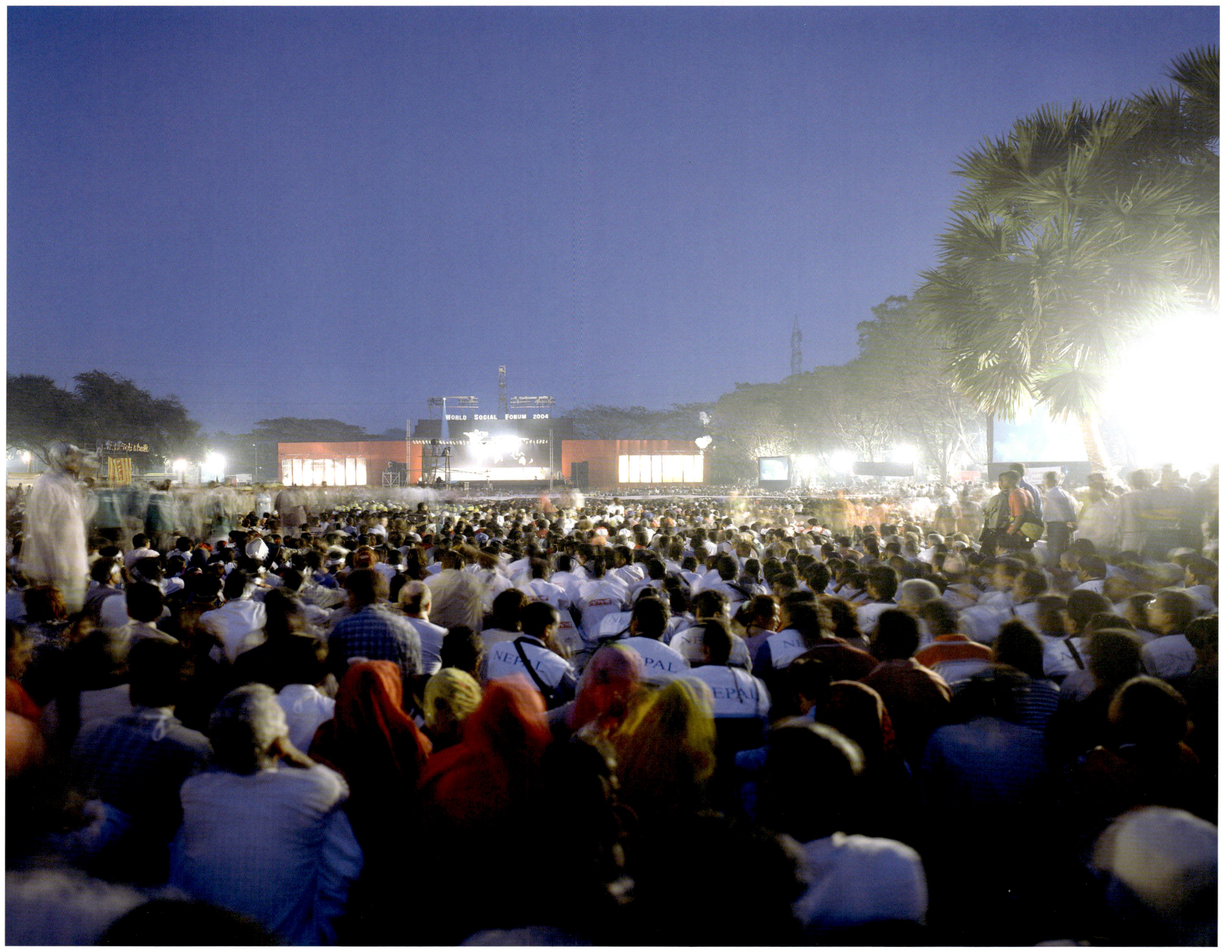
WORLD SOCIAL FORUM 2004
NEPAL

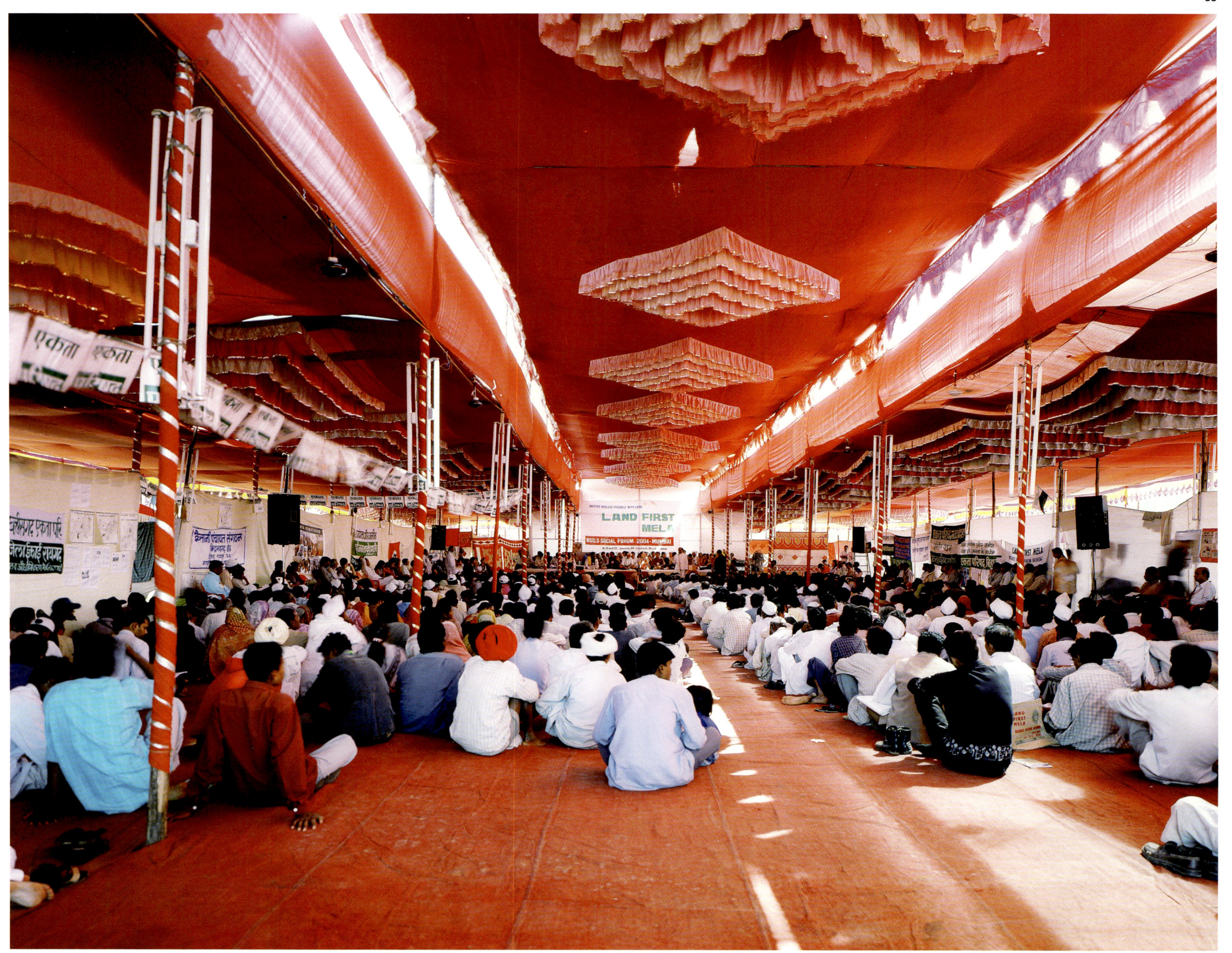
LAND FIRST
MELA
WORLD SOCIAL FORUM 2004 MUMBAI
एकता
एकता

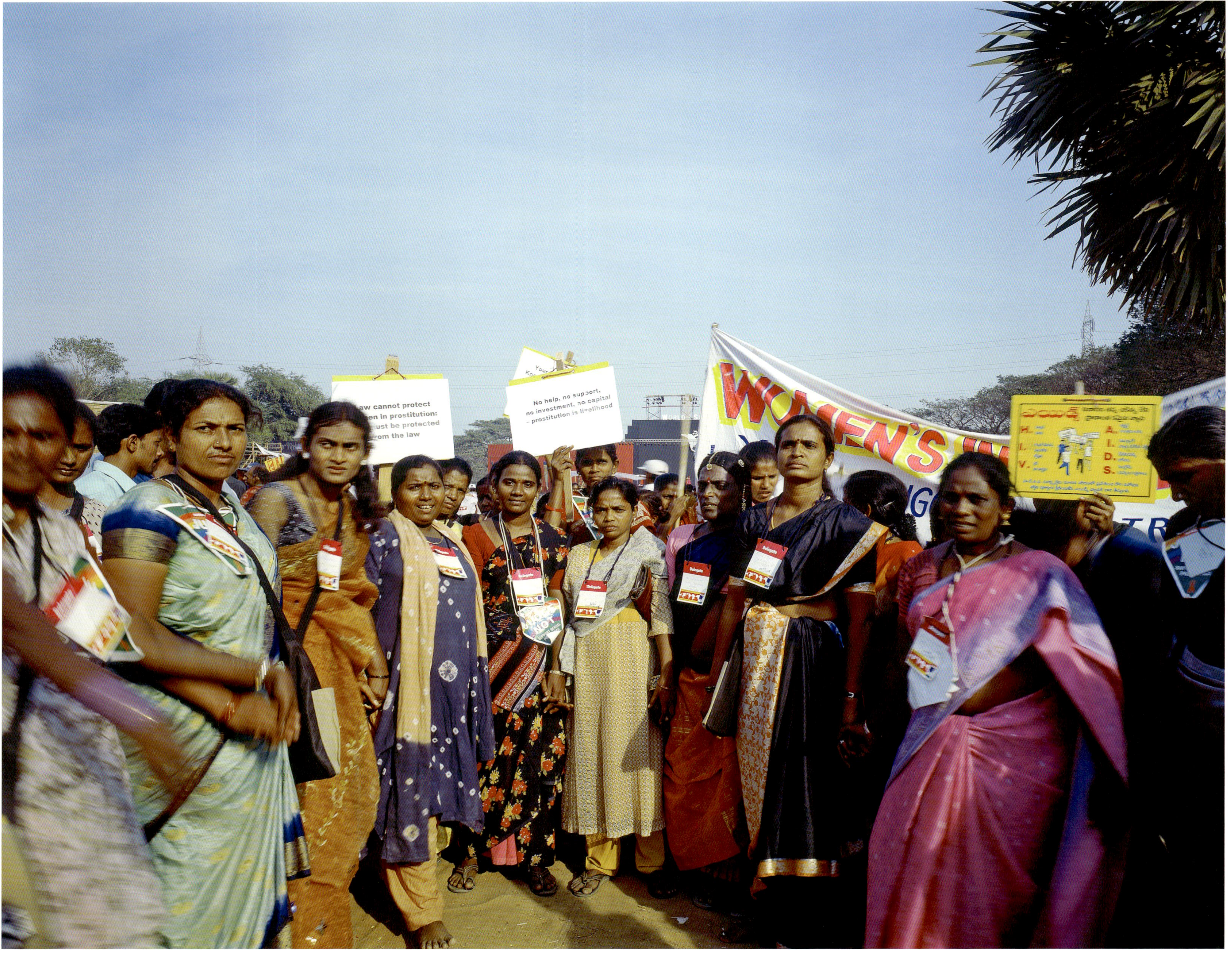
No help, no support,
no investment, no capital
– prostitution is livelihood

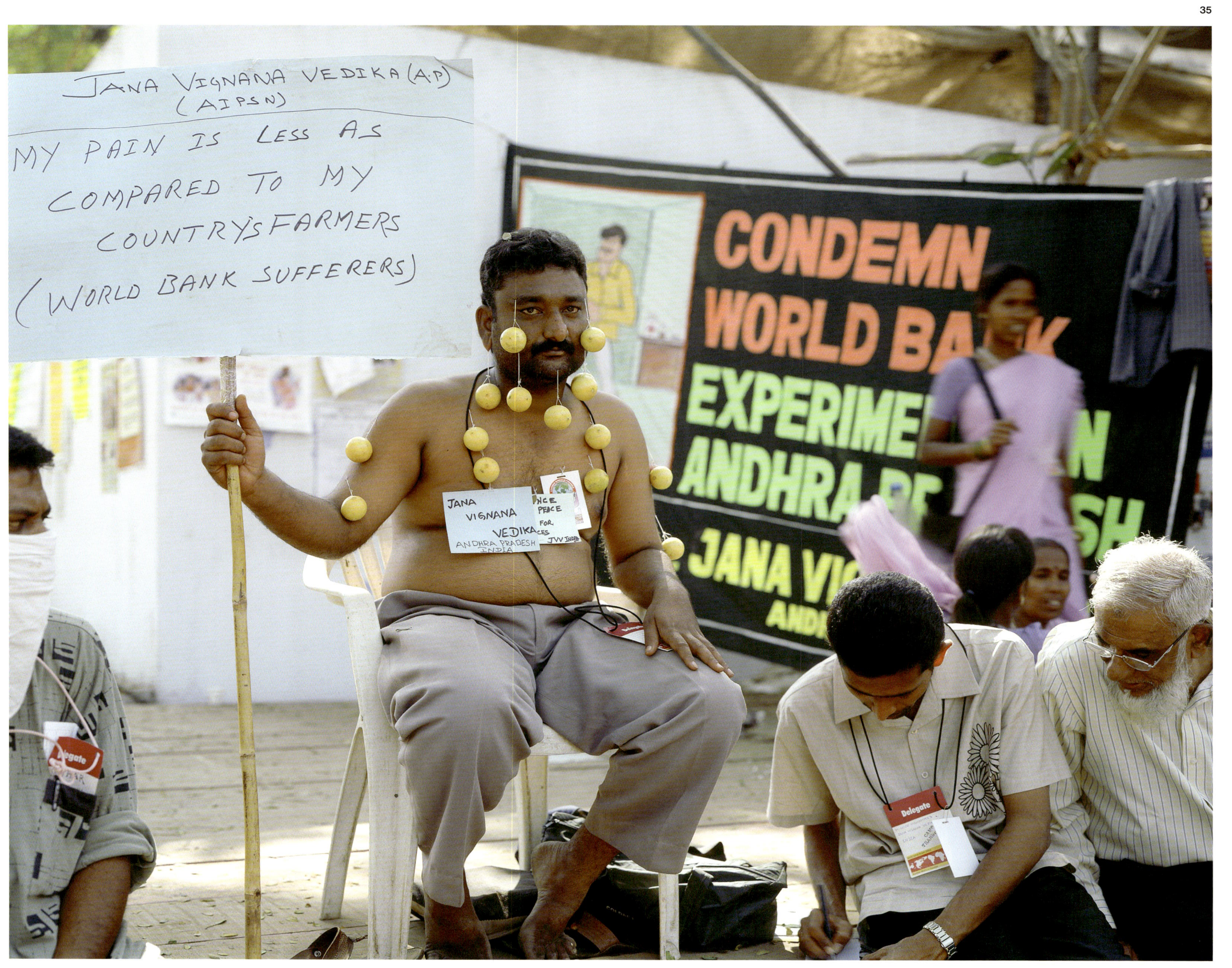
JANA VIGNANA VEDIKA (A.P)
(AIPSN)
MY PAIN IS LESS AS
COMPARED TO MY
COUNTRY'S FARMERS
(WORLD BANK SUFFERERS)
CONDEMN
WORLD BA
EXPERIME
ANDHRA
JANA VI
JANA
VIGNANA
VEDIKA
ANDHRA PRADESH
INDIA
Delegate

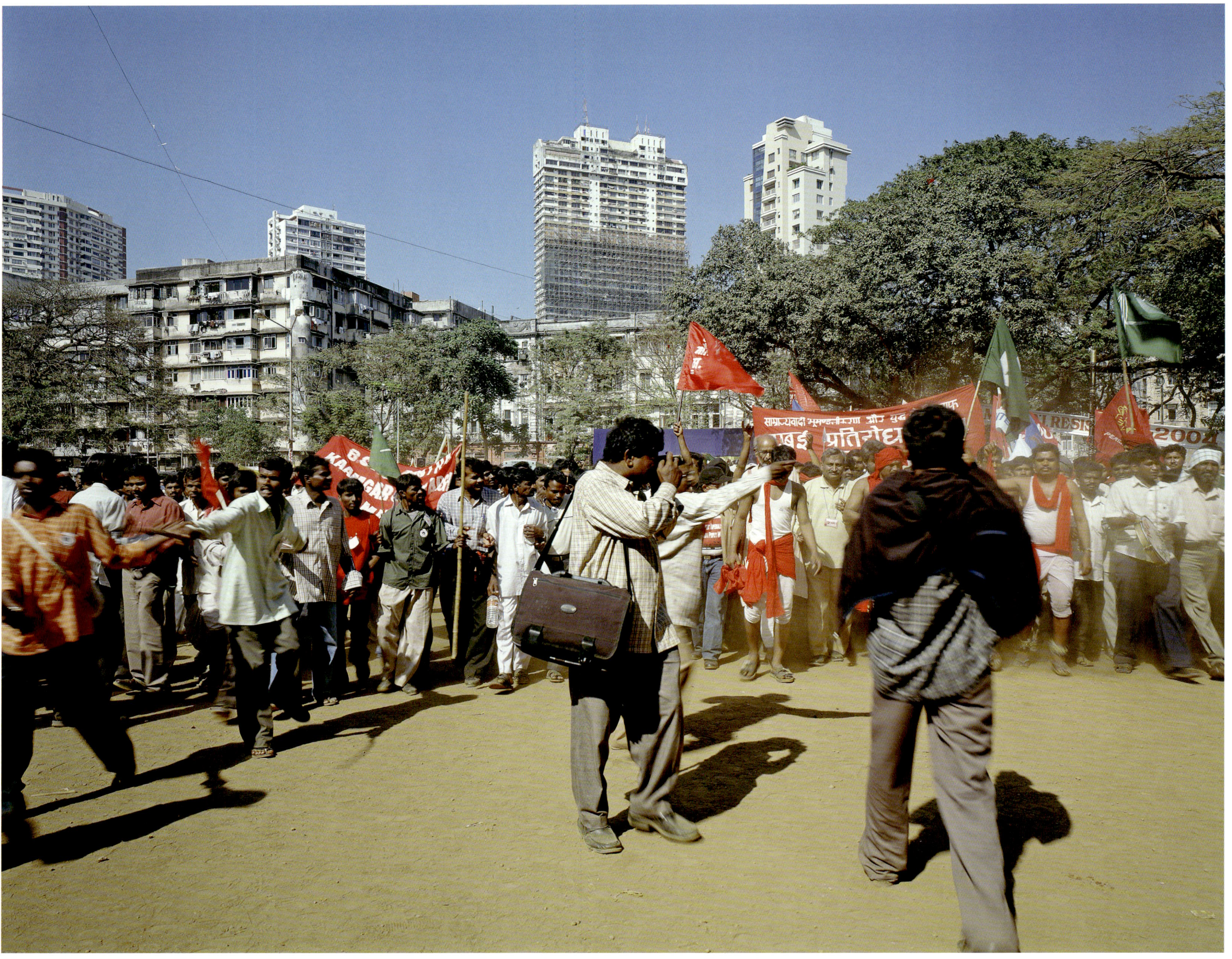

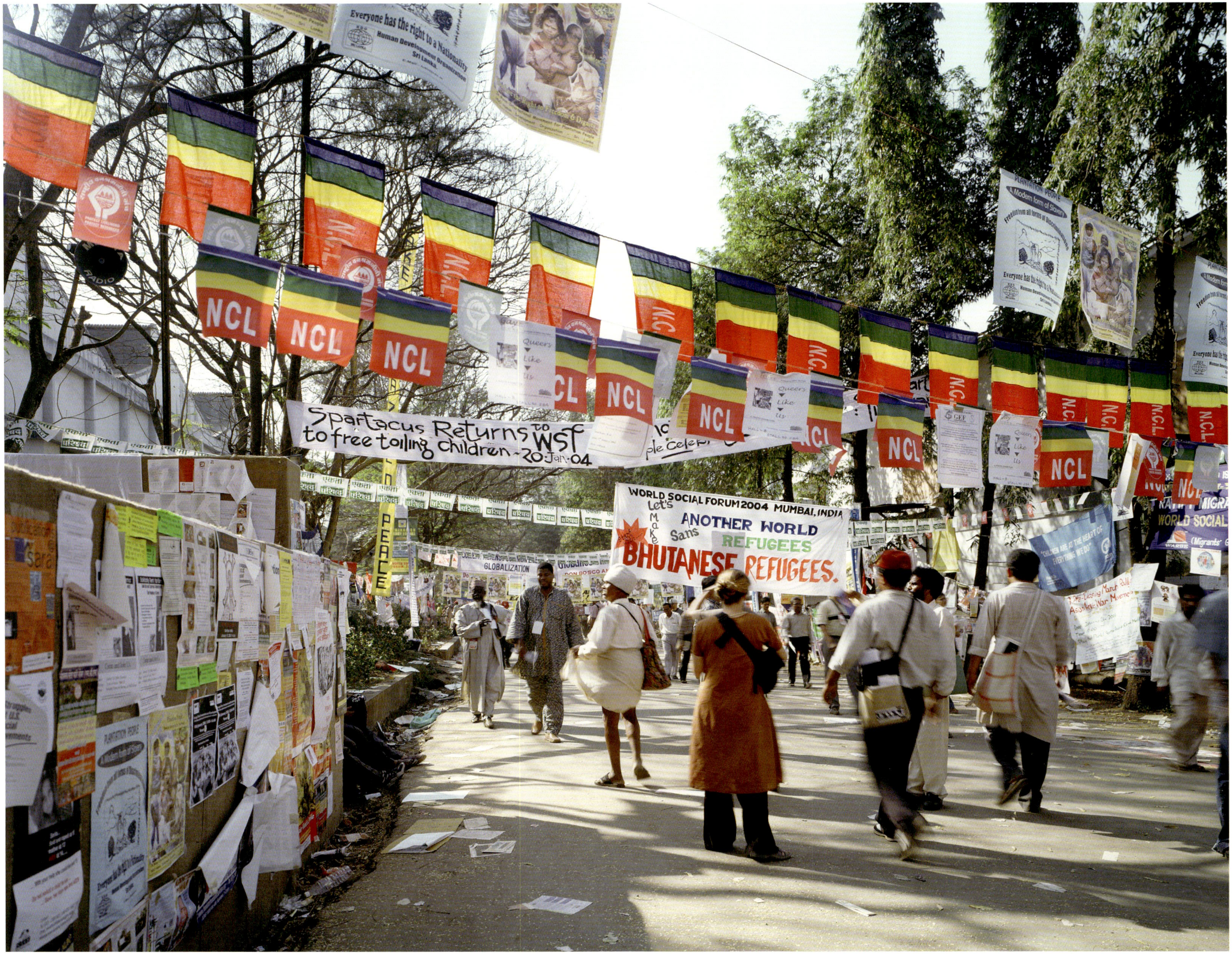
Everyone has the right to a Nationality
Human Development Organisation
Sri Lanka
NCL
Spartacus Returns to WSF
to free toiling children - 20-Jan-04
Queers
Like
Us
WORLD SOCIAL FORUM 2004 MUMBAI, INDIA
Let's Make
ANOTHER WORLD
Sans
REFUGEES
BHUTANESE REFUGEES.
GLOBALIZATION
PEACE
N.C.L.
Modern form of Slavery
WORLD SOCIAL

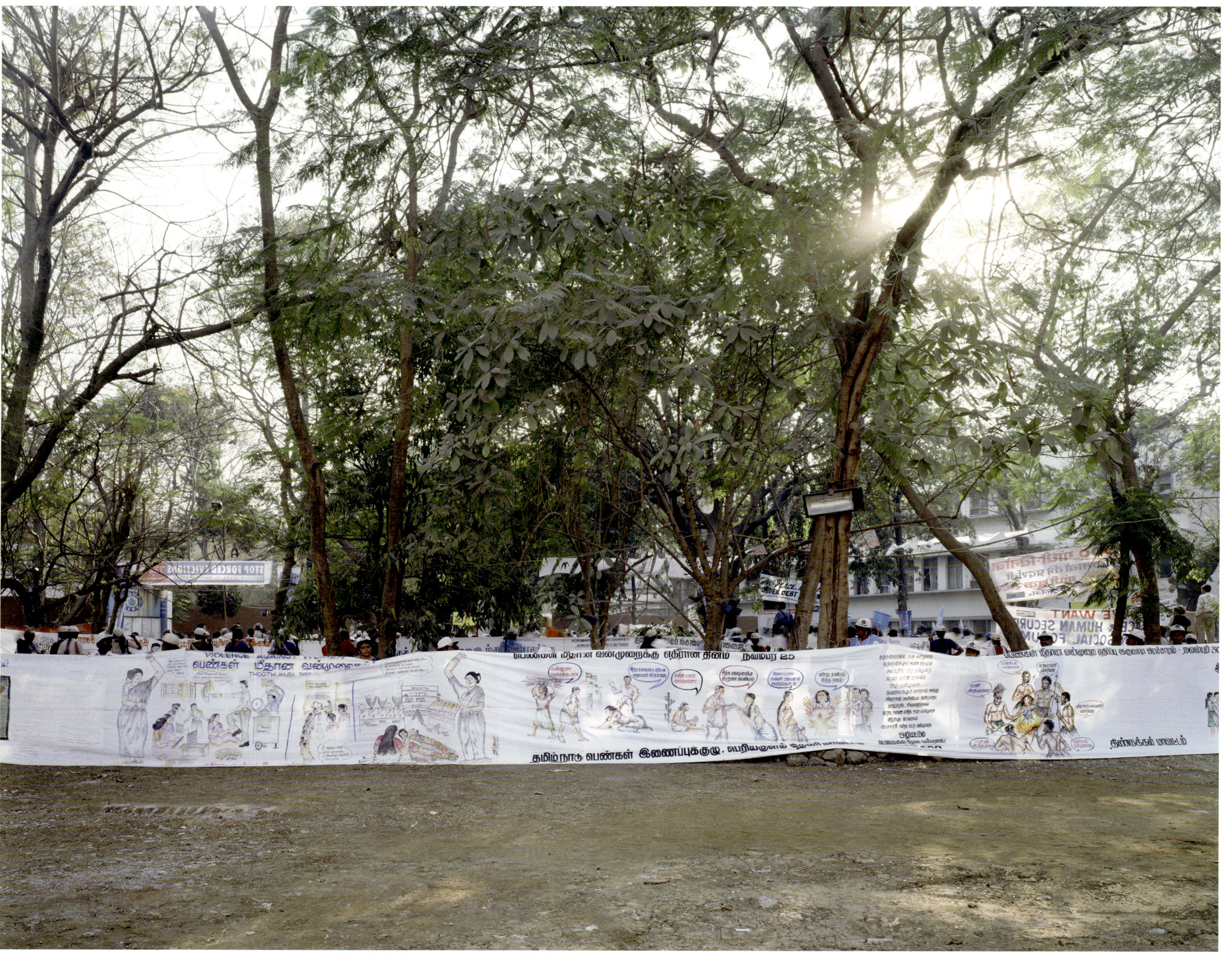
STOP FORCED EVICTIONS
பெண்கள் மீதான வன்முறைக்கு எதிரான தினம் நவம்பர் 25
தமிழ்நாடு பெண்கள் இணைப்புக்குழு

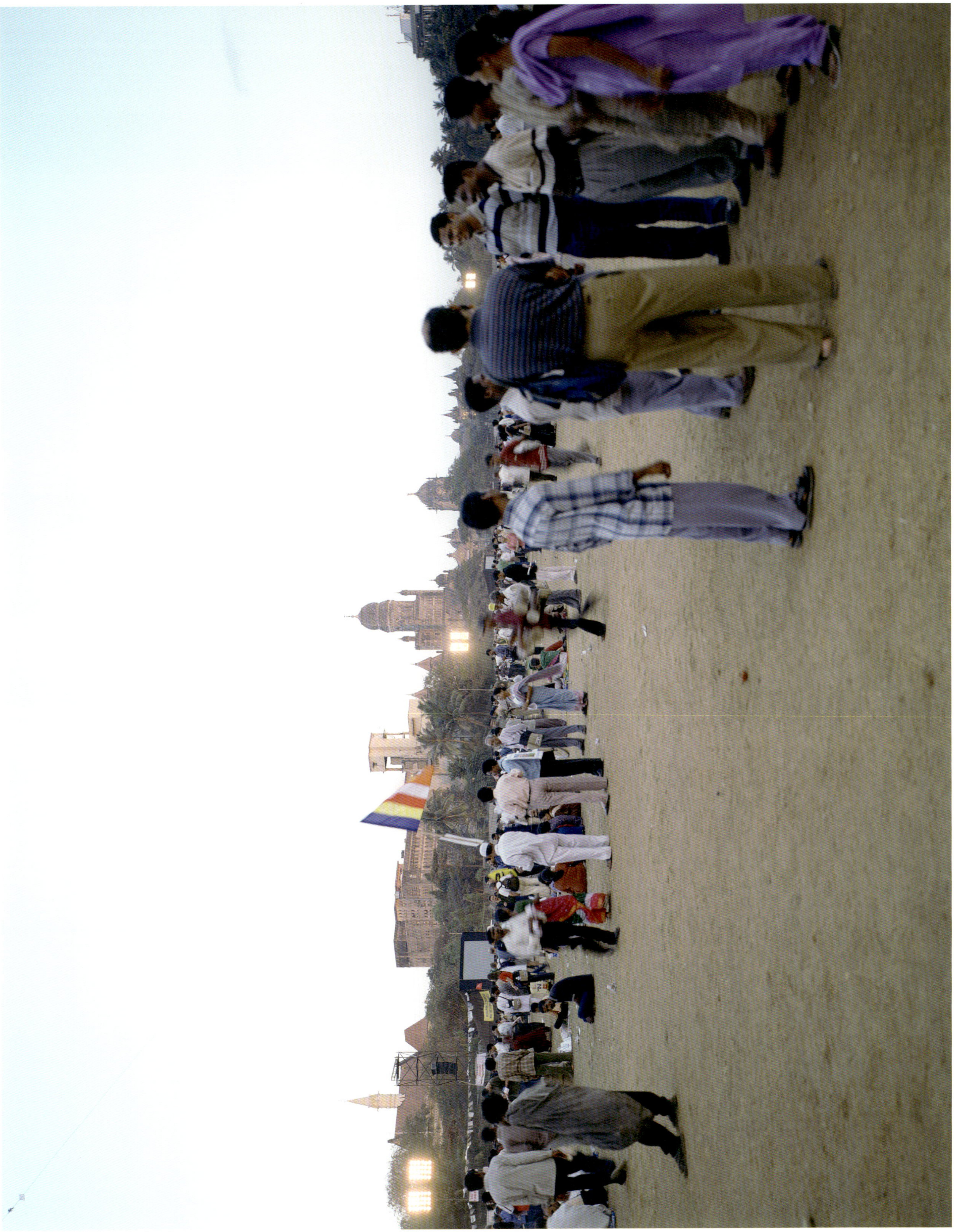

Luna Park, Bilbao
2005

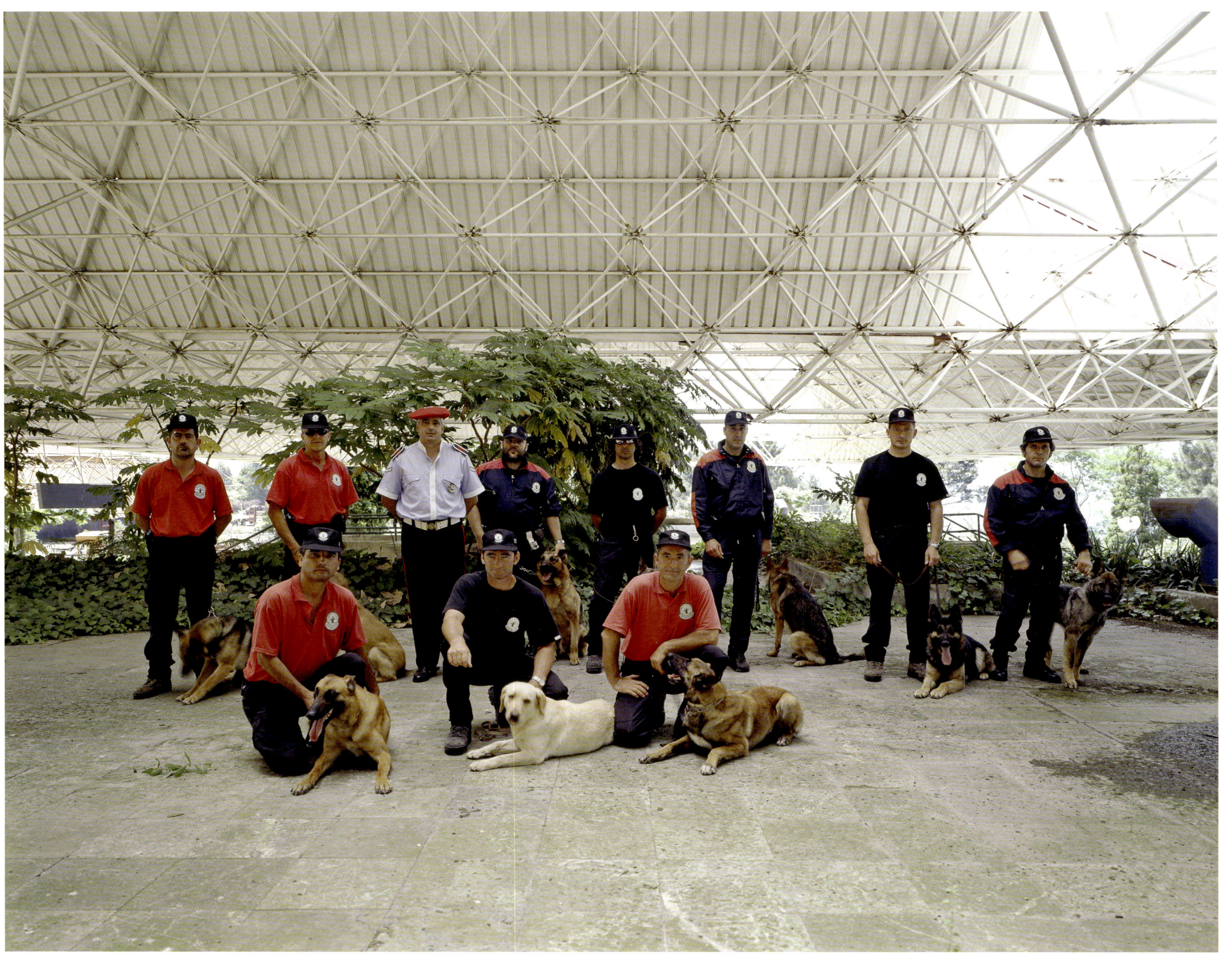

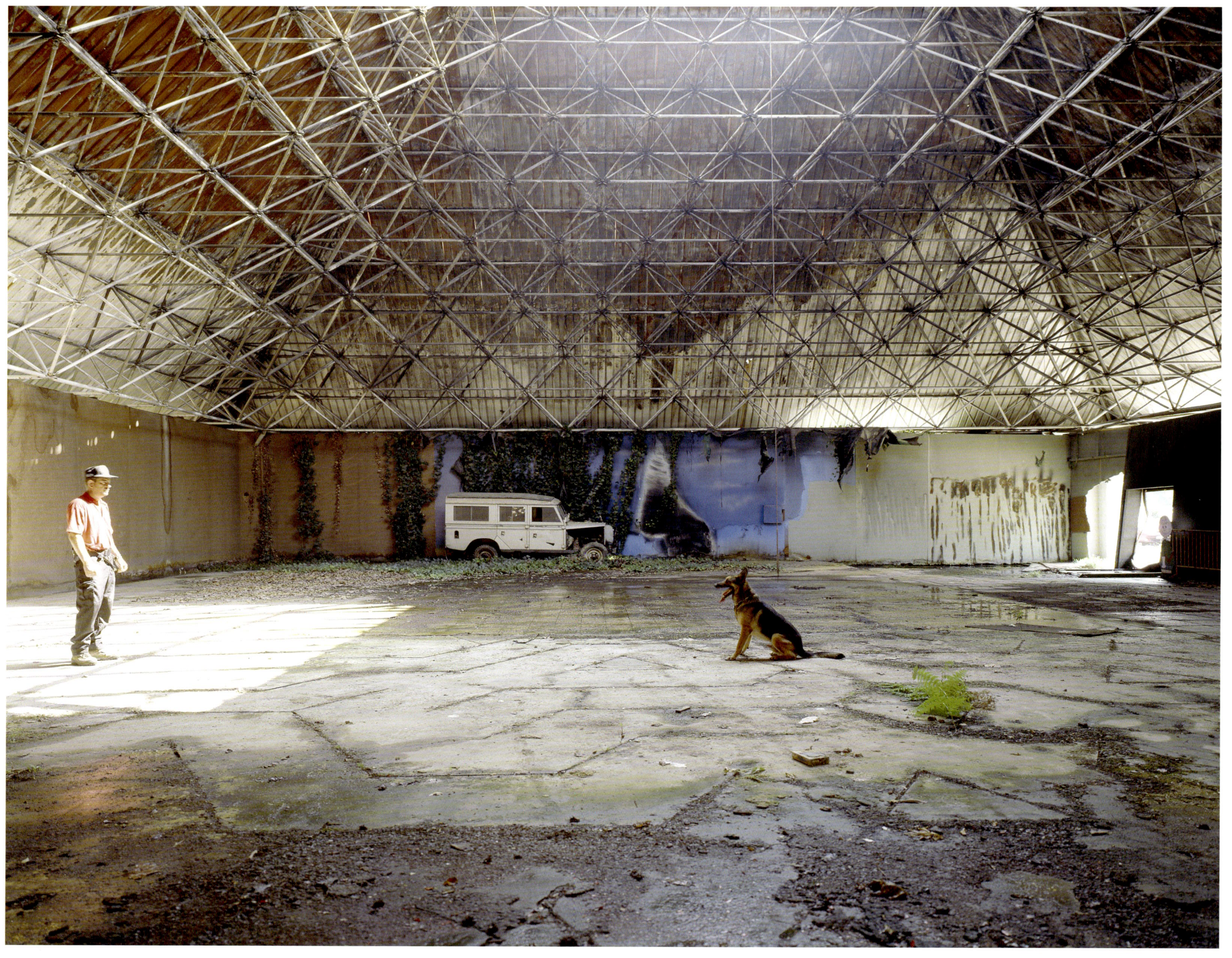

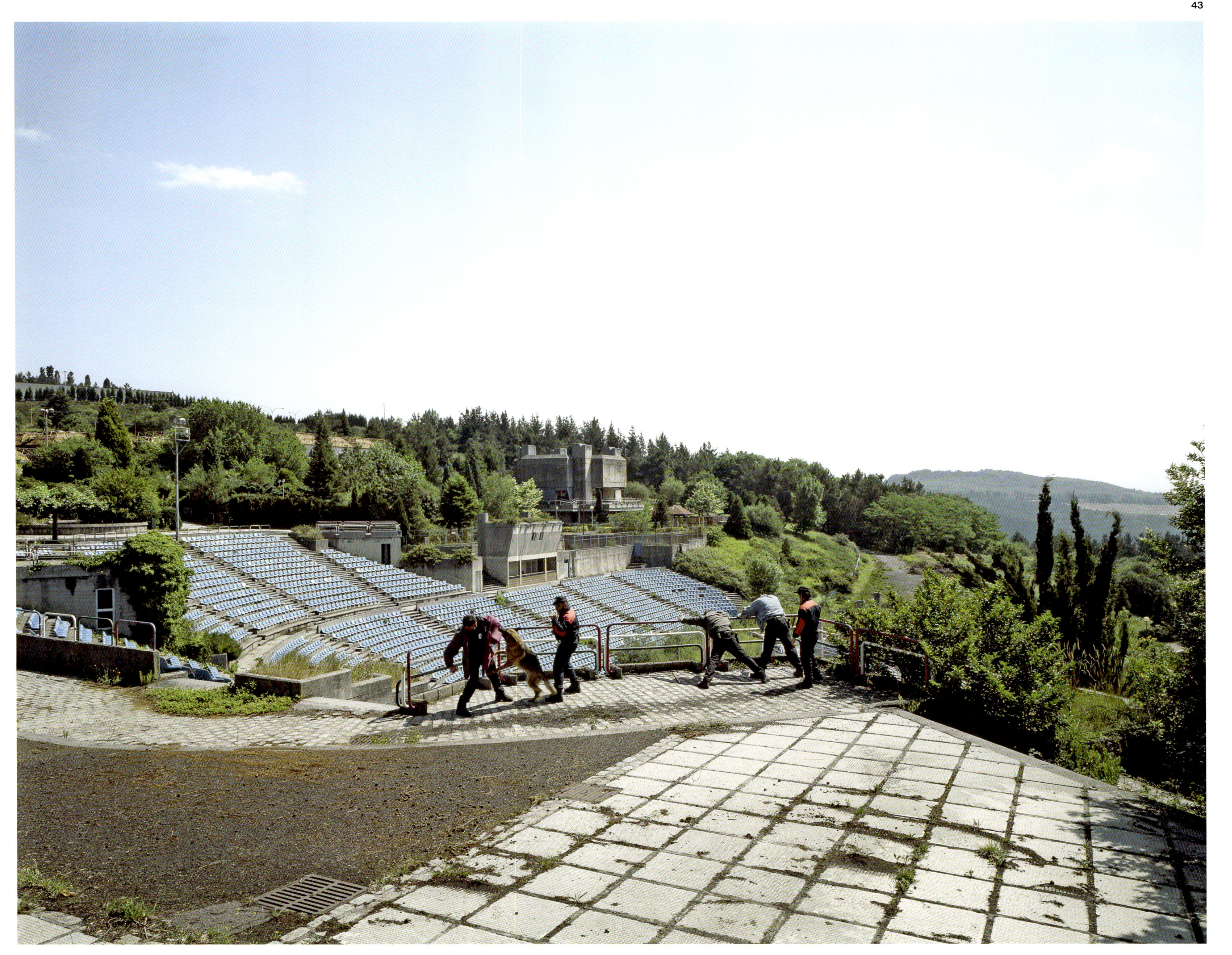

Sommet mondial sur la Société de l’information, Tunis
[World Summit on the Information Society, Tunis]
2005

The second phase of the World Summit on the Information Society was held in Tunis from November 16 to 18, 2005. Representatives from 170 participating countries reaffirmed, from the first article of the Engagement of Tunis adopted at the end of the Summit, their “unreserved support of the Declaration of Principles and the Plan of Action instituted in the first phase of the SMSI in Geneva, December 2003.” More than anything, the text establishes the foundation for a reform of the “governance” of the Internet, guiding it toward more international control. In order to do this, a new institution, the Internet Governance Forum (IGF) was founded.

Not only will world governments participate in the IGF, but also representatives from the private sector, as well as both civilian and national organizations.

At the same time, journalists and non-governmental organizations bore the brunt of certain measures implemented by the Tunisian government concerning the liberty of the press and human rights, before and during the Summit: the intimidation of certain delegates, acts of violence committed on journalists, the breaking up of civilian meetings by President Ben Ali’s thugs, the censuring of press conferences and speeches (notably that of the President of the Helvetic Confederation during the opening ceremonies). Hence the question posed by numerous observers: why this Summit in Tunisia?

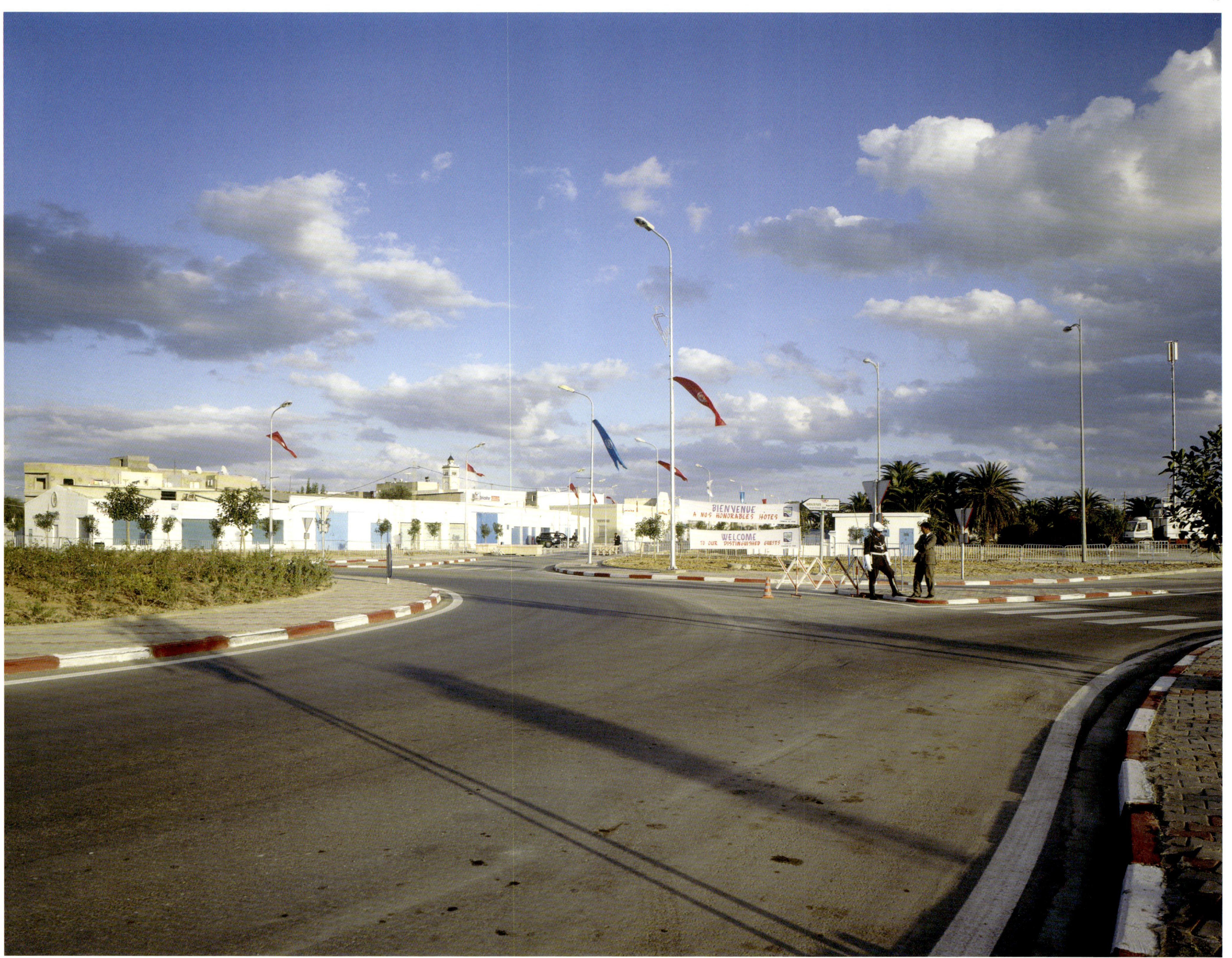
BIENVENUE
A NOS HONORABLES HOTES
WELCOME
TO OUR DISTINGUISHED GUESTS

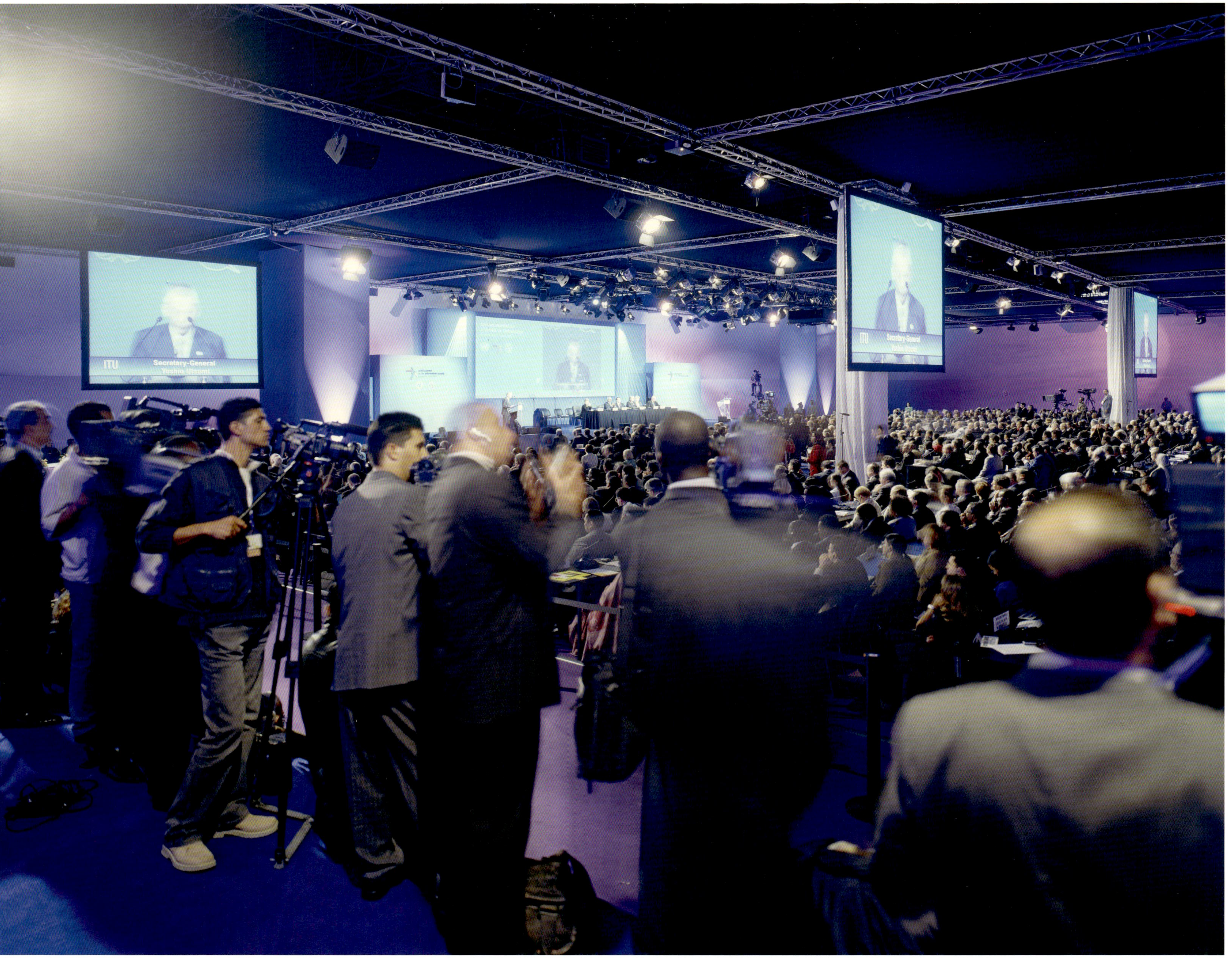
ITU
Secretary-General
Yoshio Utsumi

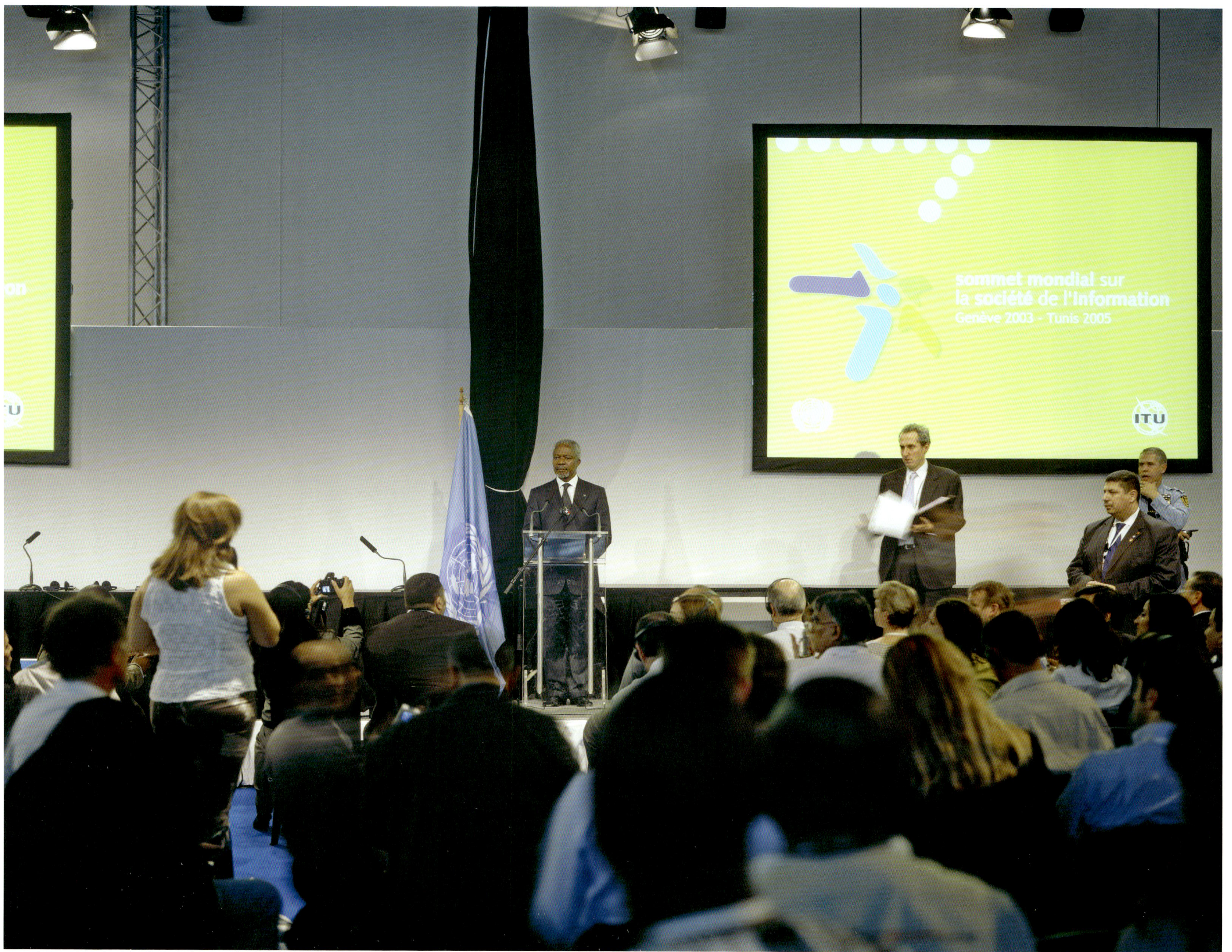
sommet mondial sur
la société de l'Information
Genève 2003 - Tunis 2005
ITU

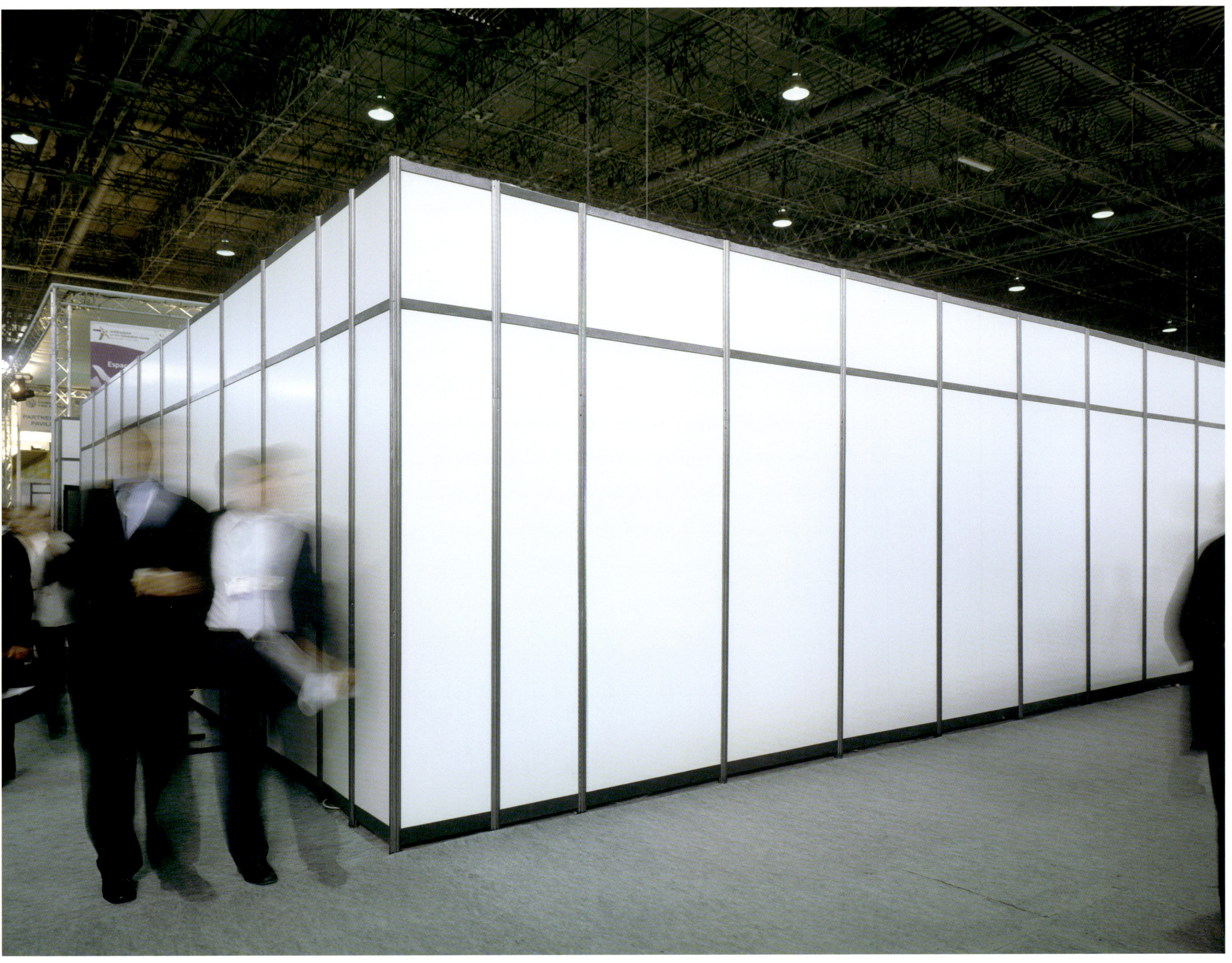

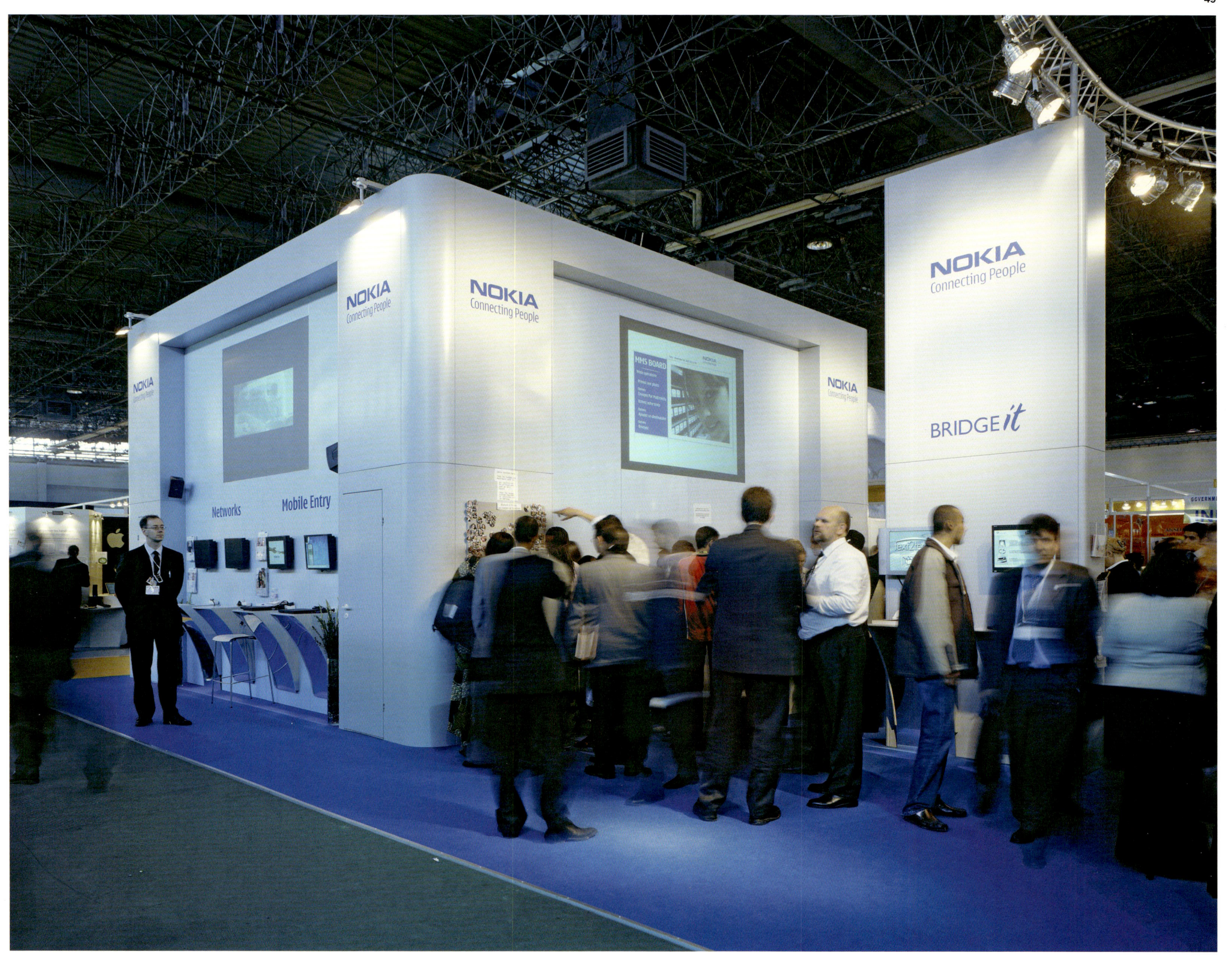
NOKIA
Connecting People
NOKIA
Connecting People
NOKIA
Connecting People
NOKIA
Connecting People
BRIDGE it
MMS BOARD
Networks
Mobile Entry

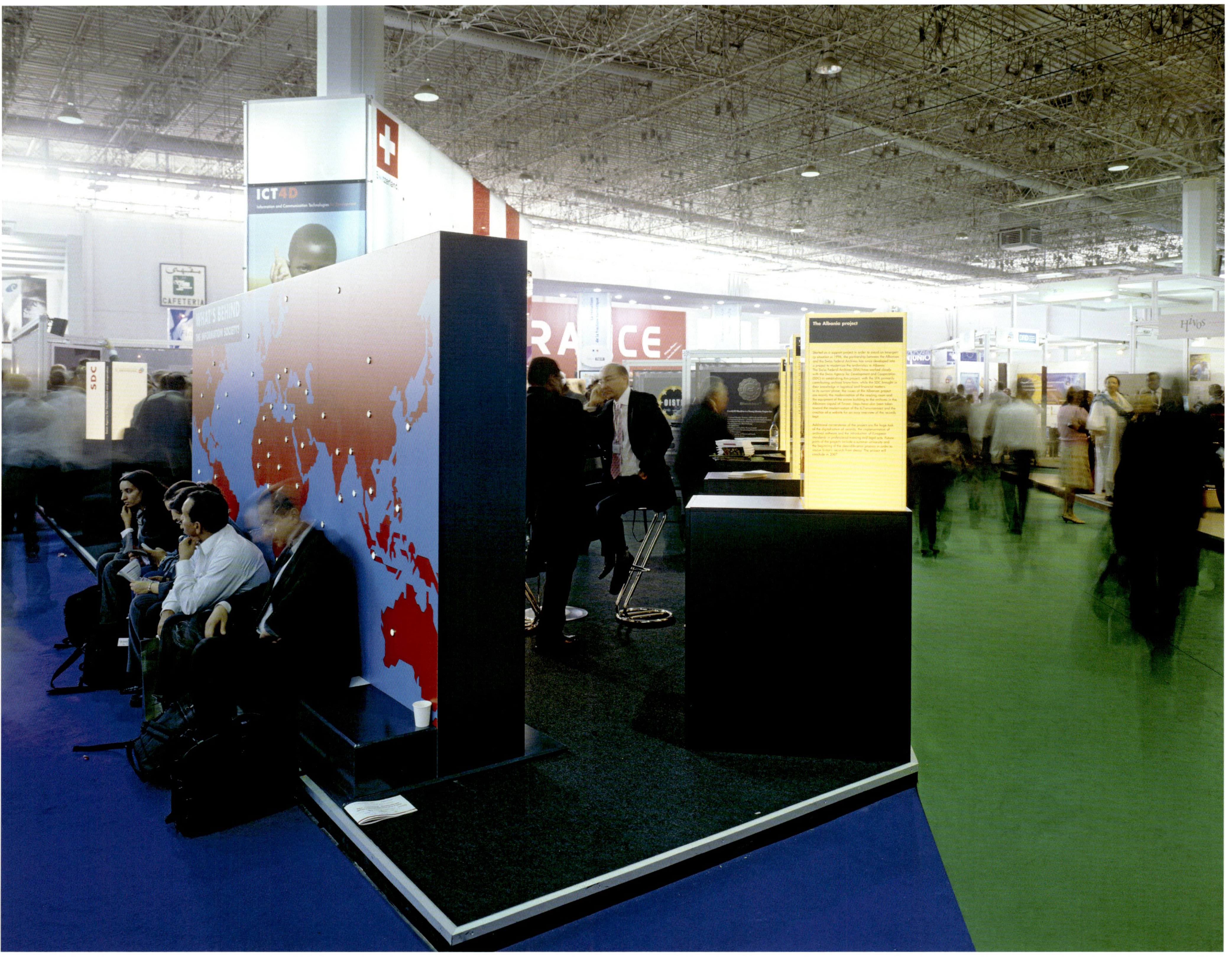
ICT4D
Information and Communication Technologies
CAFETERIA
WHAT'S BEHIND
THE INFORMATION SOCIETY?
SDC
The Albania project
Hivos

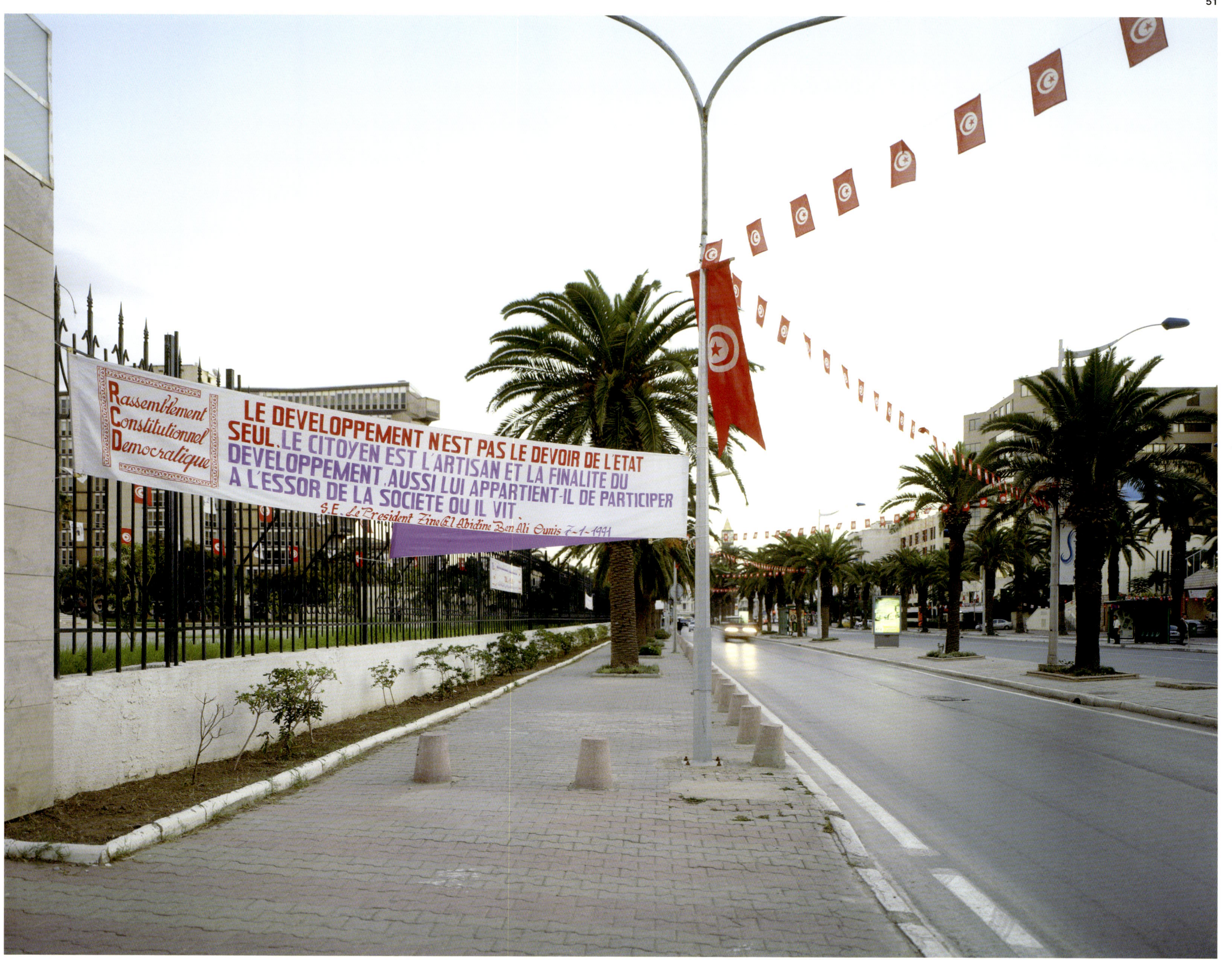
Rassemblement
Constitutionnel
Democratique
LE DEVELOPPEMENT N'EST PAS LE DEVOIR DE L'ETAT
SEUL. LE CITOYEN EST L'ARTISAN ET LA FINALITE DU
DEVELOPPEMENT. AUSSI LUI APPARTIENT-IL DE PARTICIPER
A L'ESSOR DE LA SOCIETE OU IL VIT
S.E. Le President Zine El Abidine Ben Ali Ounis 7-1-1991

La Otra
2006

On January 1, 2006, Subcomandante Marcos, the charismatic spokesperson of the Zapatista Army of National Liberation (Ejército Zapatista de Liberación Nacional, EZLN), left his southeastern Mexican enclave in order to initiate a year-long political campaign throughout the entire country. Although this, the "Other Campaign," took place at the same time as that of the official 2006 presidential election, the goal was significantly different.

The stakes for the Zapatista guerrilla were double: to strategically get the media's attention via a particular event. The Delegado Zero left Chiapas on a motorcycle just as Ernesto Guevara had mounted his to cross South America.

However, the reason for this move was also, and more importantly, to seek allies at a time when the Zapatists felt the impetus of their struggle waning due to too marked an isolation. "This is what we think and feel in our hearts, and which forces us to say that we have come to the threshold of something and that it is possible that we have been losing everything we have (…) Well, the time has once again come to take risks (…) And perhaps only through being linked with other social sectors, which lack the same things as us, will it become possible to obtain what we both need and deserve. A new step forward in the indigenous struggle is only possible if the indigenous peoples unite with the farmers, students, professors, and blue-collar workers, which is to say, workers in the cities and in the fields." This is what could be read in the press statement of the EZLN in June 2005.

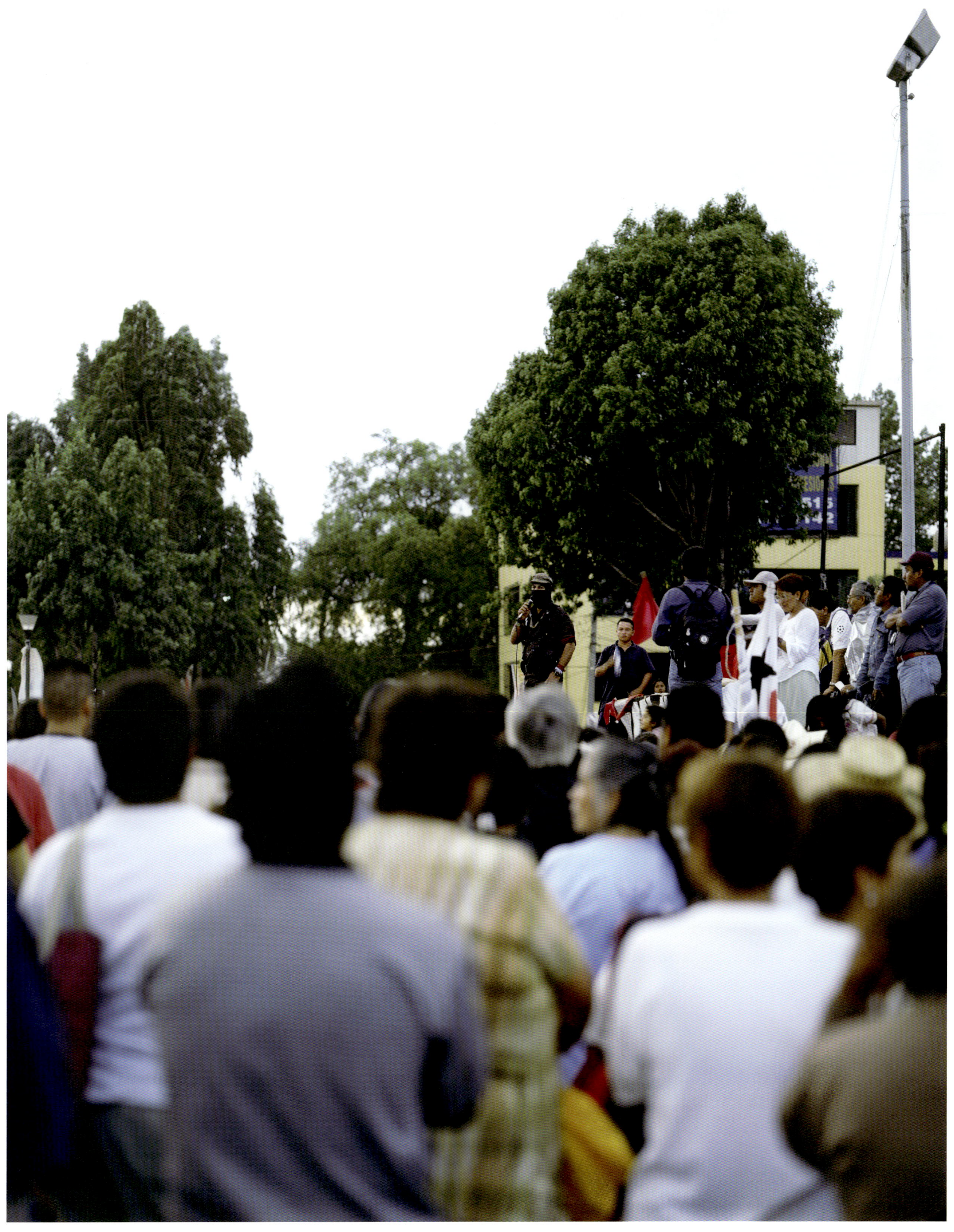

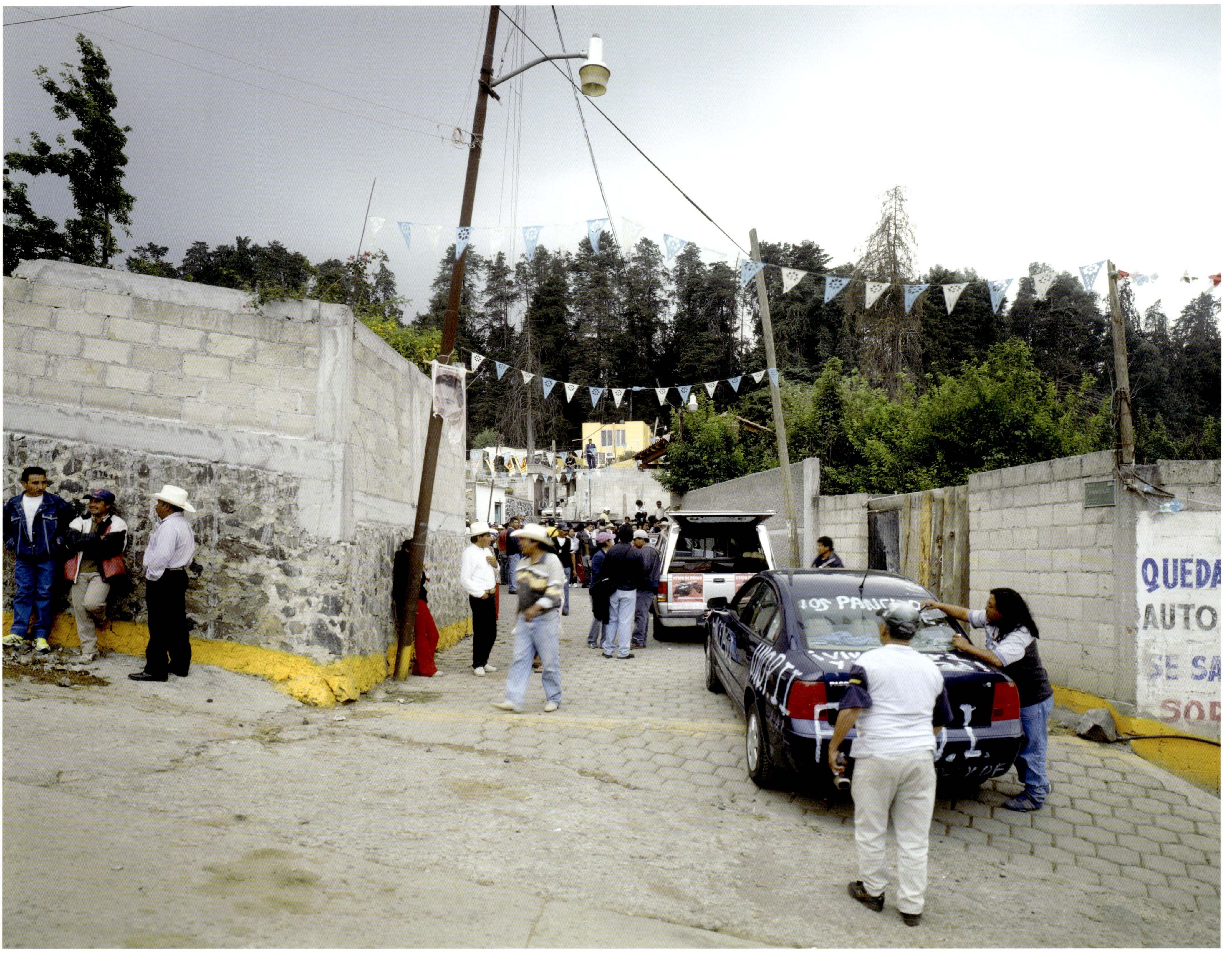

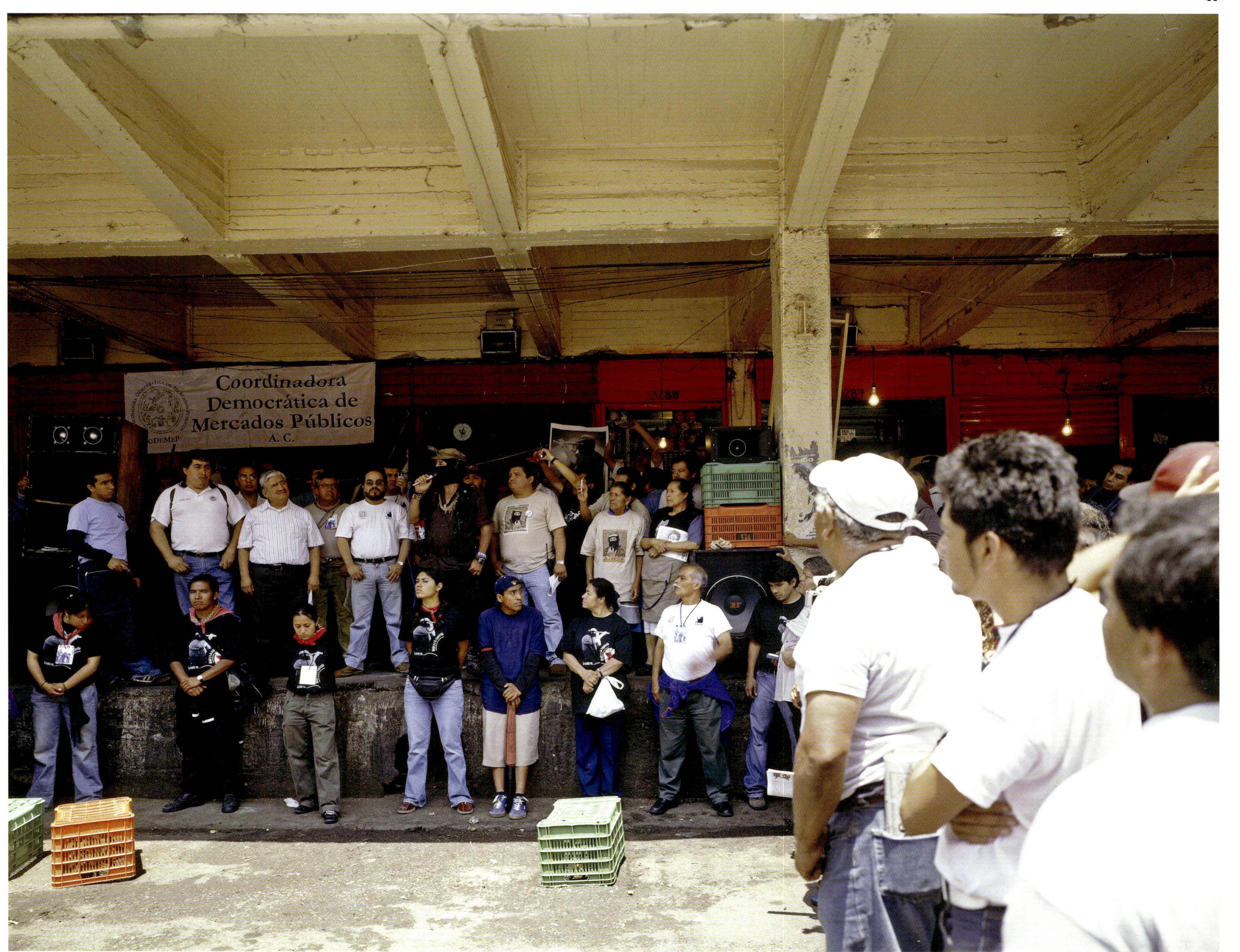
Coordinadora
Democrática de
Mercados Públicos
A. C.

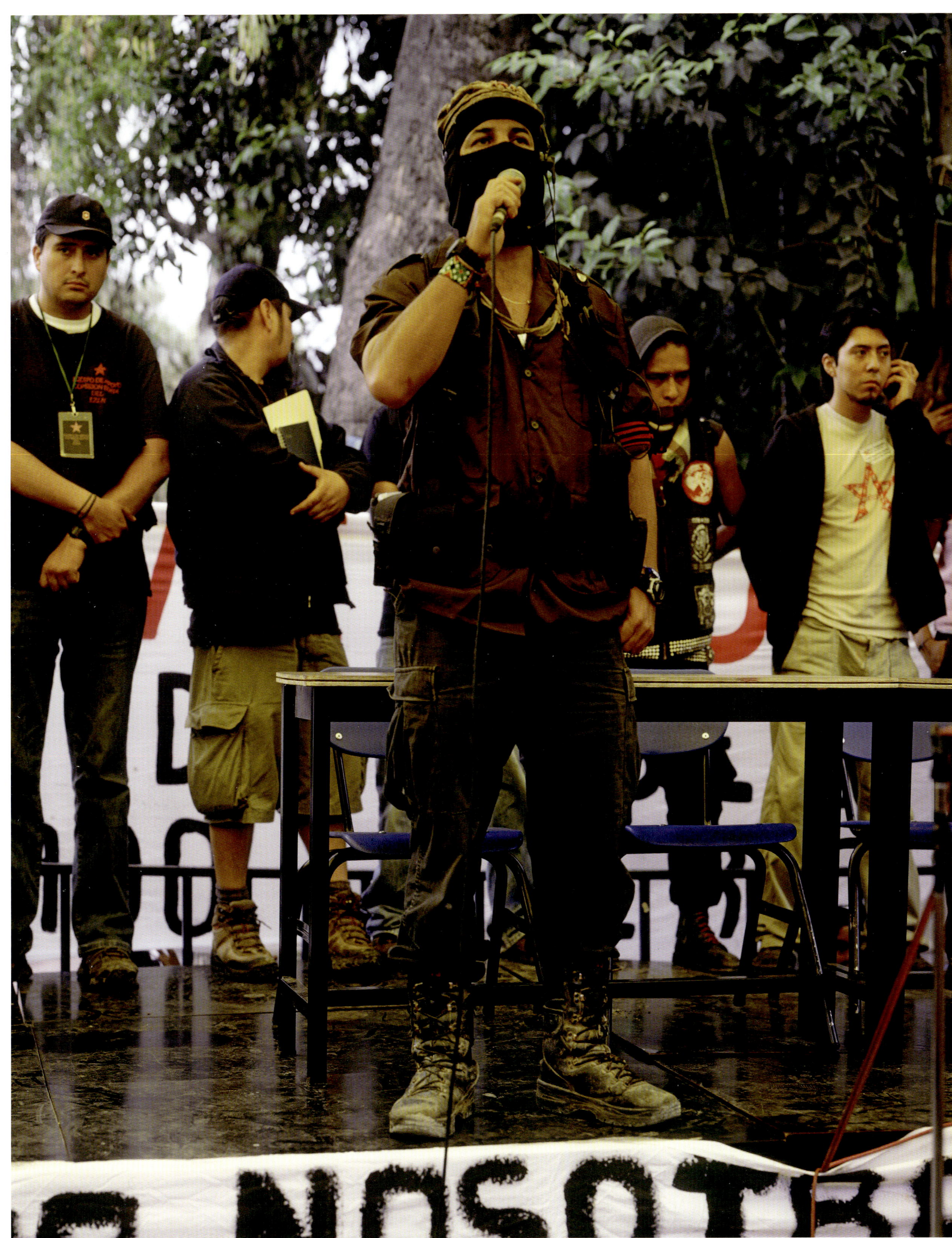

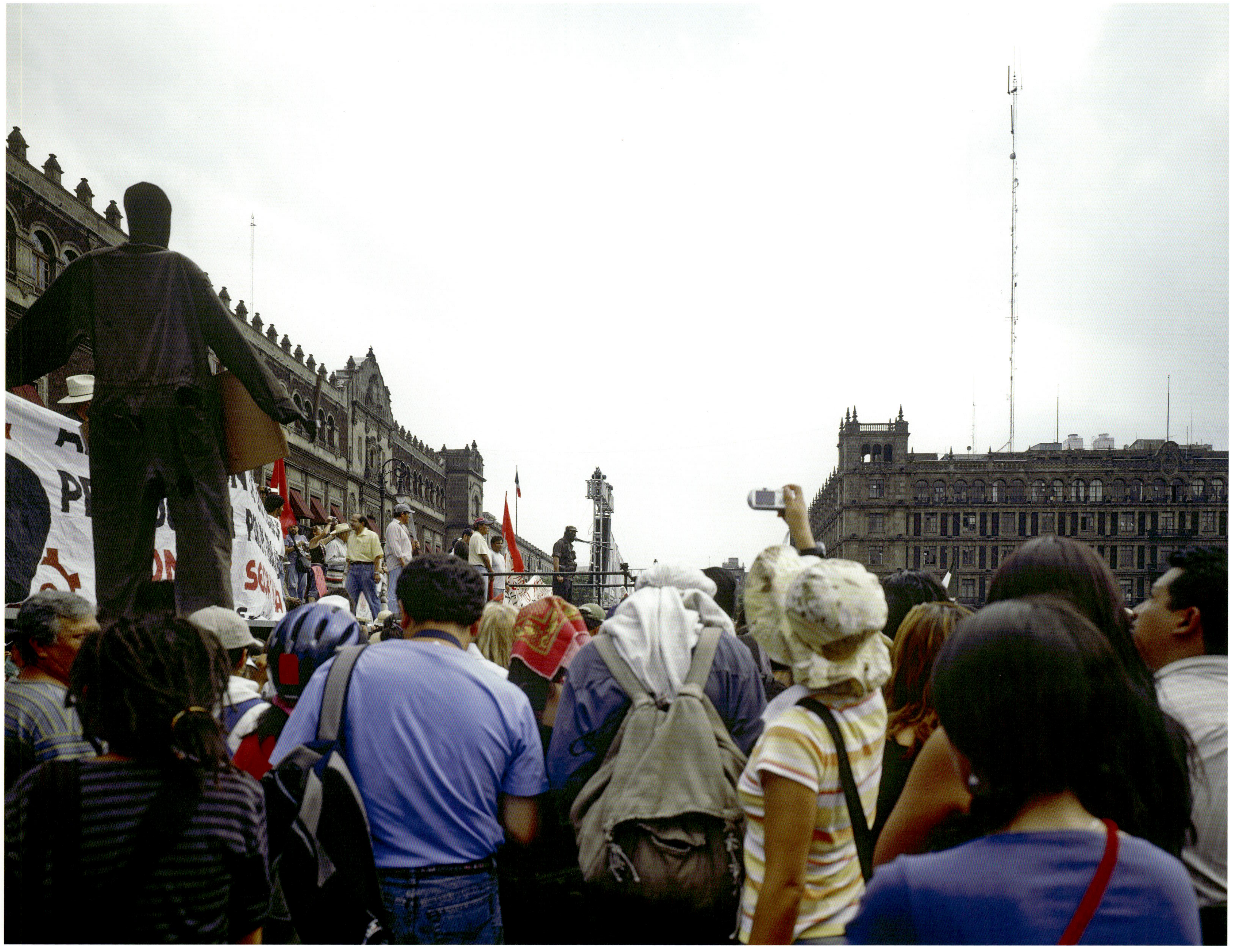

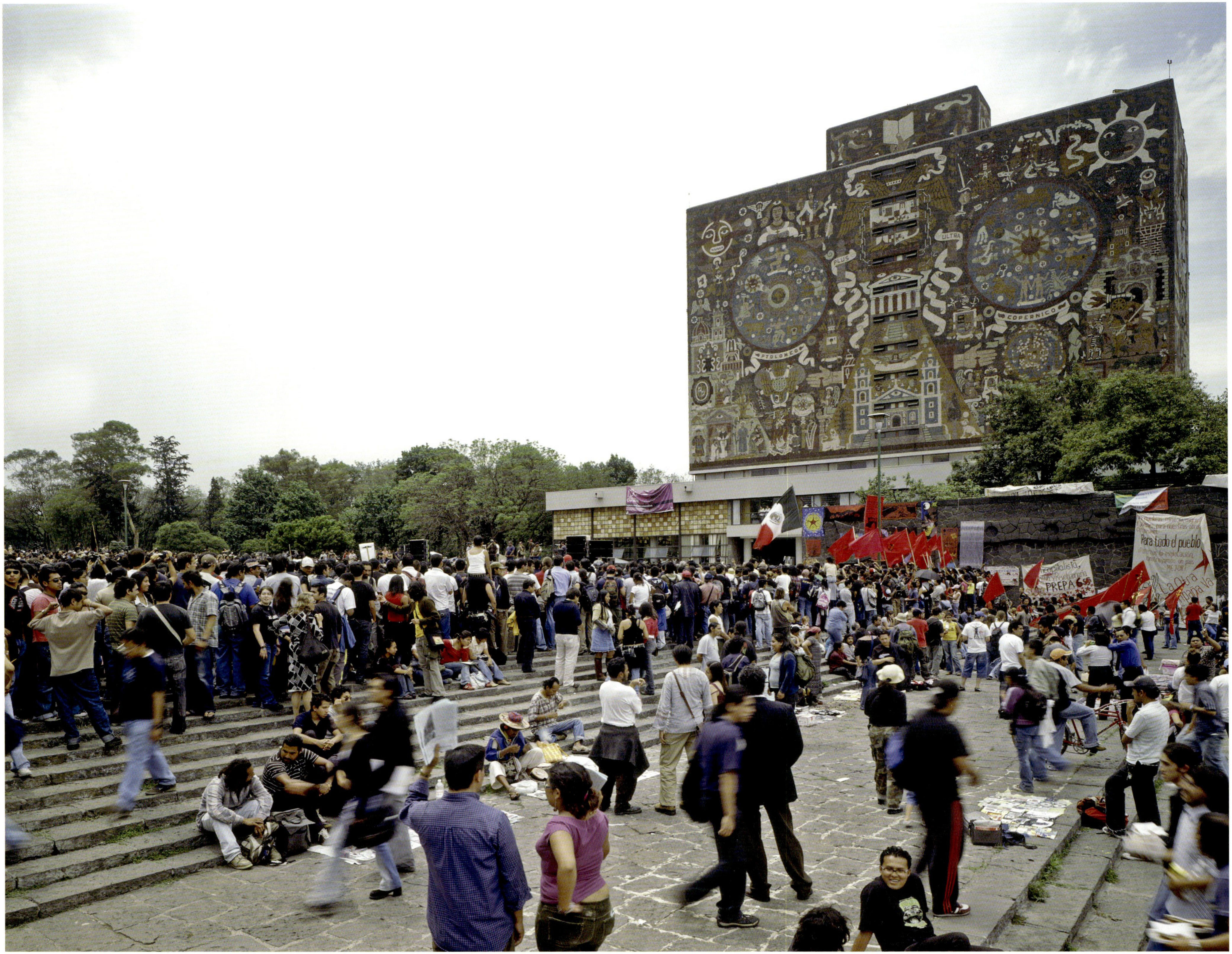
Para todo el pueblo
PREPA

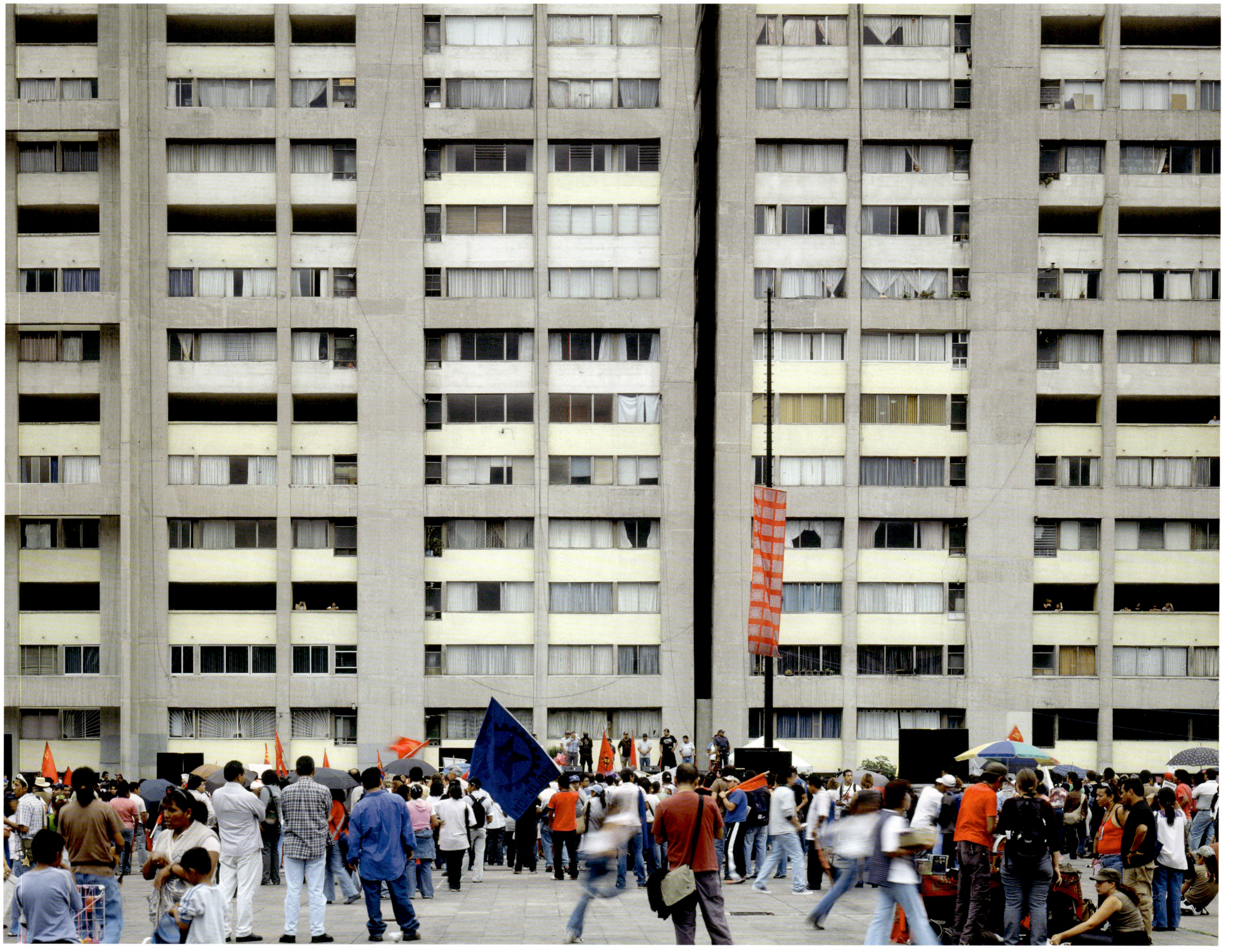

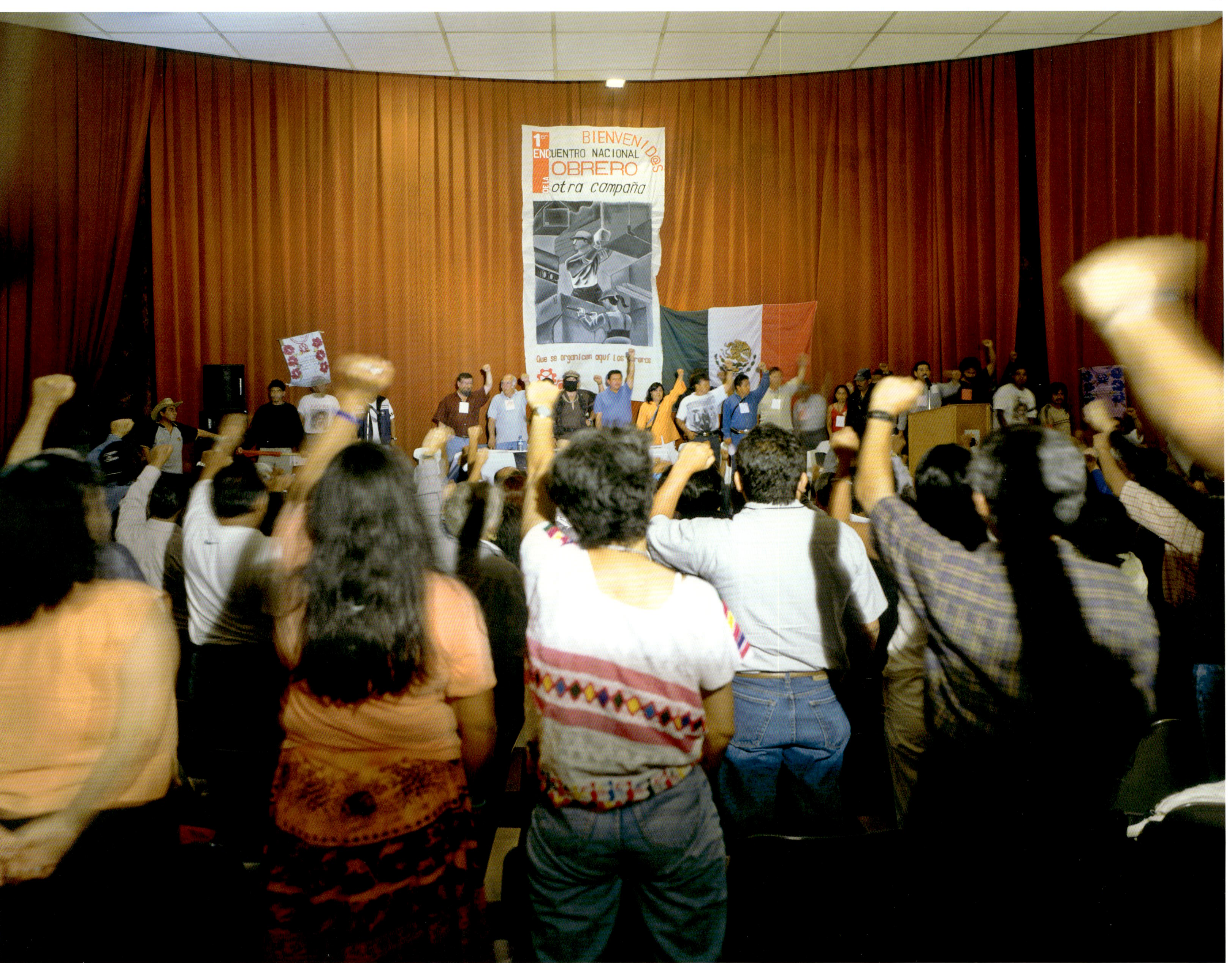
BIENVENID@S
1er ENCUENTRO NACIONAL
OBRERO
DE LA otra campaña
Que se organicen aquí los

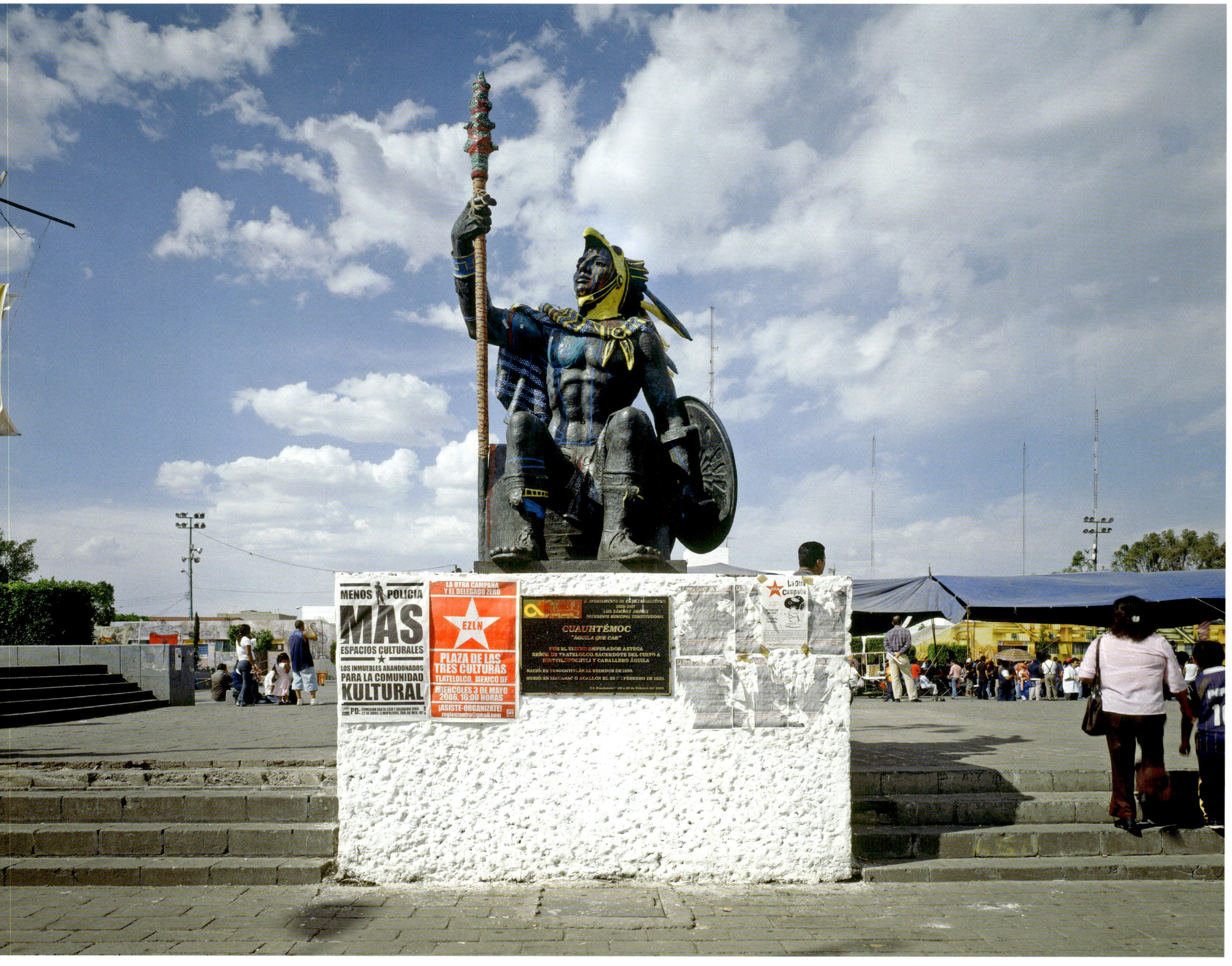
MENOS POLICIA
MAS
ESPACIOS CULTURALES
LOS INMUEBLES ABANDONADOS
PARA LA COMUNIDAD
KULTURAL
PD: COMISION SEXTA EZLN Y DELEGADO ZERO
22 DE ABRIL-3 MAYO2006, EDO. DE MEX.-DF
LA OTRA CAMPANA
Y EL DELEGADO ZERO
EZLN
PLAZA DE LAS
TRES CULTURAS
TLATELOLCO, MEXICO DF
MIERCOLES 3 DE MAYO
2006, 16:00 HORAS
¡ASISTE-ORGANIZATE!
regionzentro@gmail.com
PRESIDENTE MUNICIPAL CONSTITUCIONAL
CUAUHTÉMOC
"ÁGUILA QUE CAE"
La Otra Campaña

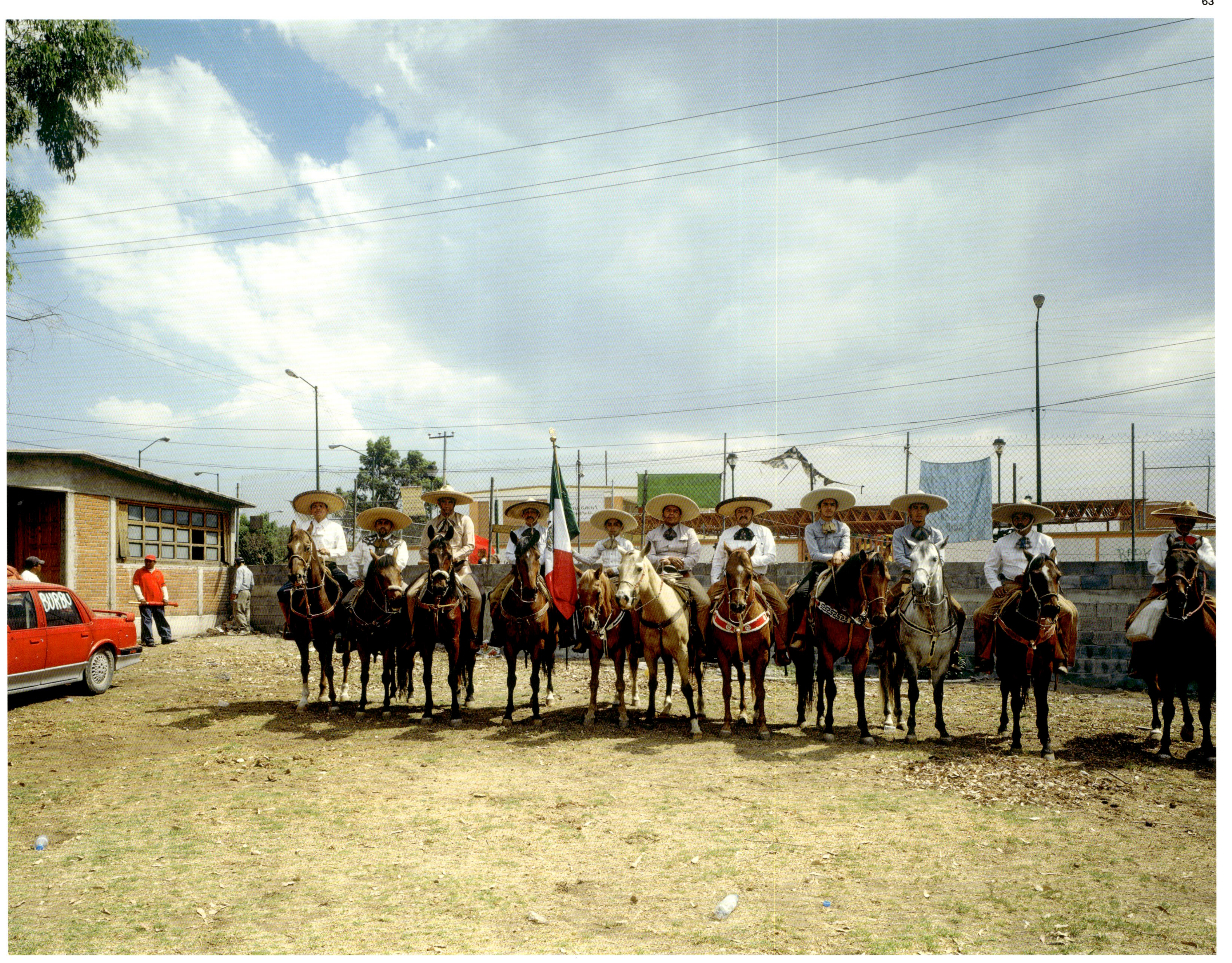

Calais
2006–2008

On November 5, 2002, the refugee camp at Sangatte, in France's Pas-de-Calais department, was closed by Nicolas Sarkozy, Minister of the Interior. The French and British governments hailed the event as a great victory in the fight against illegal immigration and the crime it was said to be generating. First opened in September 1999 and run by the Red Cross, the center—in what was originally a depot for the machines used to dig the Channel Tunnel—housed up to 1 200 migrants at a time, mainly Afghans, Kosovars, Iraqis, and Iranians in search of a passage to England.

Neither the closure of the camp nor the intensified police repression that followed did anything to stem the flow of migrants: Calais remains the French city nearest to England and its port's capacity for trucks in transit is constantly being increased. Local community associations helping the migrants estimate that there are currently some 400–600 people living on wasteland and in the woods around the city.

On September 26, 2009, the biggest of the improvised camps, known as "The Jungle"—close to the ferry port and with a mainly Afghan population—was broken up by the police. 276 "illegal" migrants were taken away.

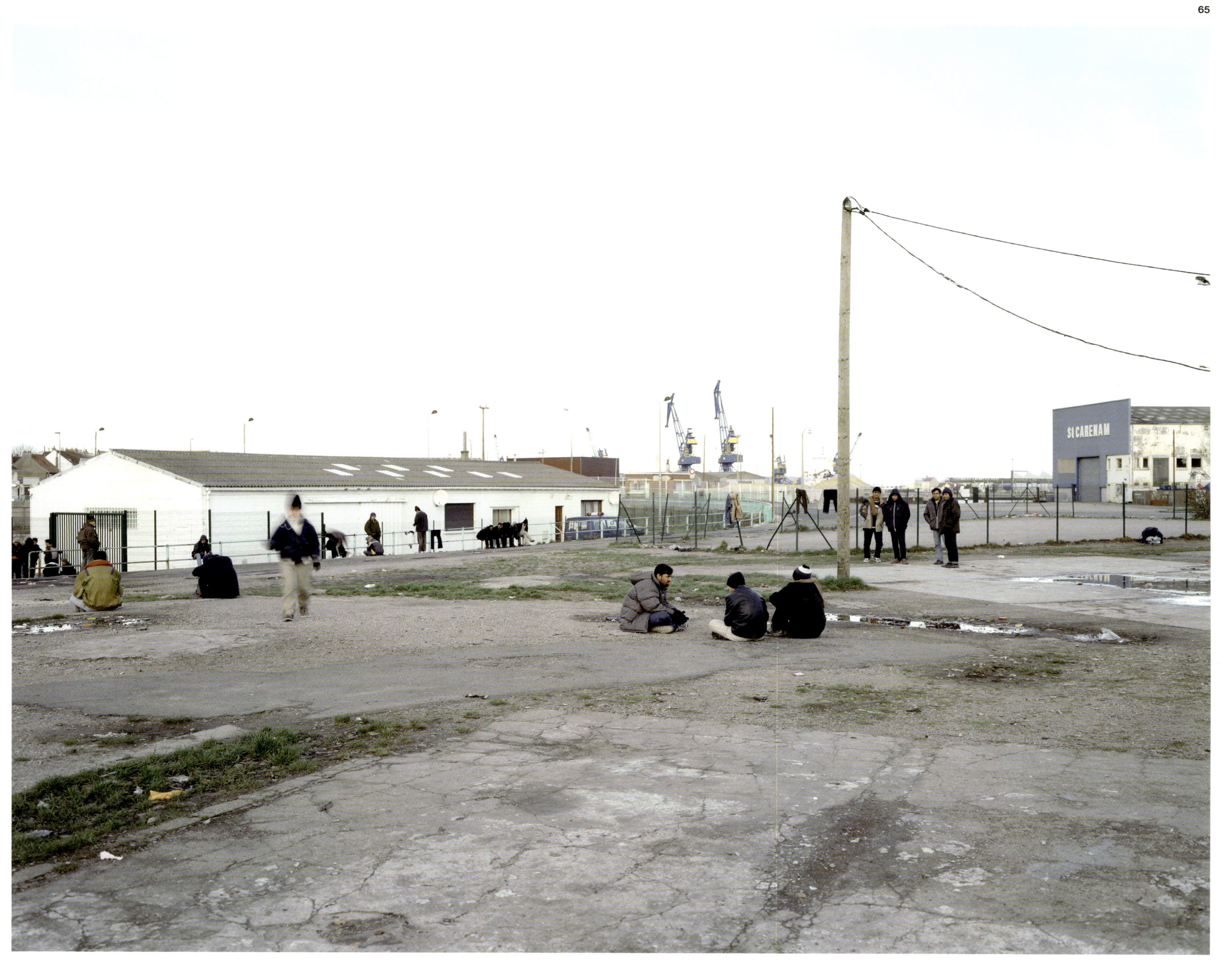
SI CARENAM

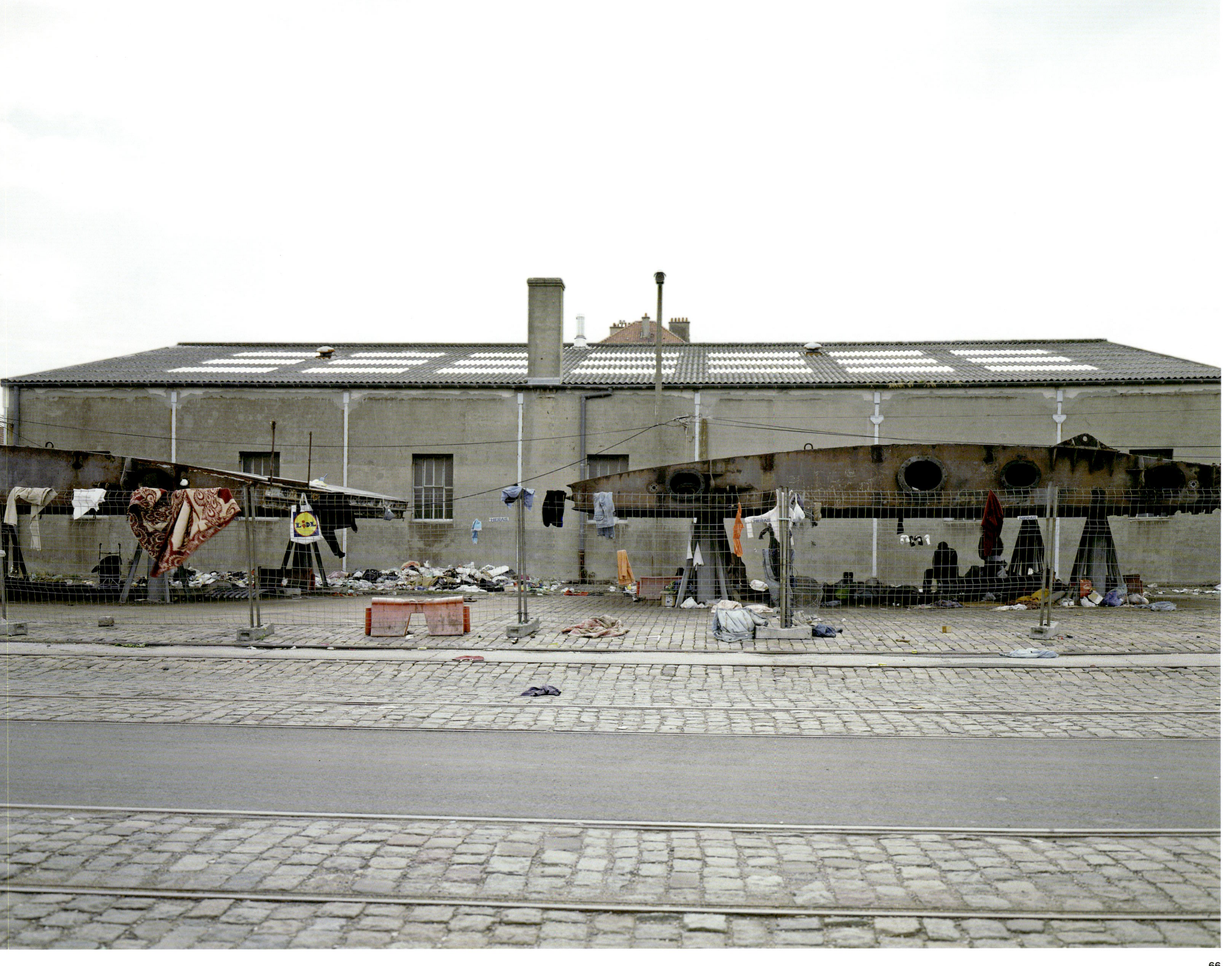
LIDL

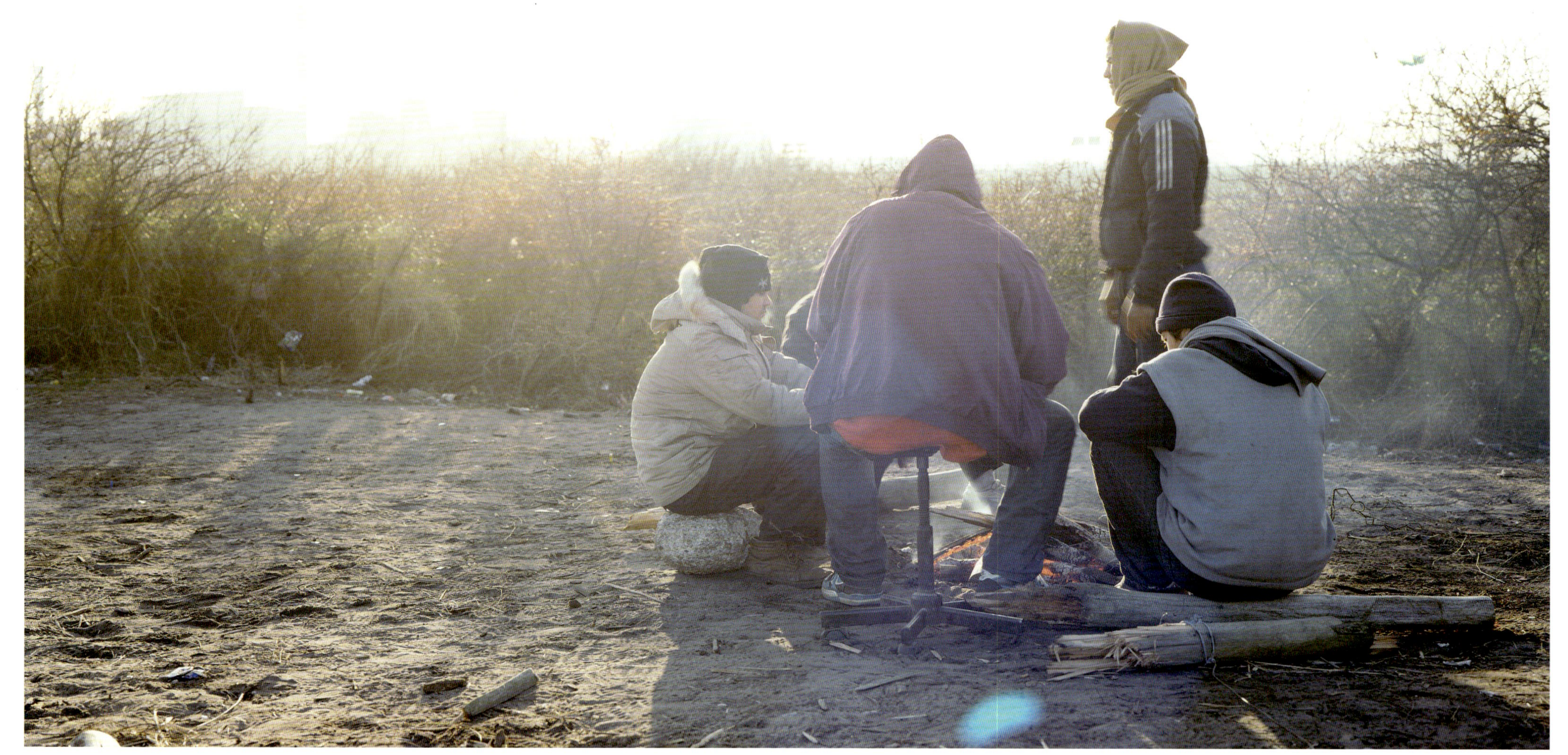

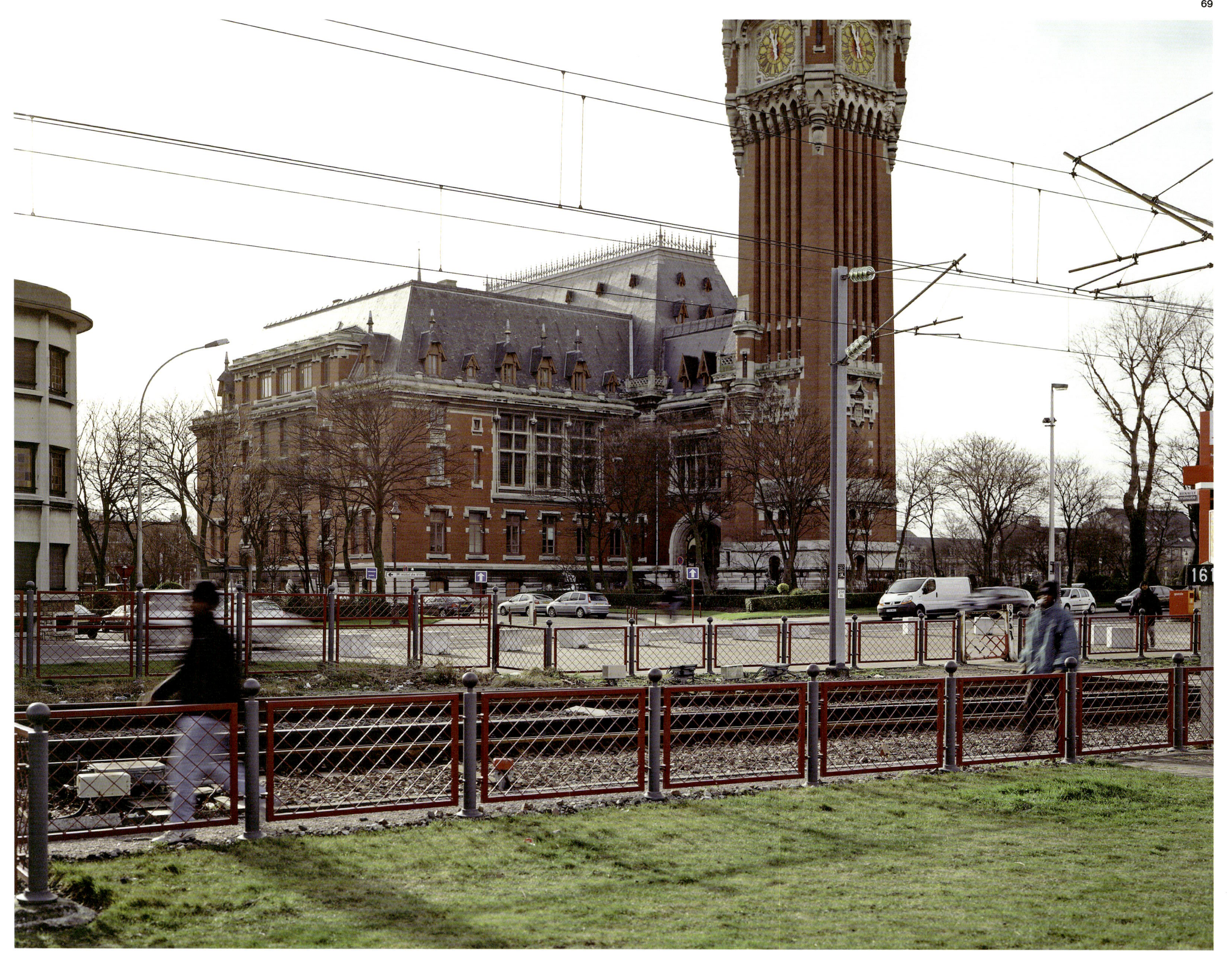

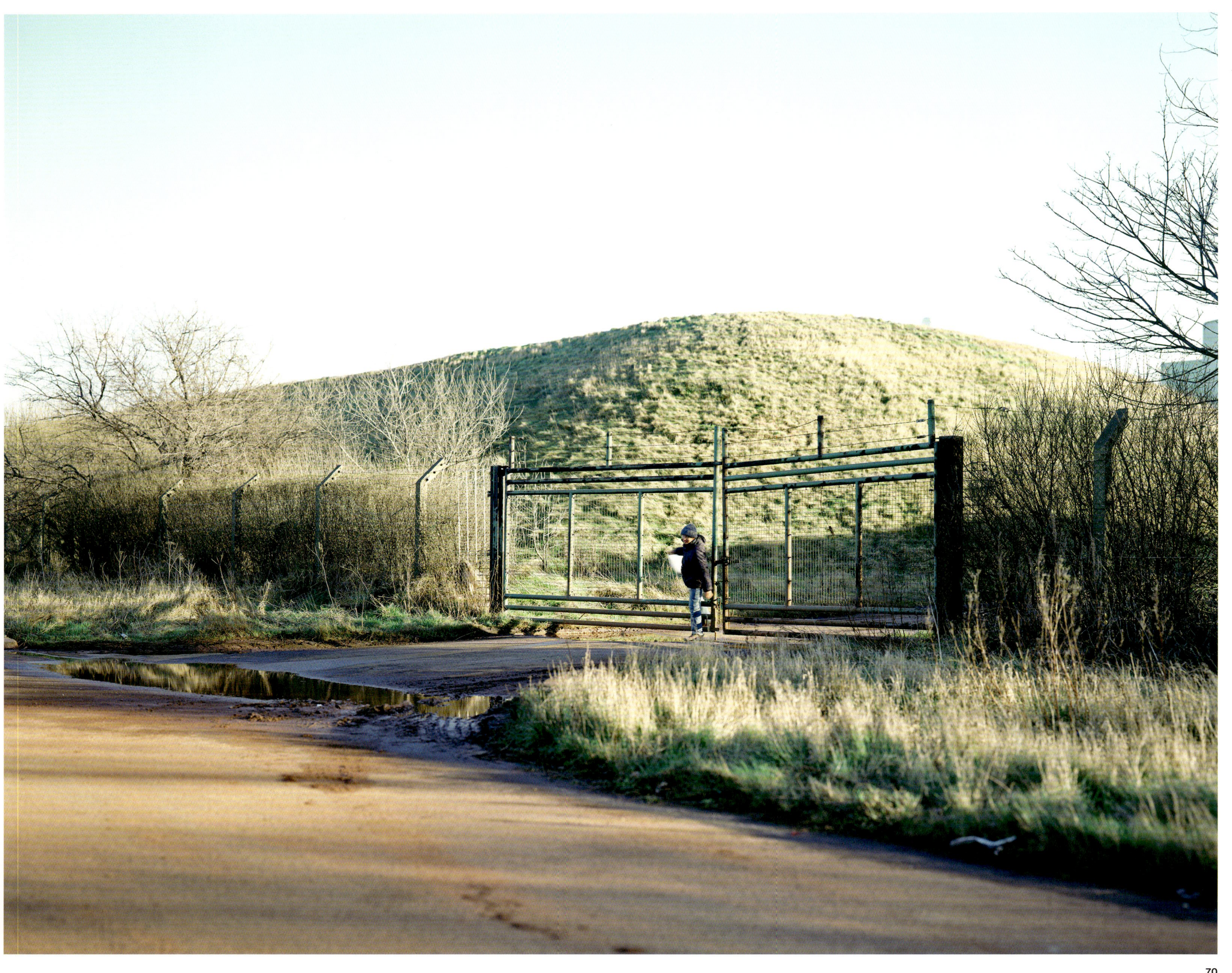

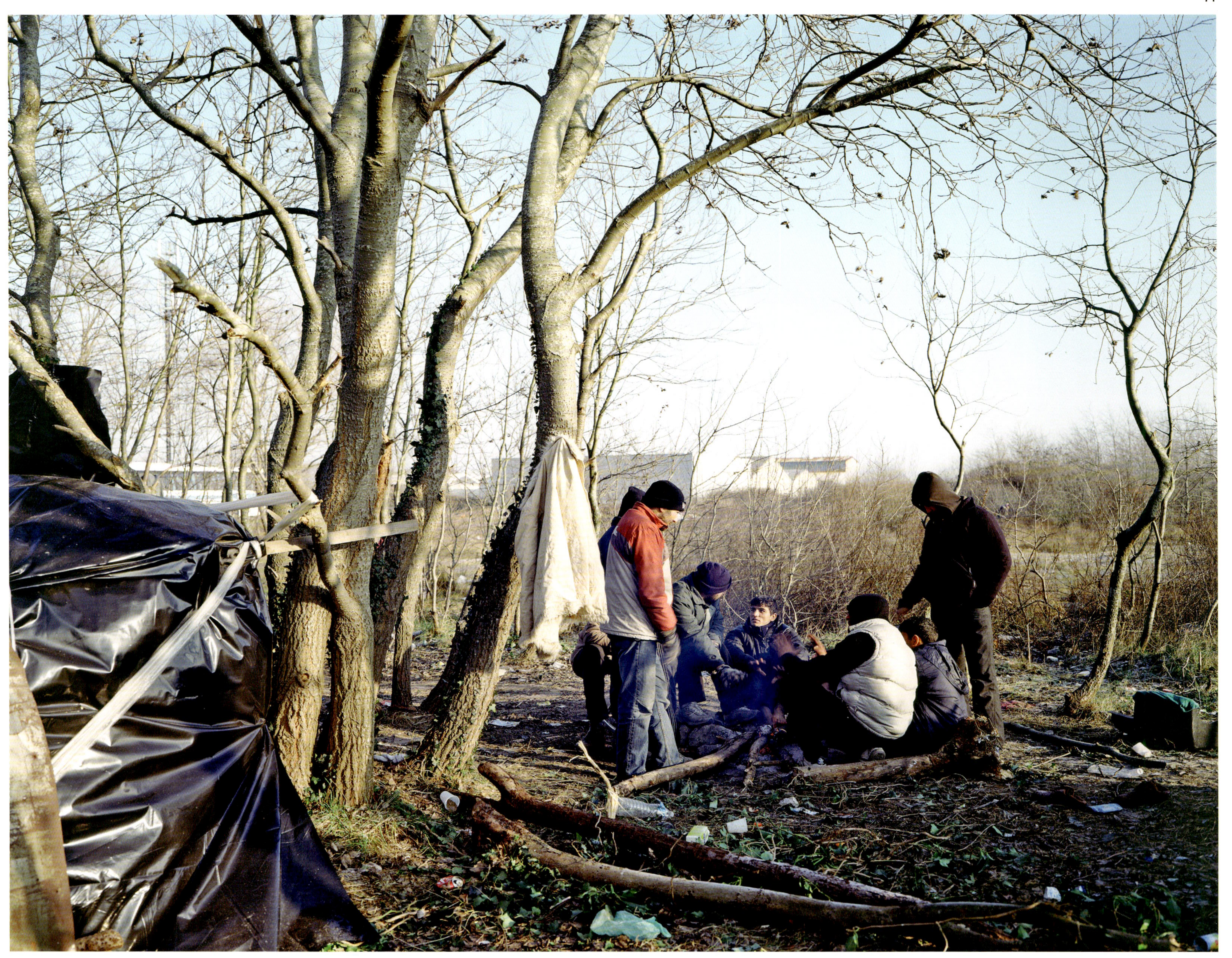

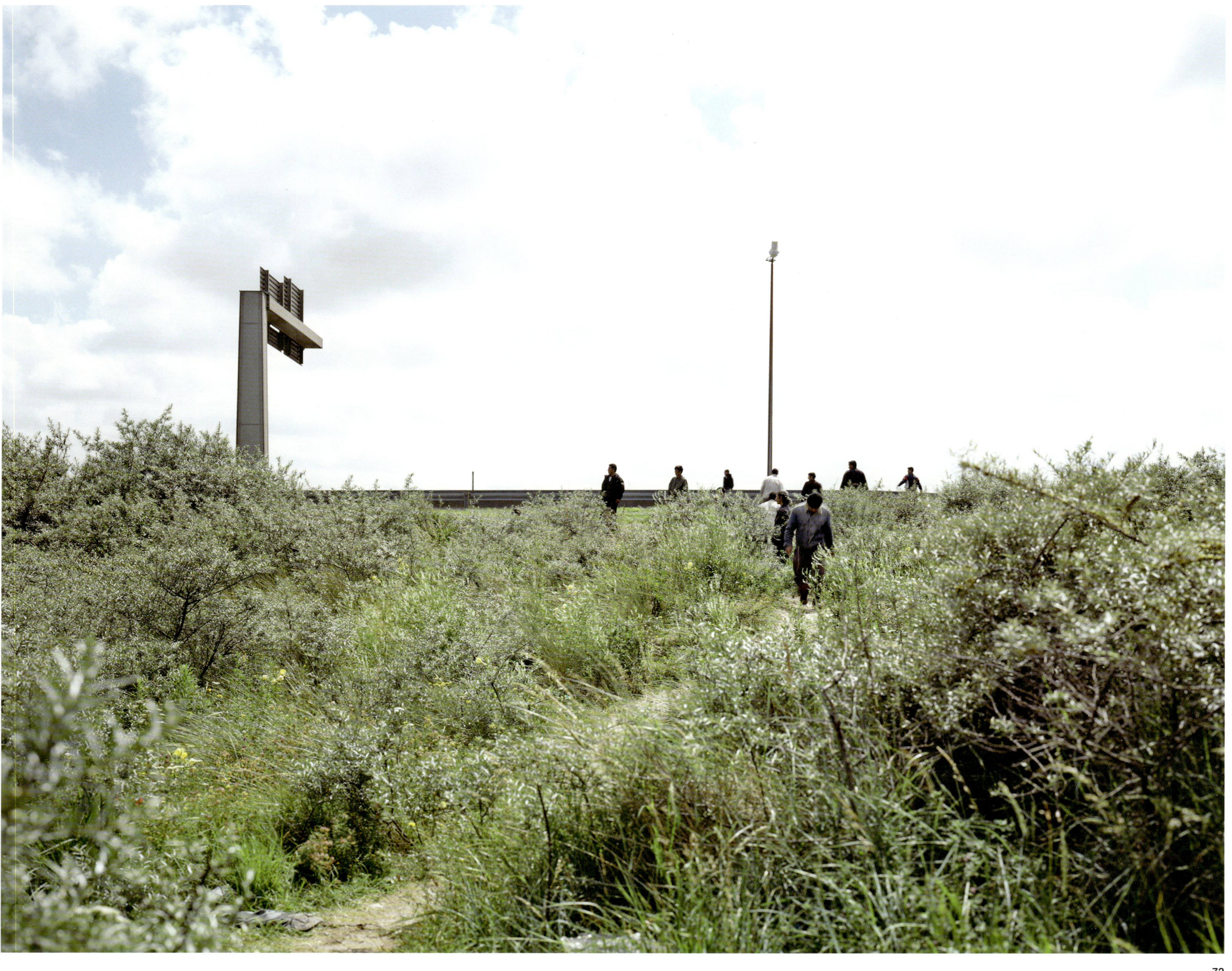

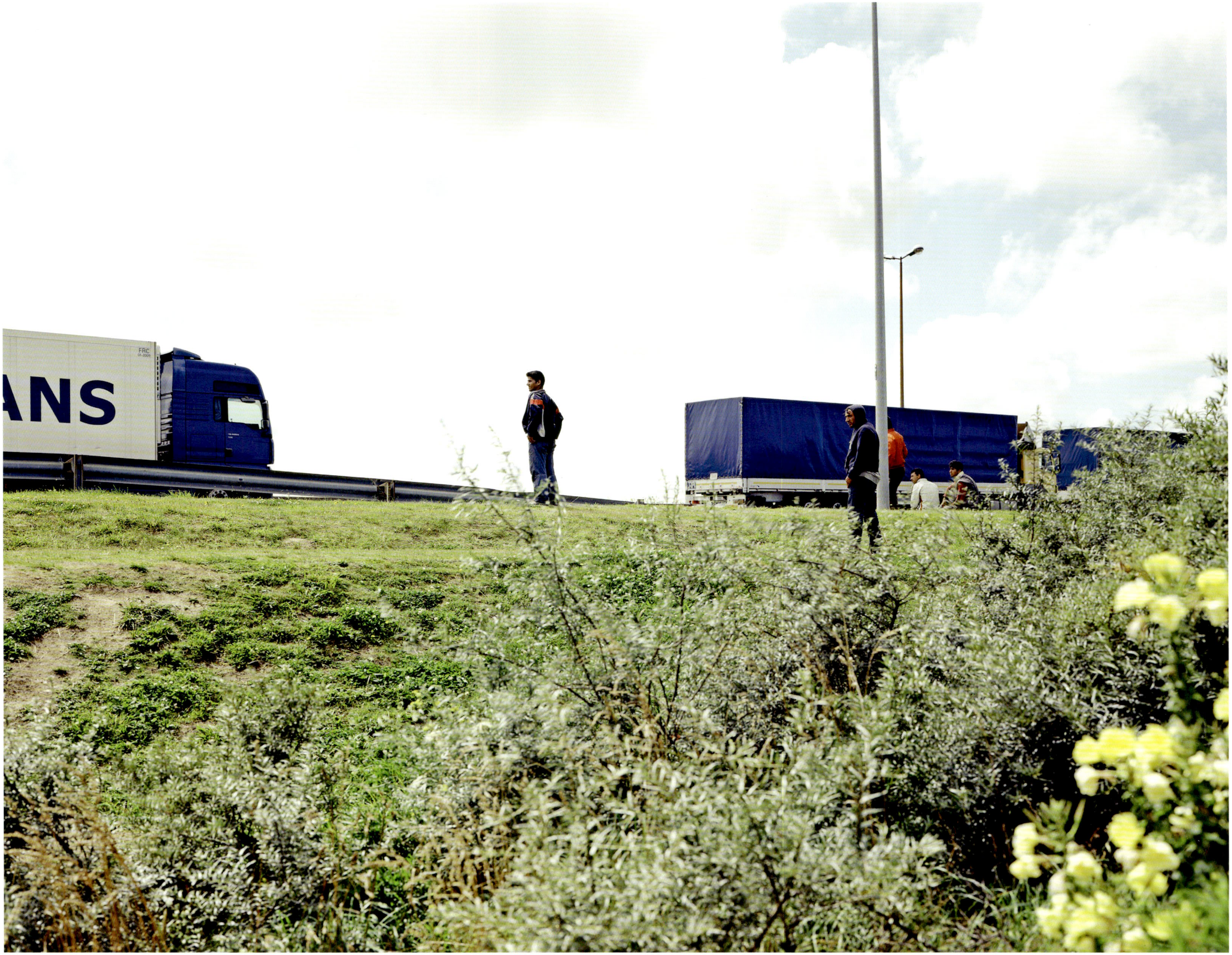

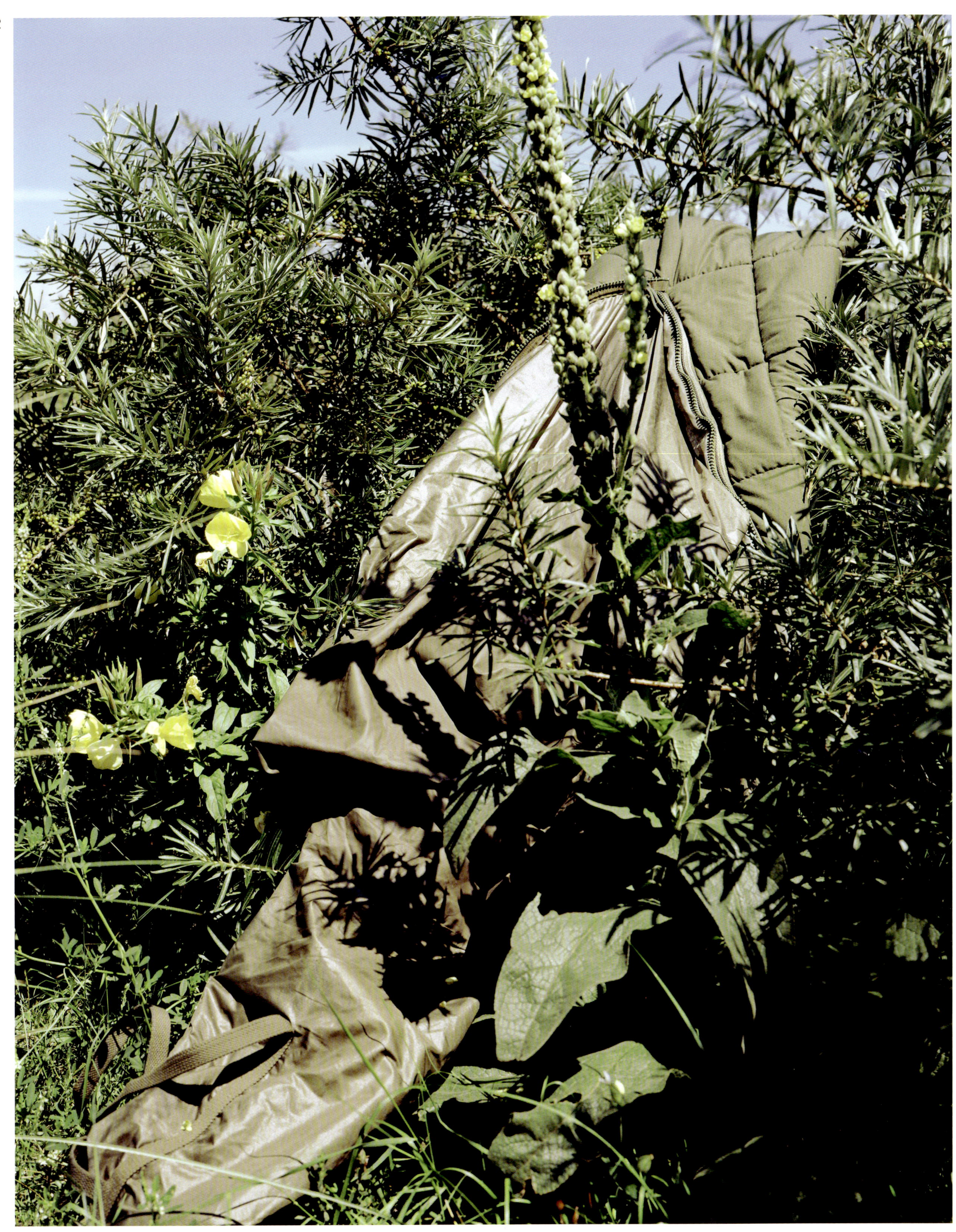

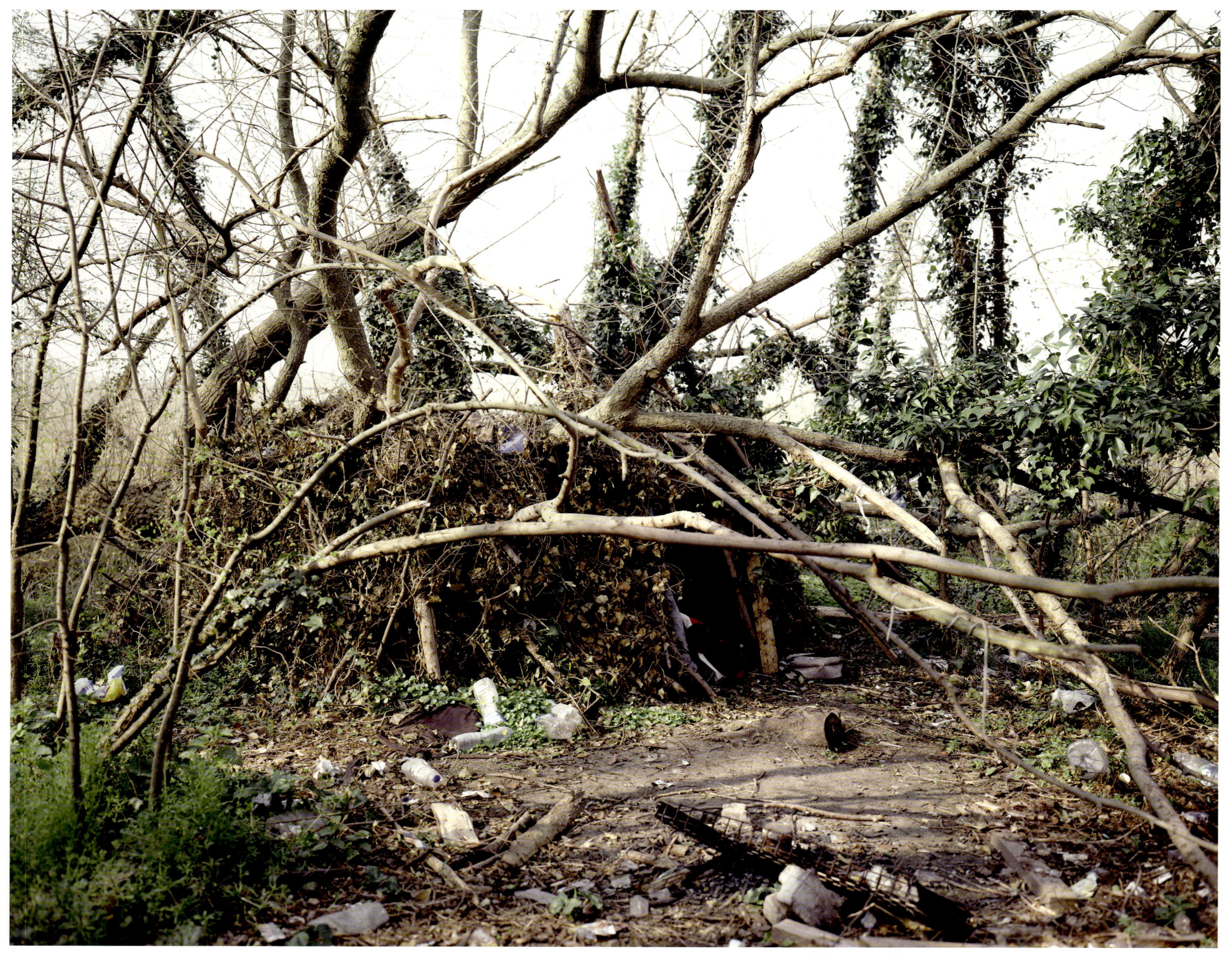

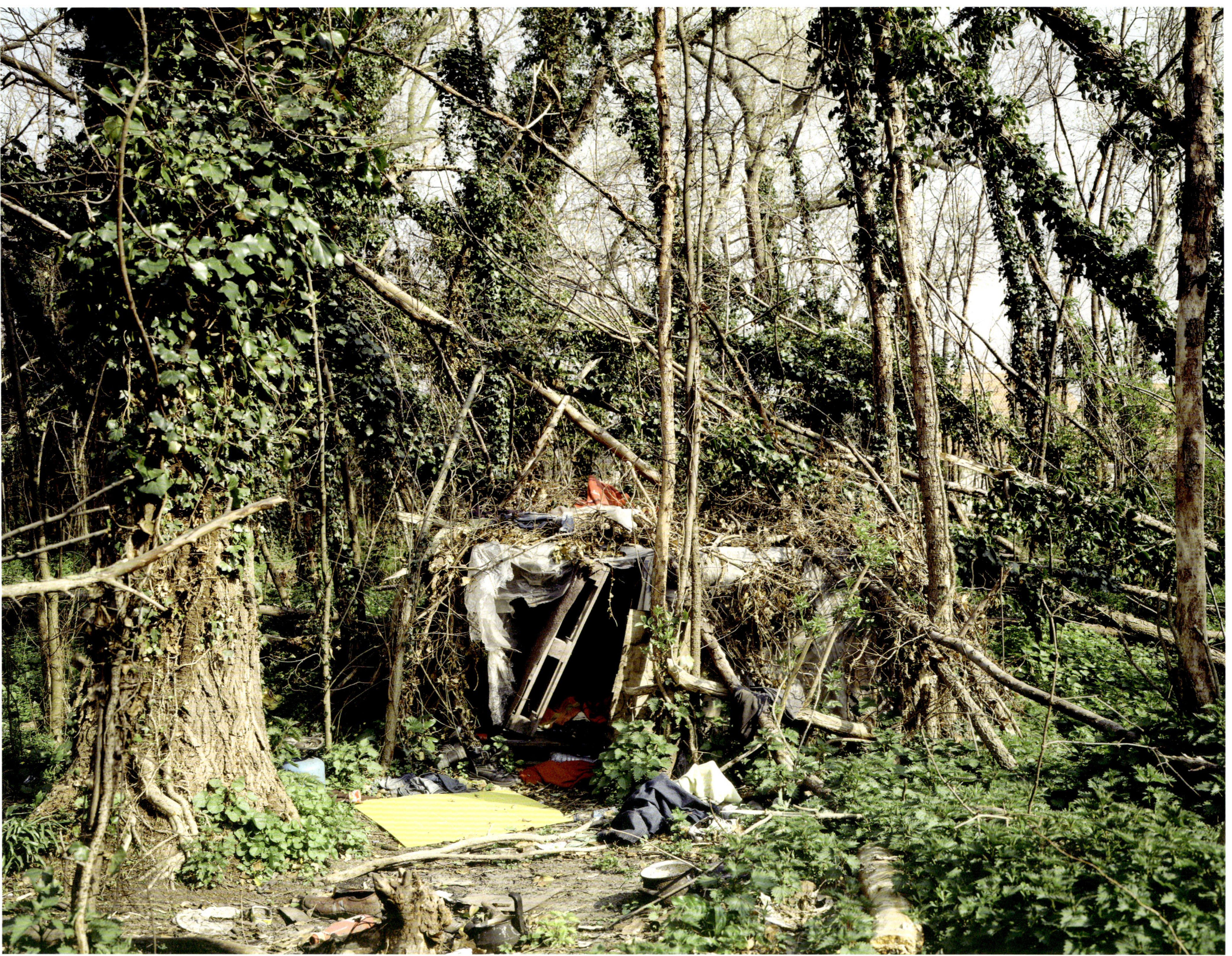

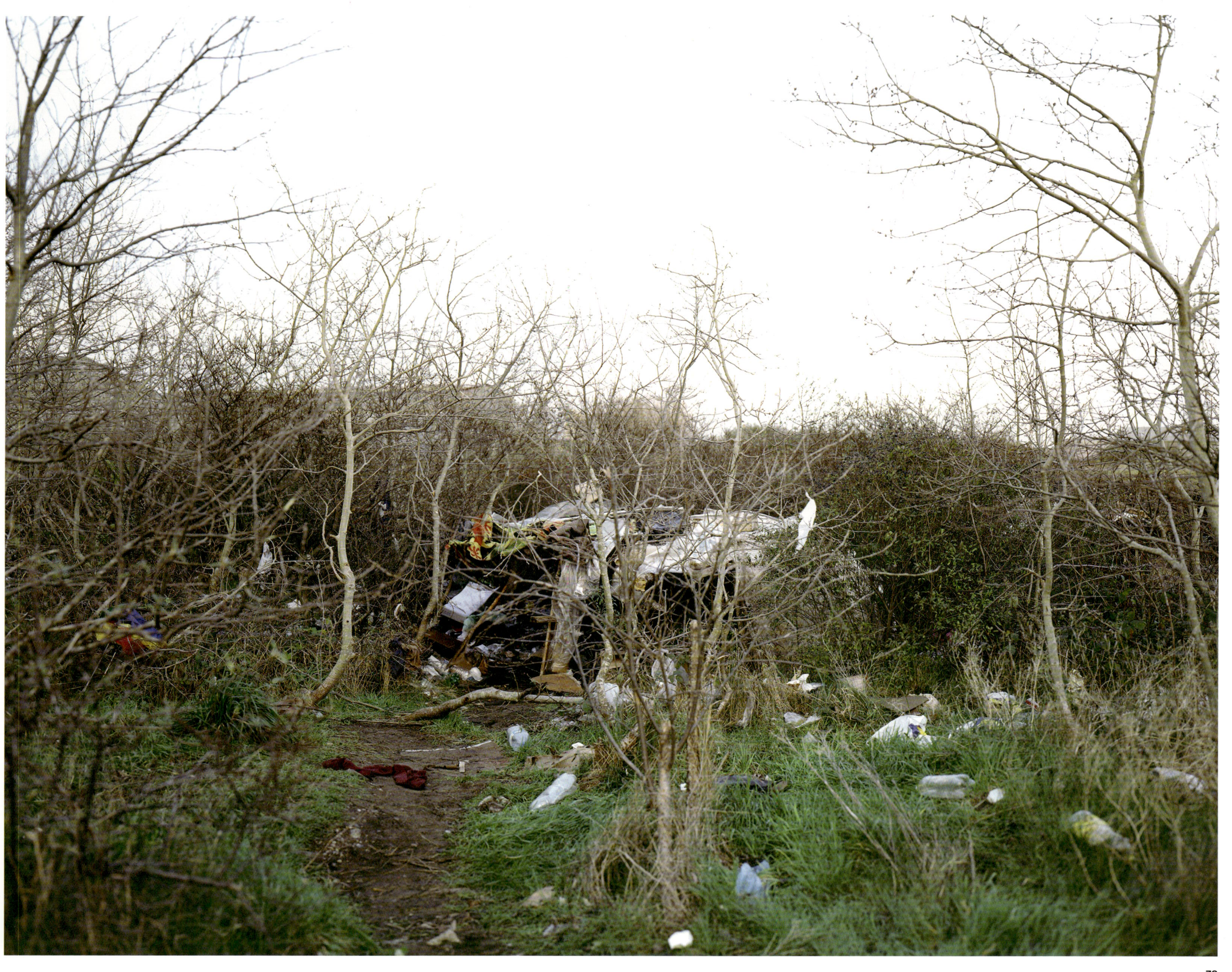

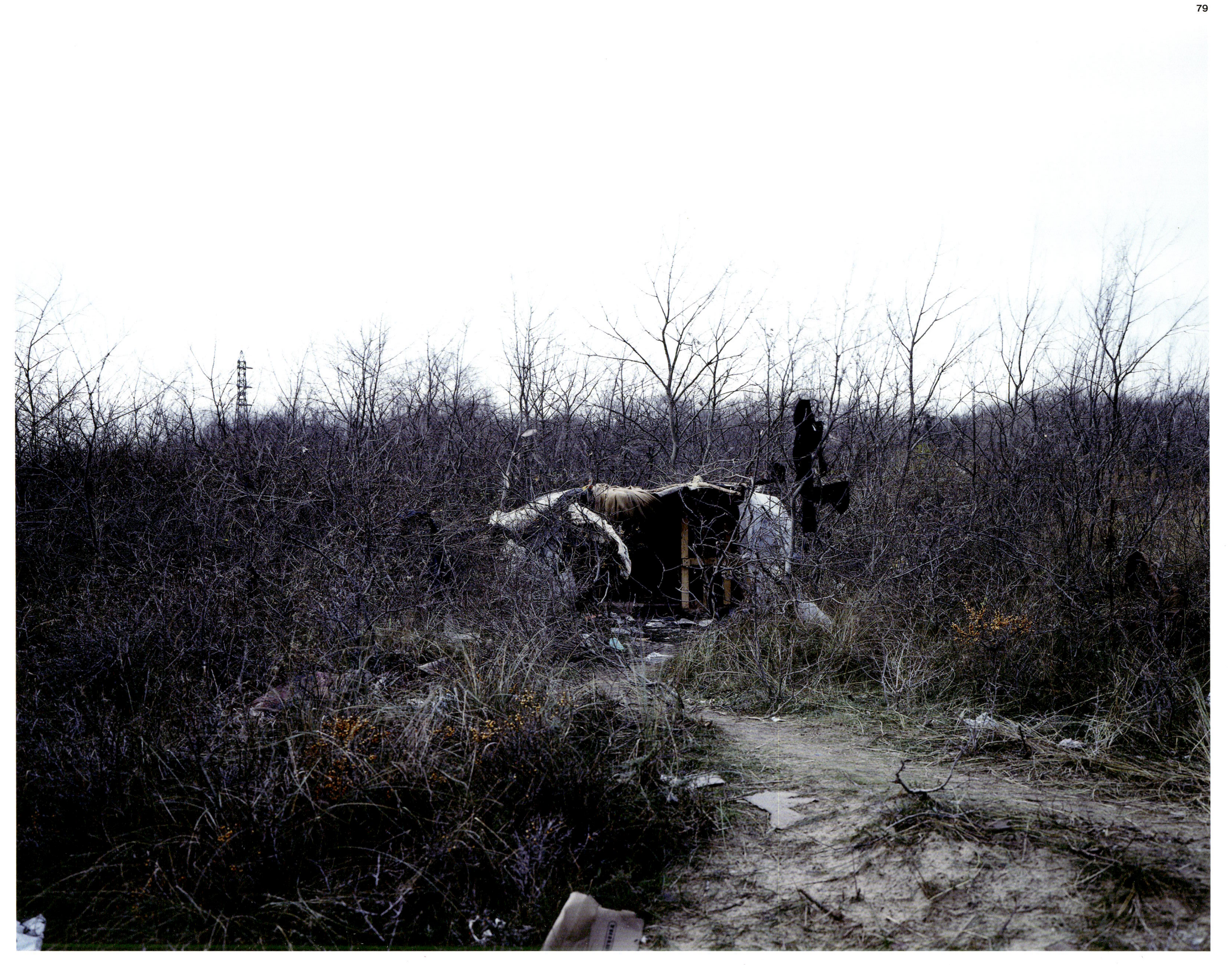

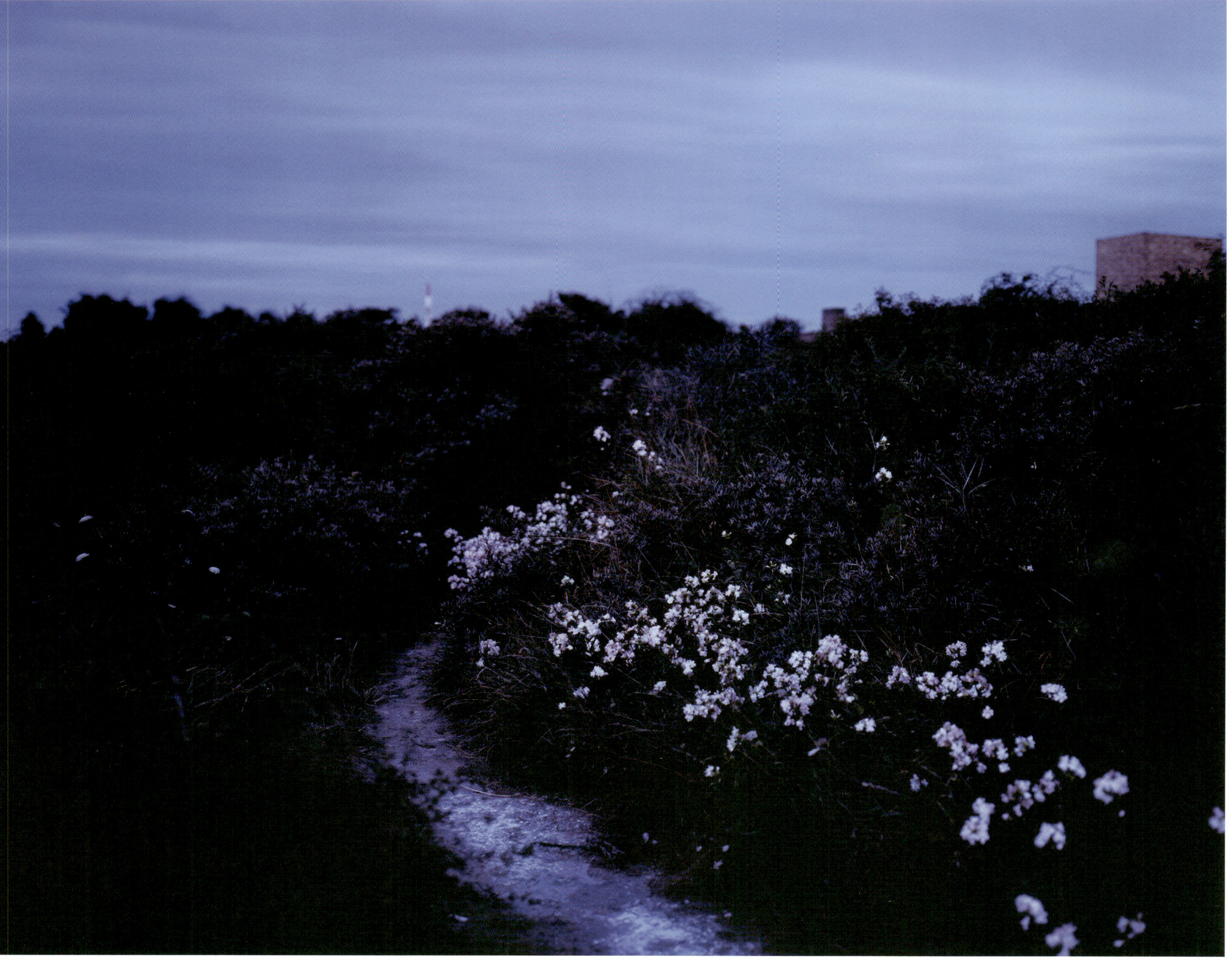

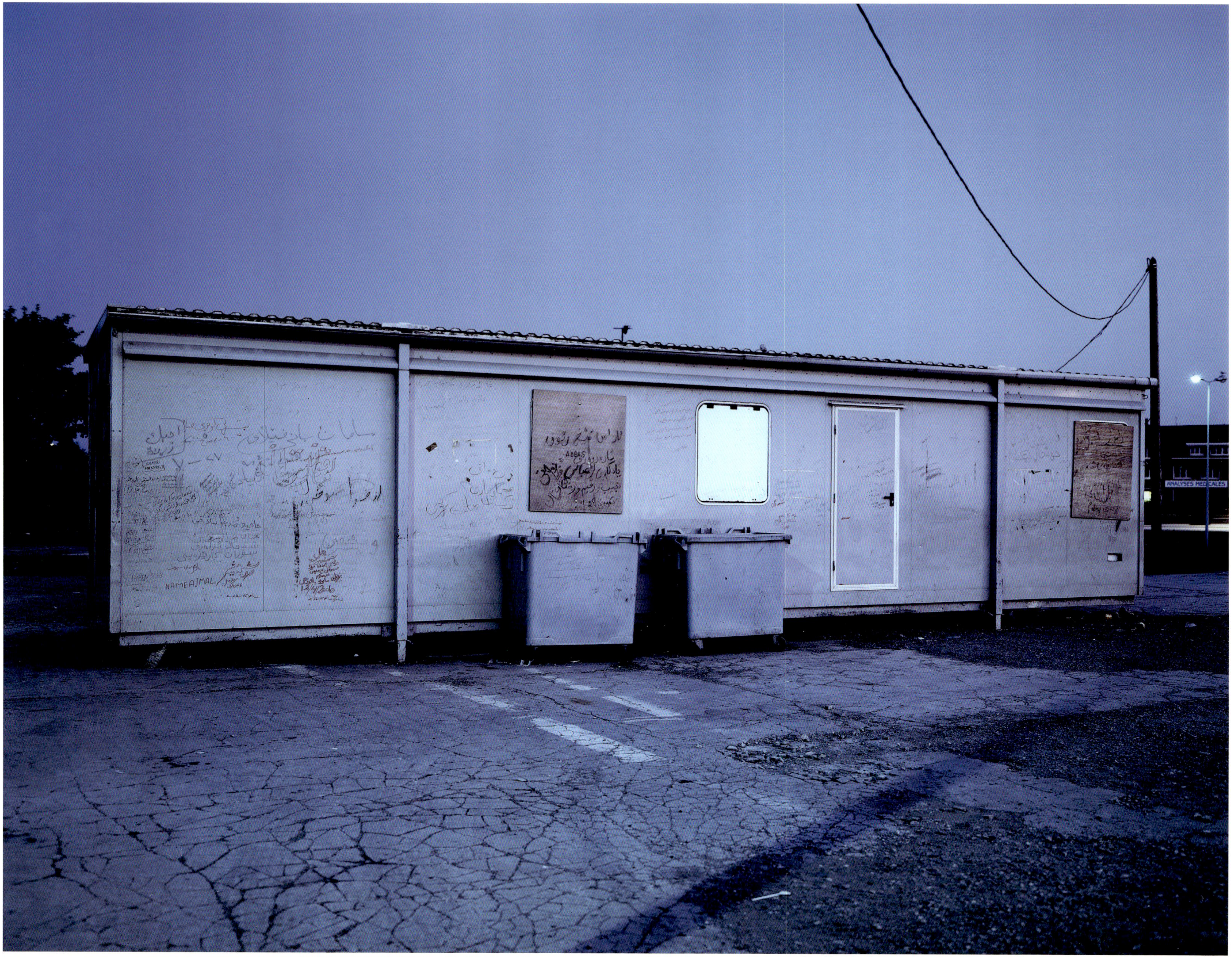
ANALYSES MEDICALES
ABBAS
NAMEAJMAL

Rise Up, Resist, Return (New Delhi & Dharamsala)
2008

In 2008 China hosted the Summer Olympic Games. The Olympic Torch left Greece on March 24, reaching Beijing on July 6. All along the route through Europe, the United States, and Asia, demonstrators took advantage of the important media attention to protest against the violations of human rights and the lack of freedom of speech in China. The Tibetan exiles took this unique opportunity to organize big demonstrations in different countries all over the world. In Lhasa these demonstrations were brutally suppressed by the Chinese army, and hundreds were killed. The Tibetans gave this worldwide operation the name "2008 People's Uprising Movement."

On April 16, 17, and 18, 2008, the Olympic Torch was in New Delhi. Under the slogan "No Torch in Tibet," thousands of Tibetan exiles in India came together in the city to protest against the Olympic Torch crossing Tibet. In a powerful symbolical gesture, the Chinese took the Olympic Torch to the top of Mount Everest.

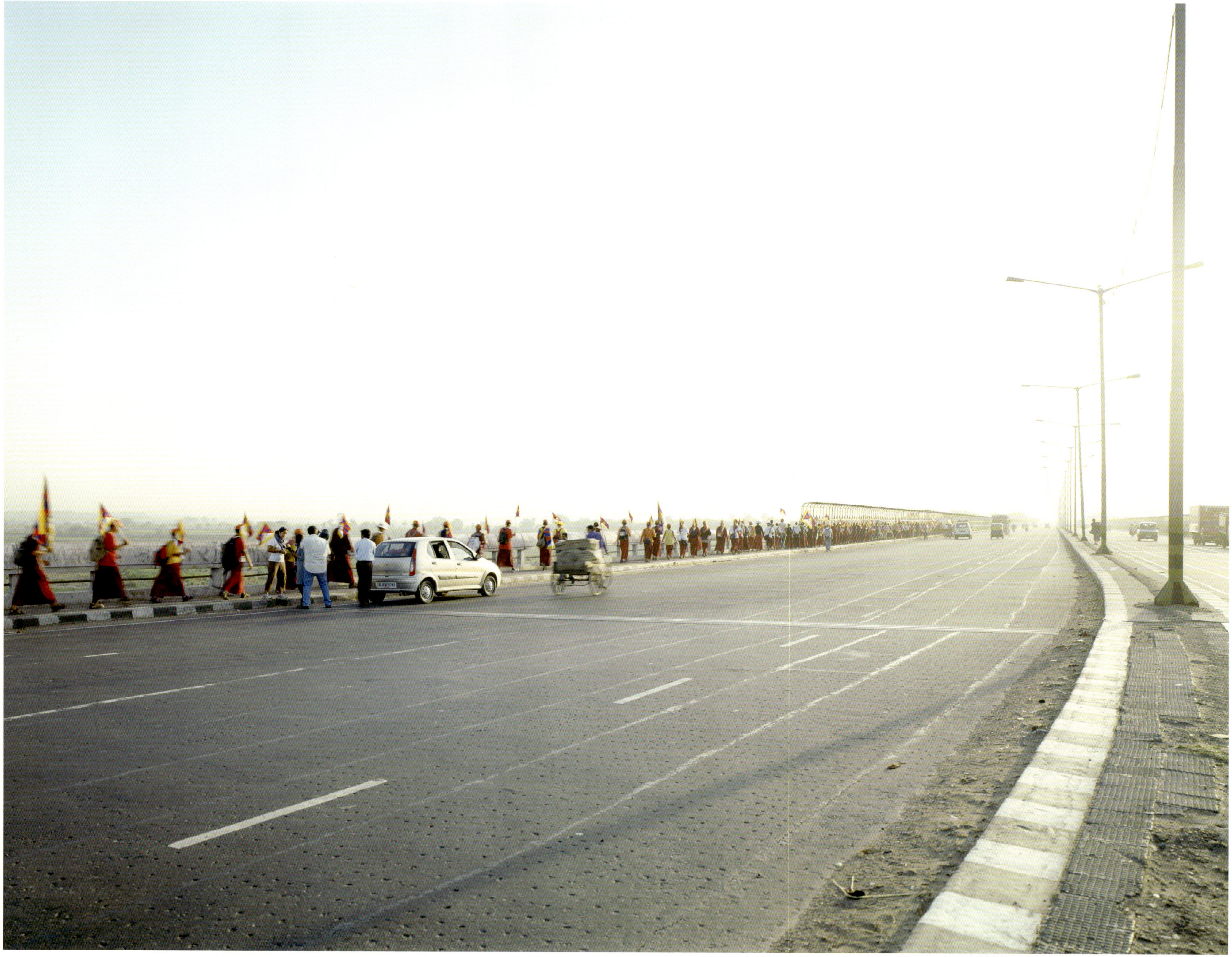

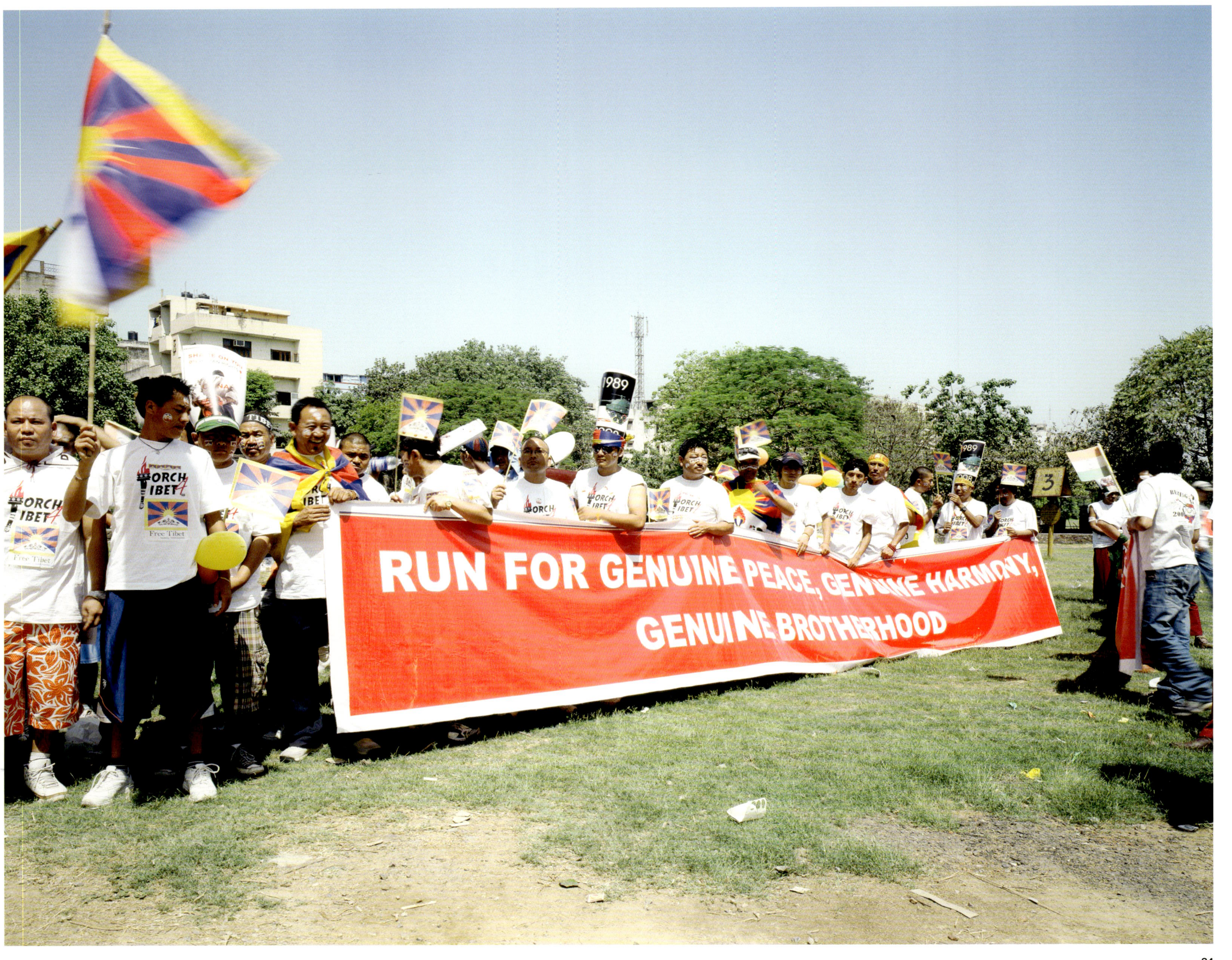
RUN FOR GENUINE PEACE, GENUINE HARMONY,
GENUINE BROTHERHOOD
1989
Free Tibet

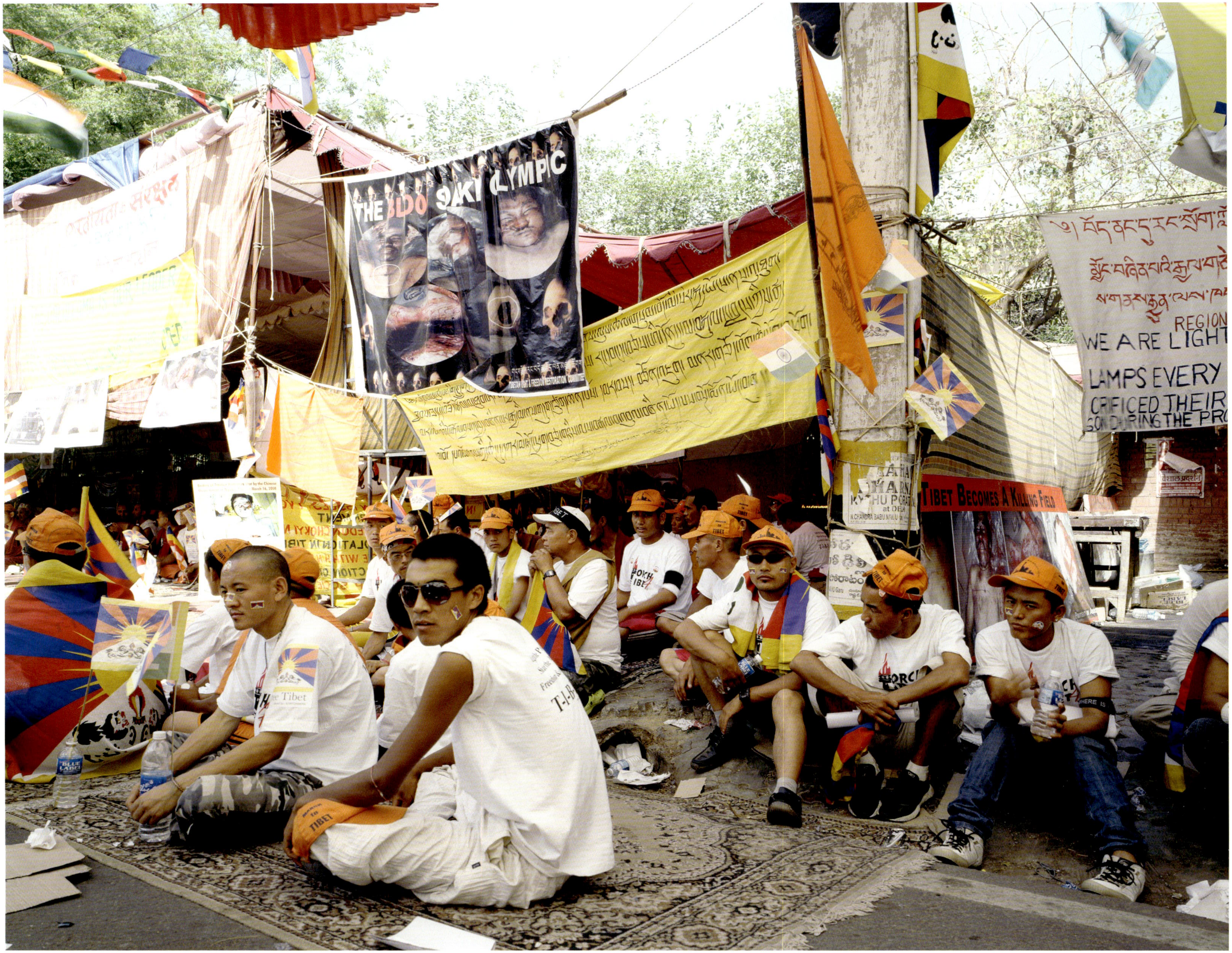
WE ARE LIGHT
LAMPS EVERY
CRIFICED THEIR
TIBET BECOMES A KILLING FIELD

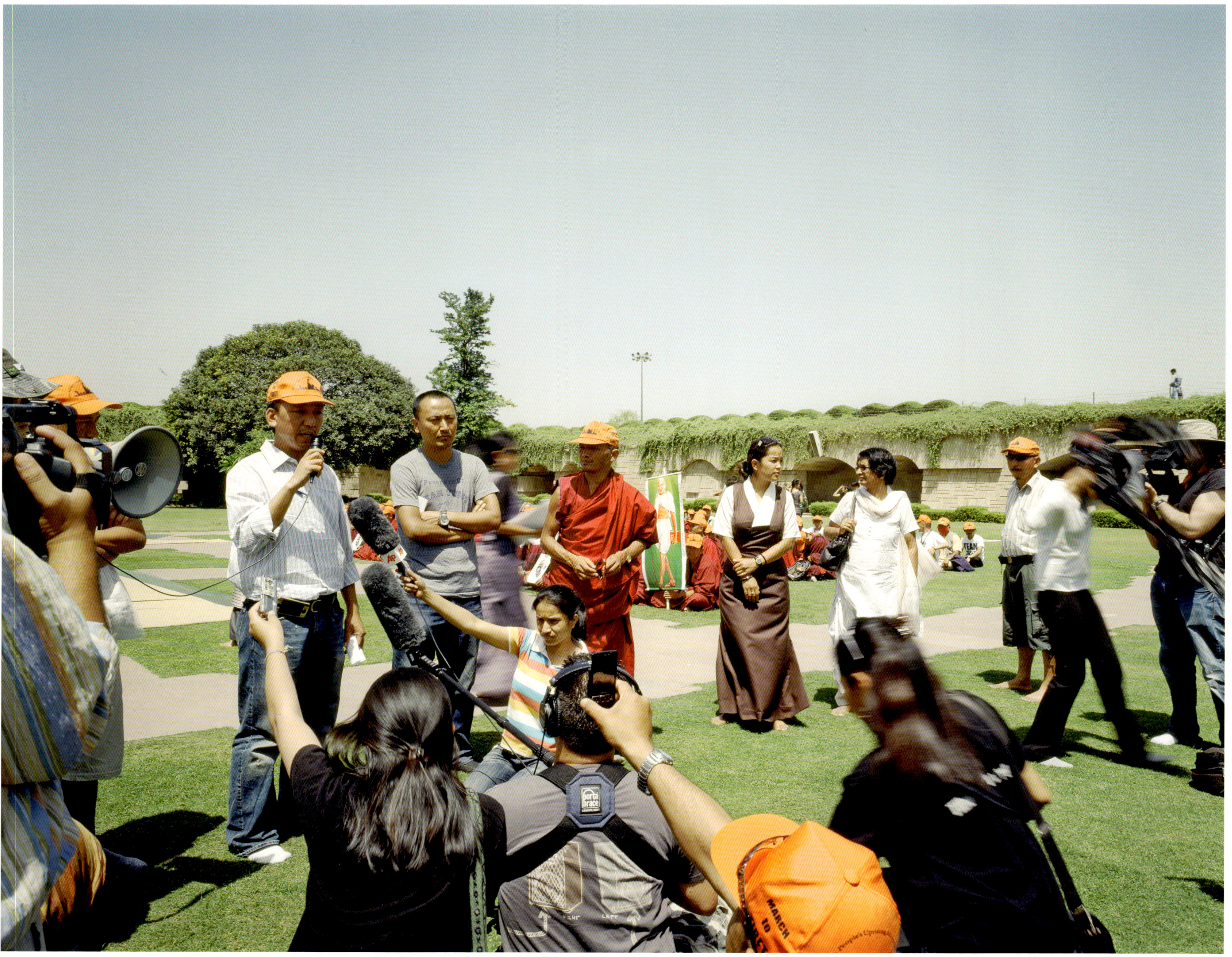
MARCH
to

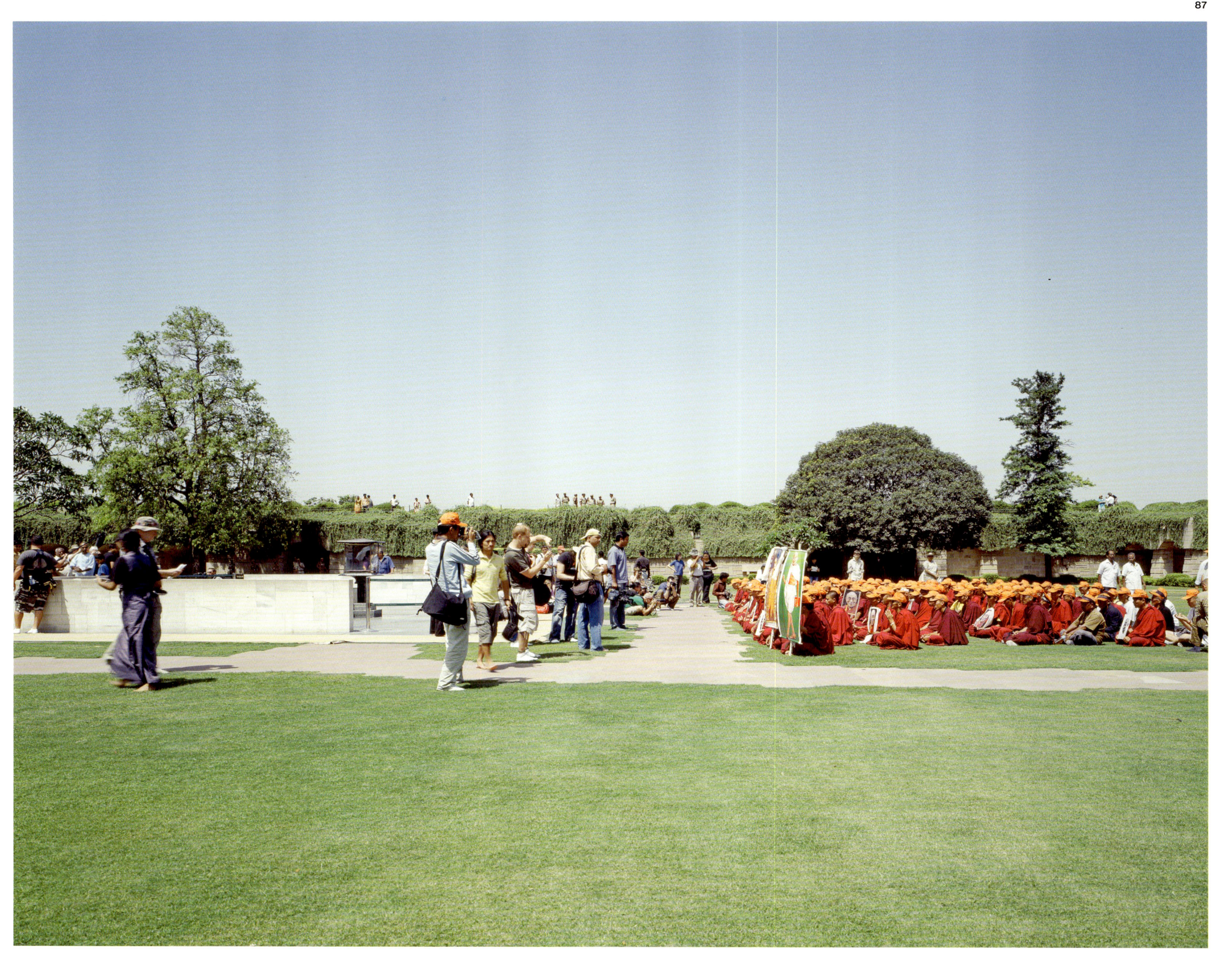

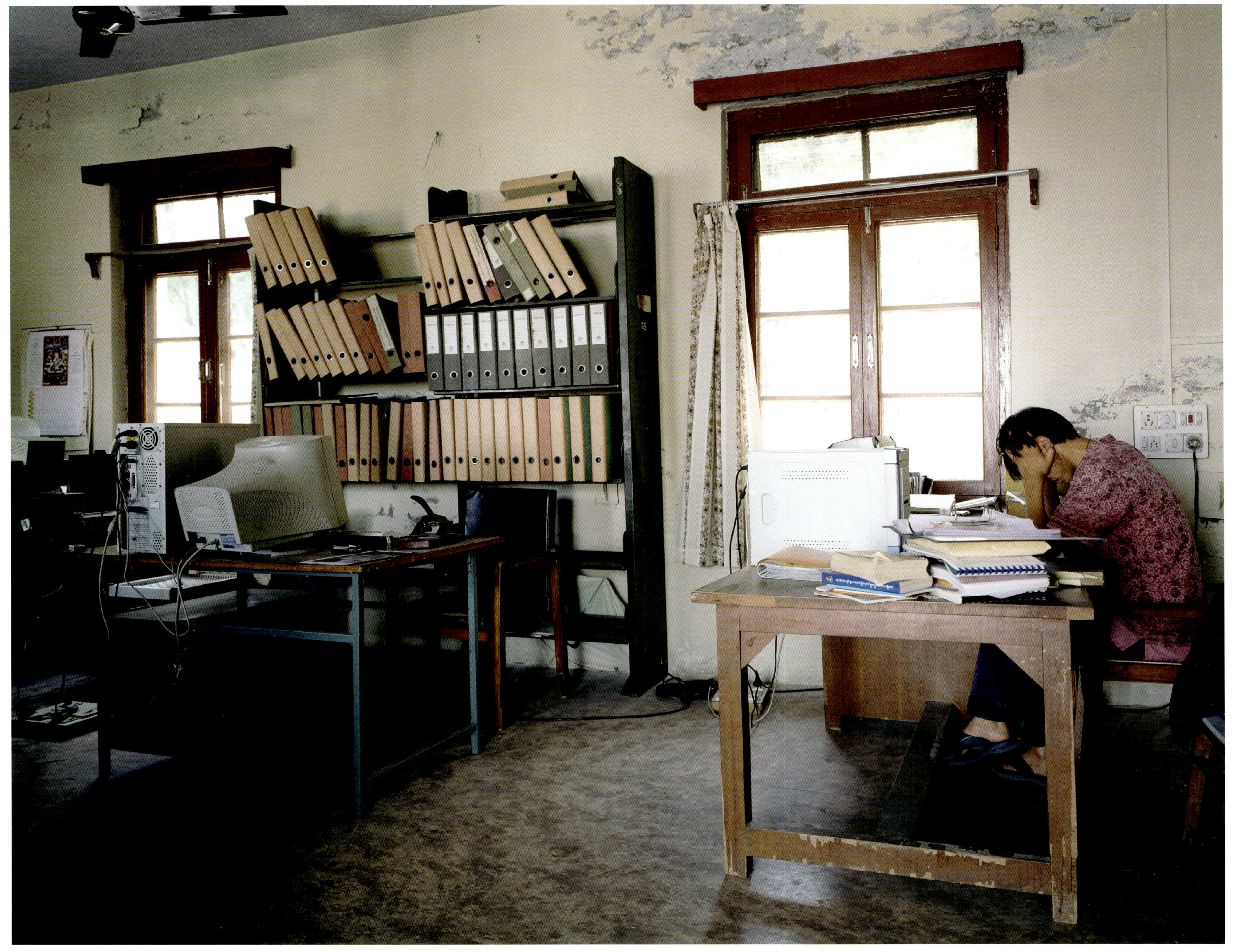

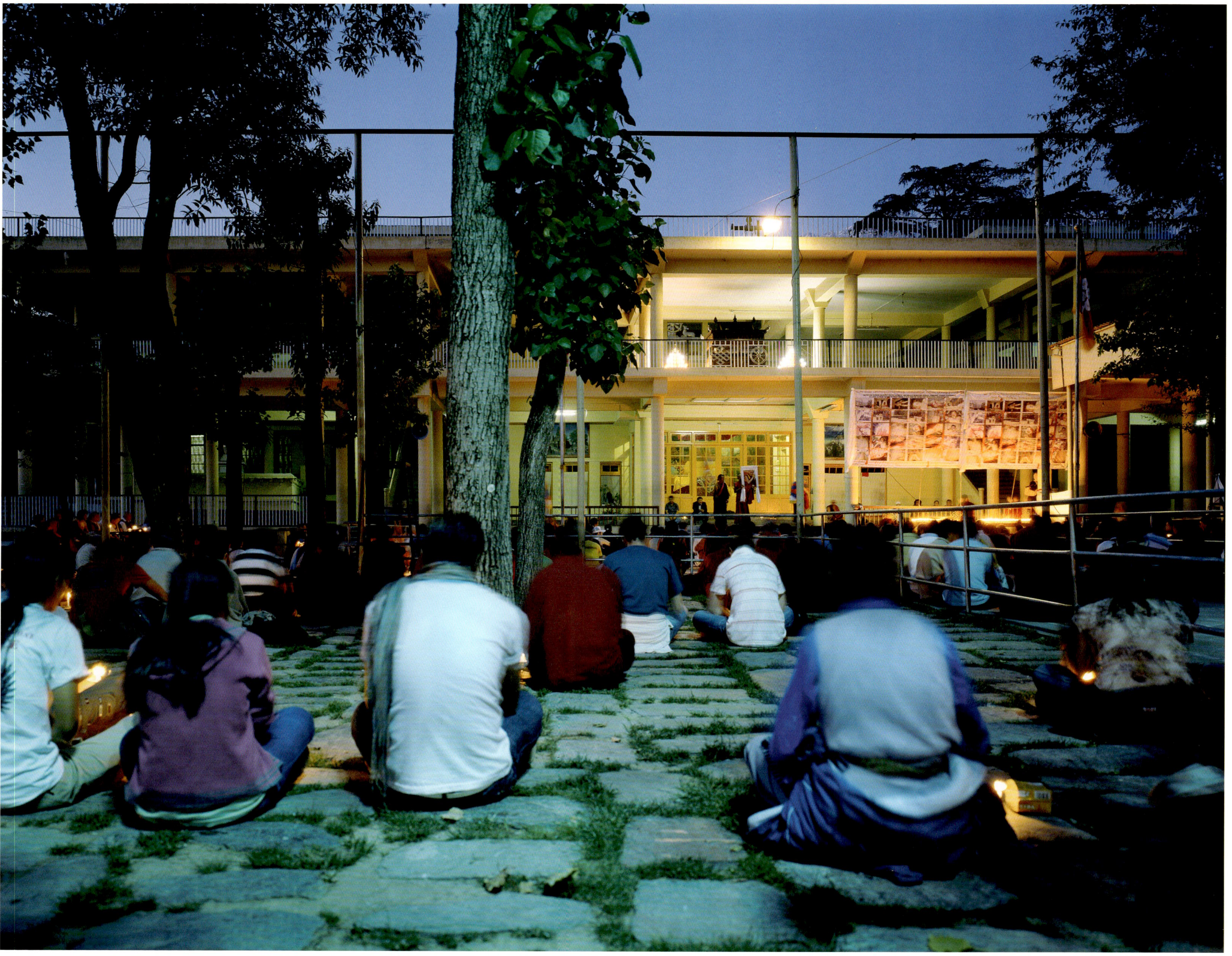

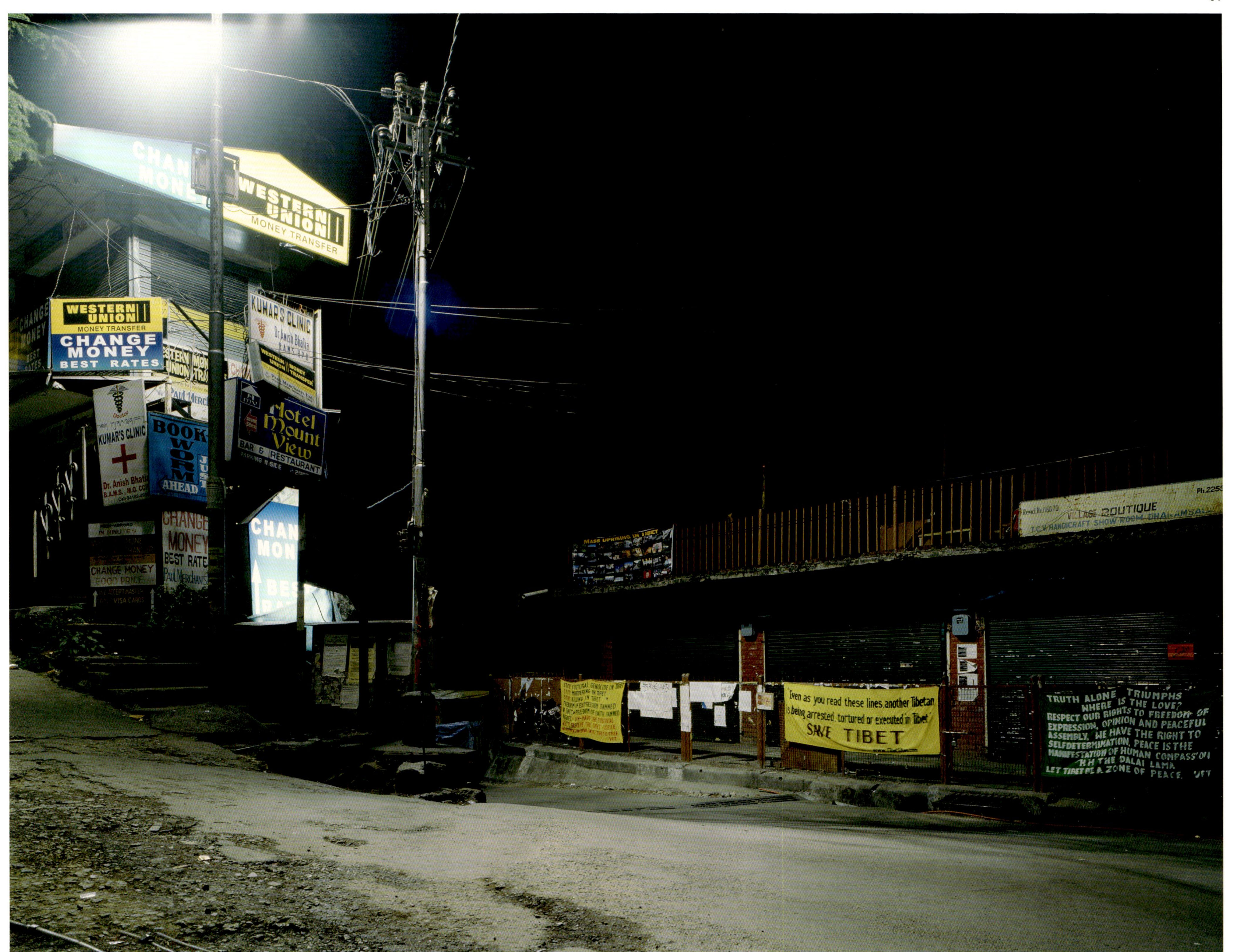
WESTERN UNION
MONEY TRANSFER
WESTERN UNION
MONEY TRANSFER
CHANGE MONEY
BEST RATES
KUMAR'S CLINIC
Dr. Anish Bhatia
B.A.M.S., M.O.C.
Hotel Mount View
BAR & RESTAURANT
PARKING INSIDE
BOOK WORM
AHEAD
KUMAR'S CLINIC
Doctor
CHANGE MONEY
BEST RATES
Paul Merchants
CHANGE MONEY
FOOD PRICE
MASS UPRISING IN TIBET
VILLAGE BOUTIQUE
T.C.V. HANDICRAFT SHOW ROOM
Even as you read these lines another Tibetan is being arrested, tortured or executed in Tibet
SAVE TIBET
TRUTH ALONE TRIUMPHS
WHERE IS THE LOVE?
RESPECT OUR RIGHTS TO FREEDOM OF EXPRESSION, OPINION AND PEACEFUL ASSEMBLY. WE HAVE THE RIGHT TO SELFDETERMINATION. PEACE IS THE MANIFESTATION OF HUMAN COMPASSION
H.H THE DALAI LAMA
LET TIBET BE A ZONE OF PEACE.

Tibet in Exile (Dharamsala)
2008

The series "Tibet in Exile (Dharamsala)" from September 2008 takes as its starting point the opening of the sixth session of the 14th assembly of the Tibetan deputies in exile. Meeting twice a year since 1960, the 43 deputies who are elected for five years are the representatives of the Tibetan communities in exile around the world. But beyond their function as a bond between the various communities in exile, the deputies maintain and develop exchanges with the parliaments of other countries (English deputies attended the opening of the sixth session). By adopting a democratic political system, the Dalai Lama has allowed Tibet not to only exist in the past, in the books and in the memory of the exiles, but in the present and in the future of internationally recognized institutions.

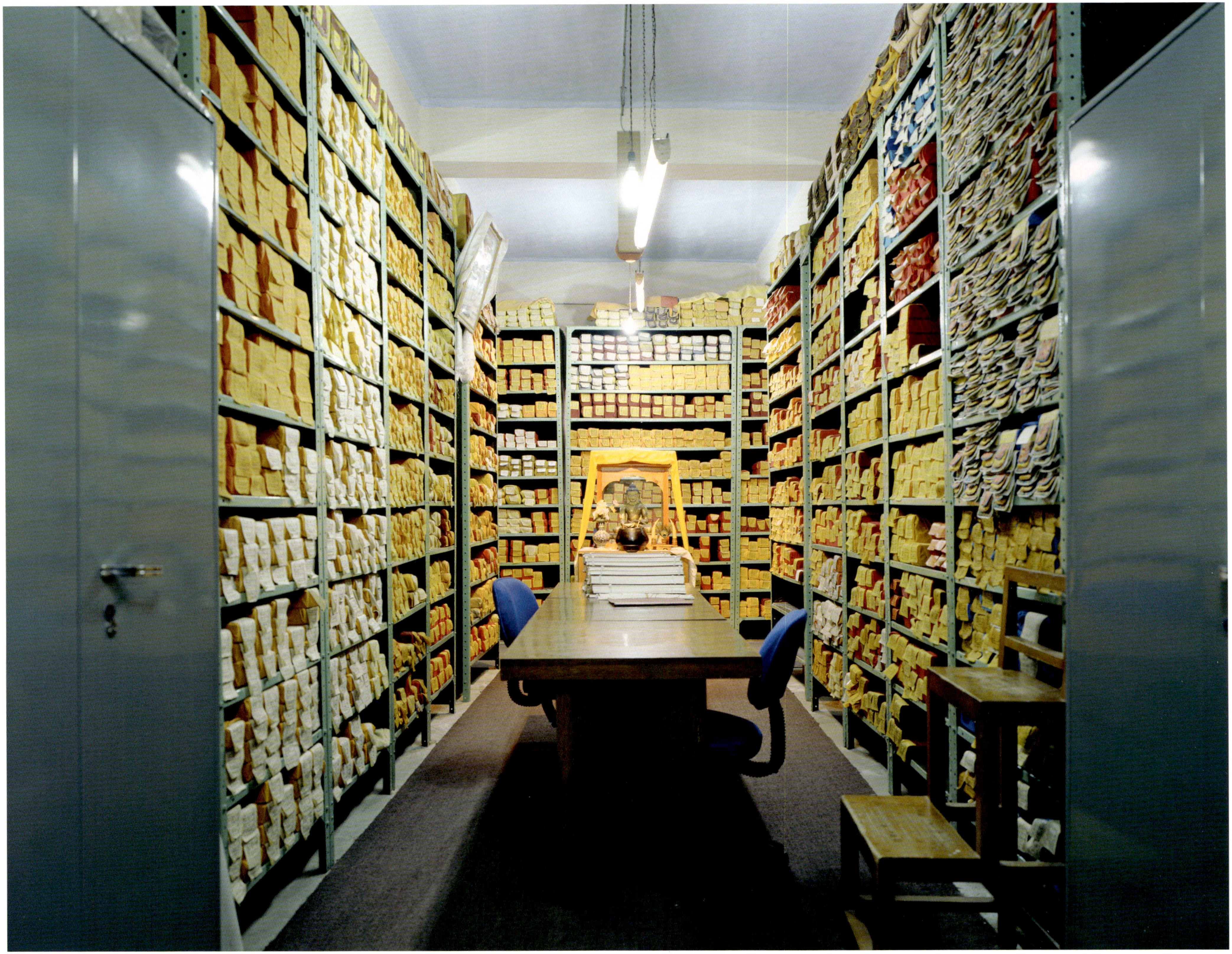

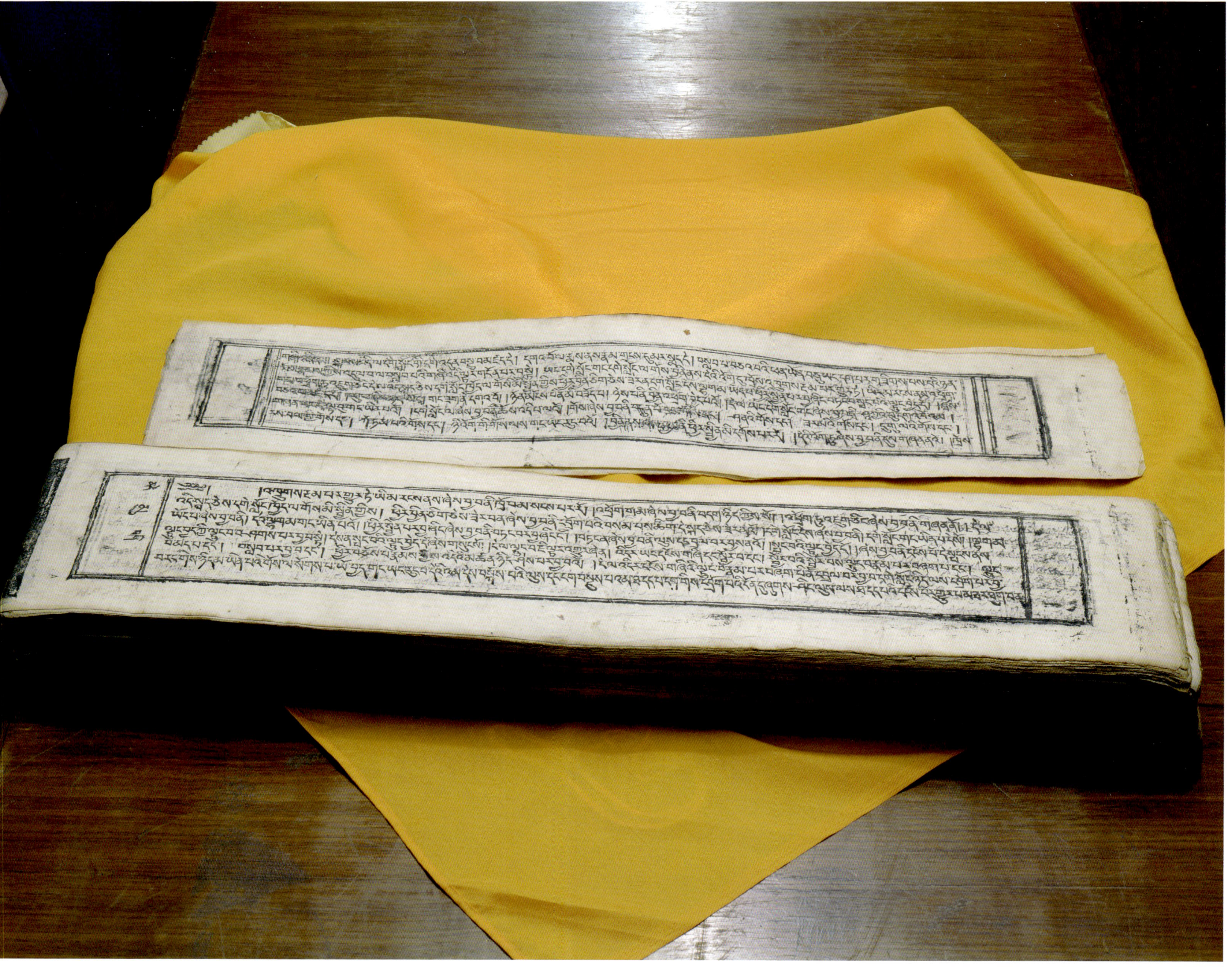

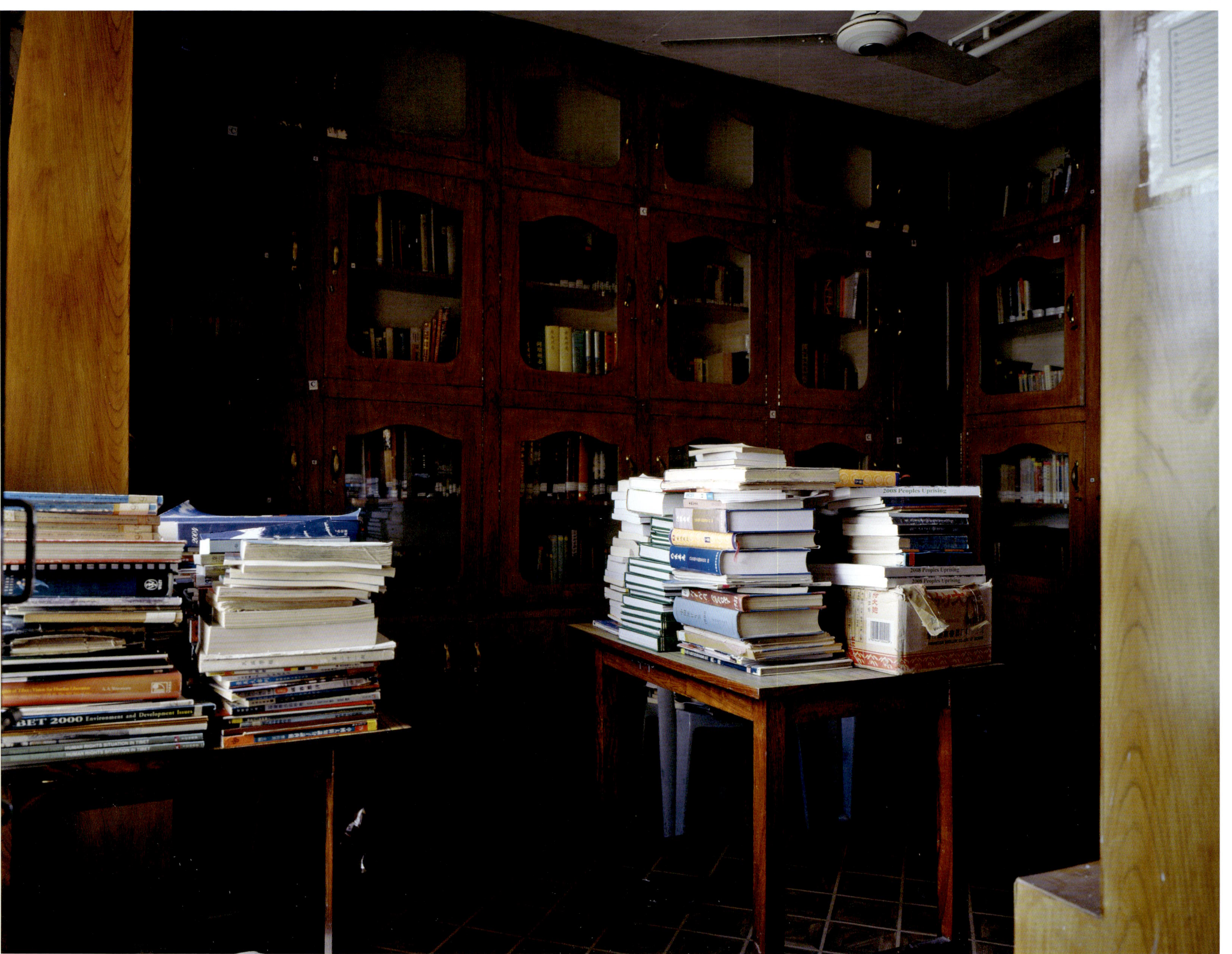
2004
BET 2000 Environment and Development Issues
2008 Peoples Uprising
2008 Peoples Uprising
2008 Peoples Uprising

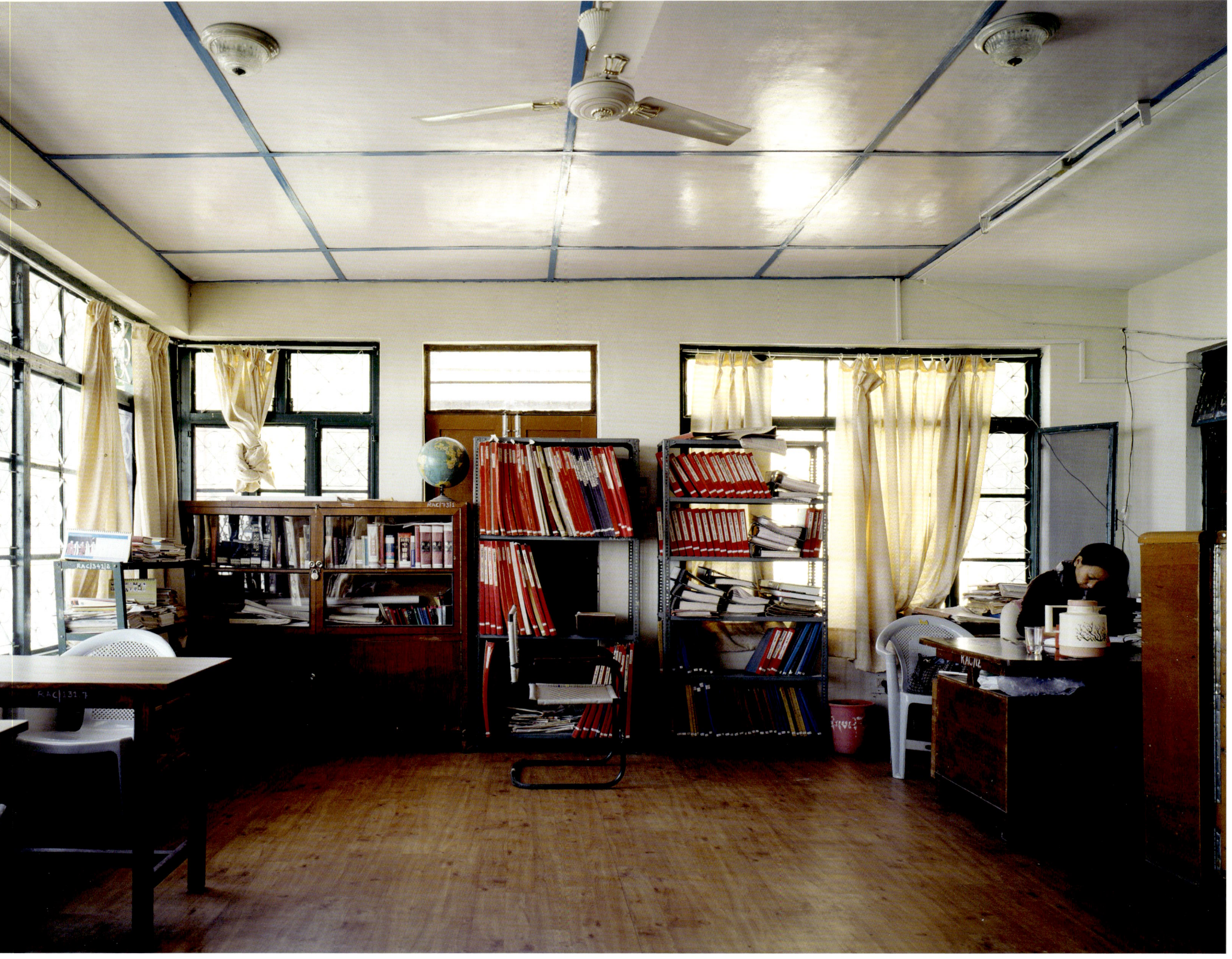

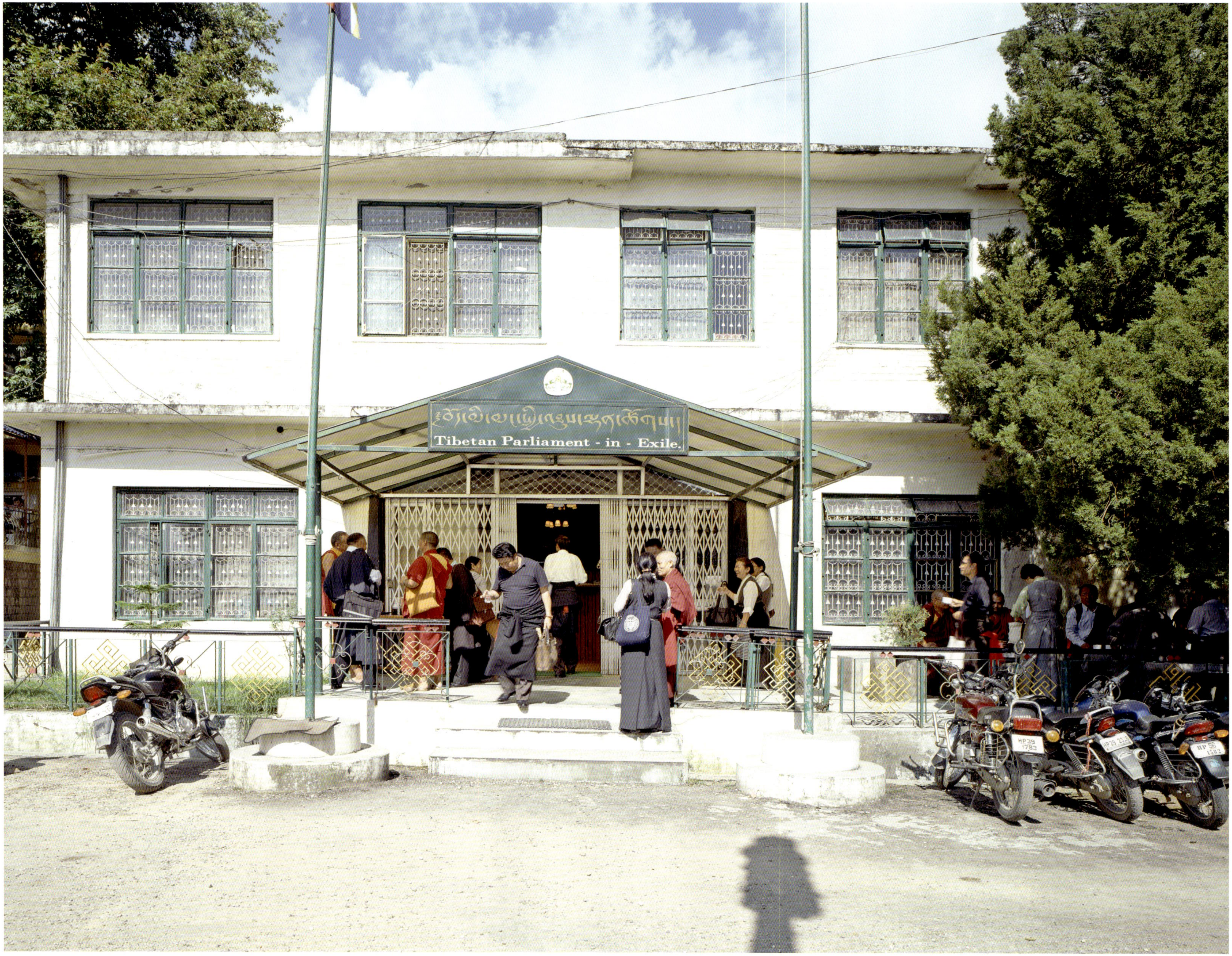
Tibetan Parliament - in - Exile.

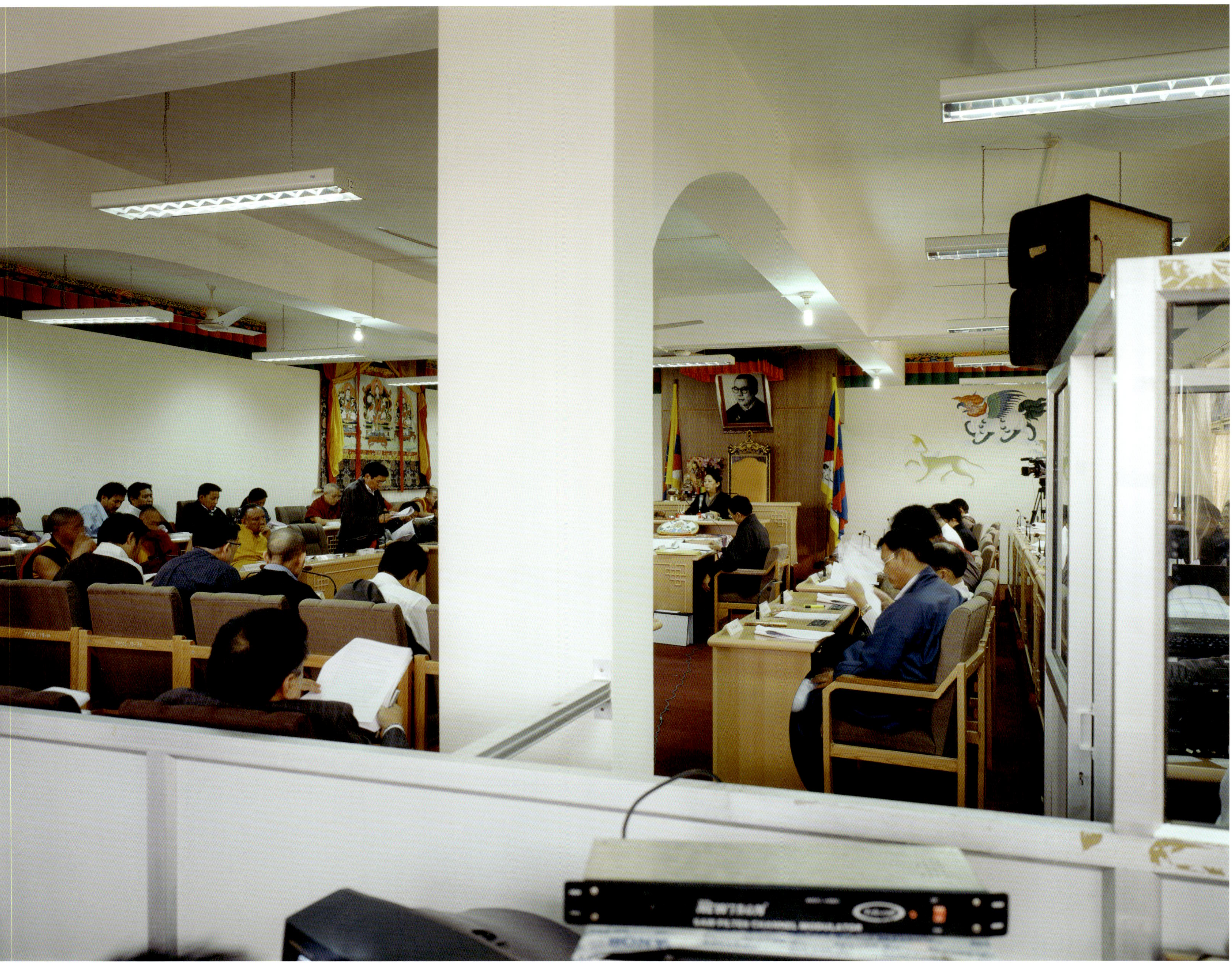

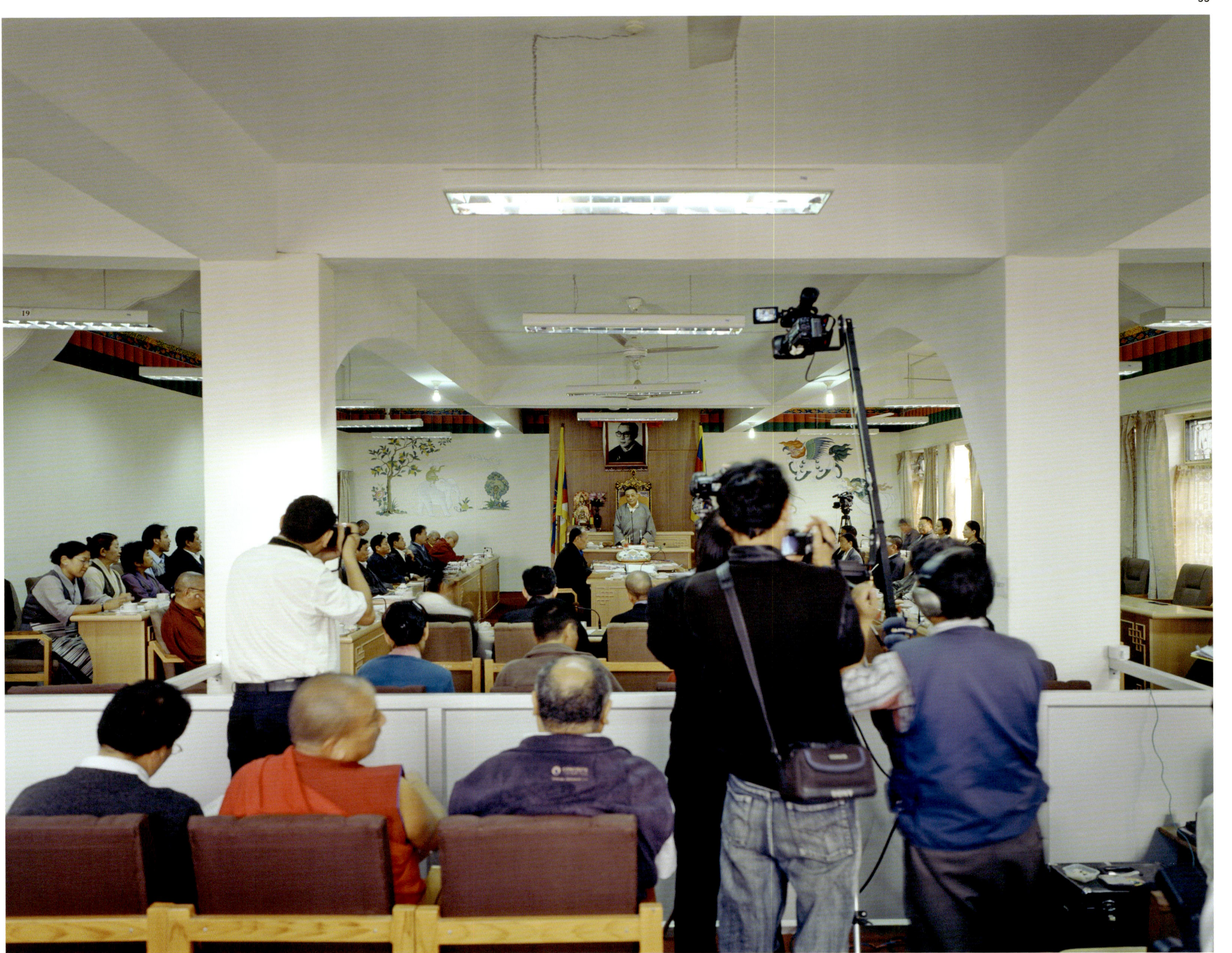

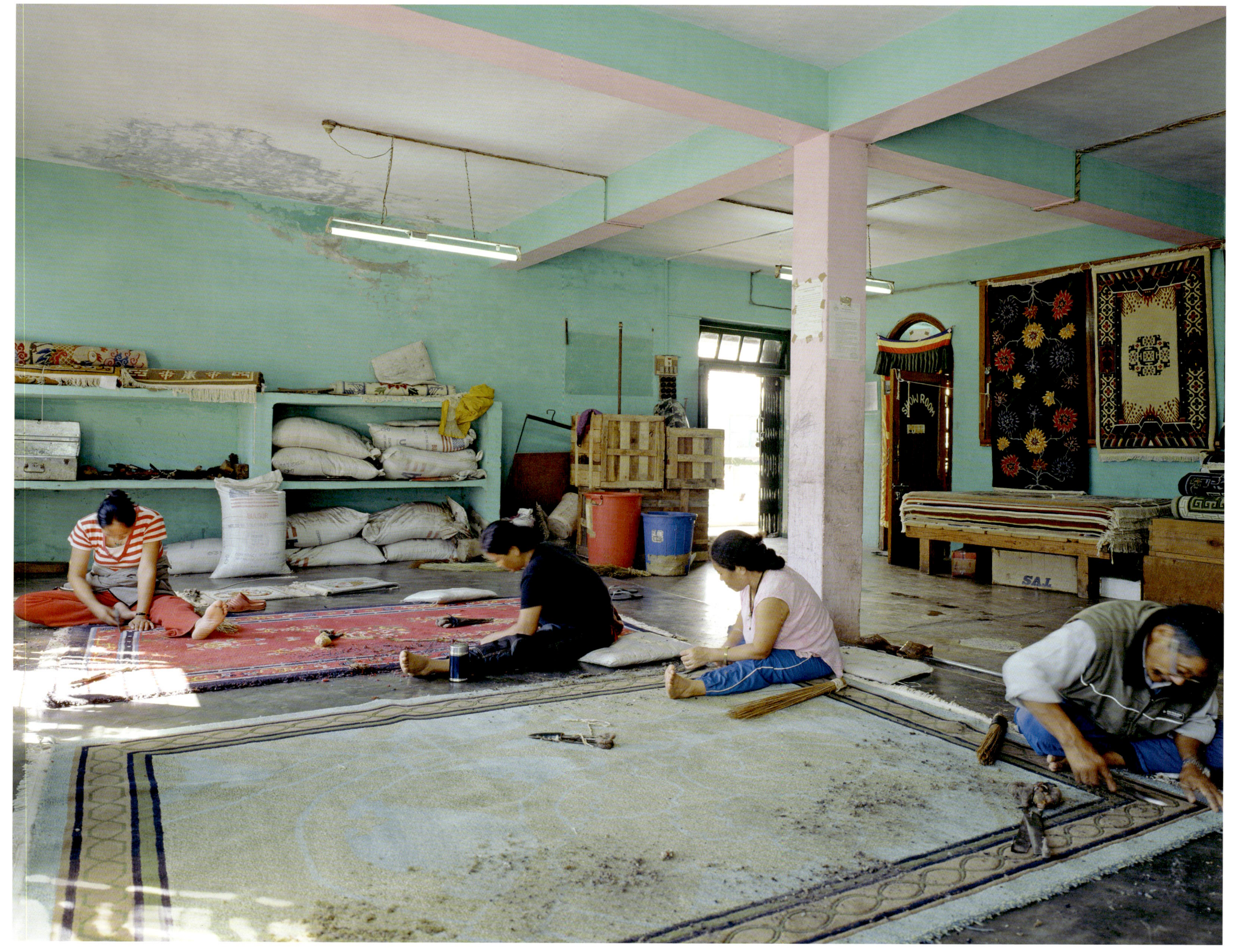
SHOW ROOM
SAL

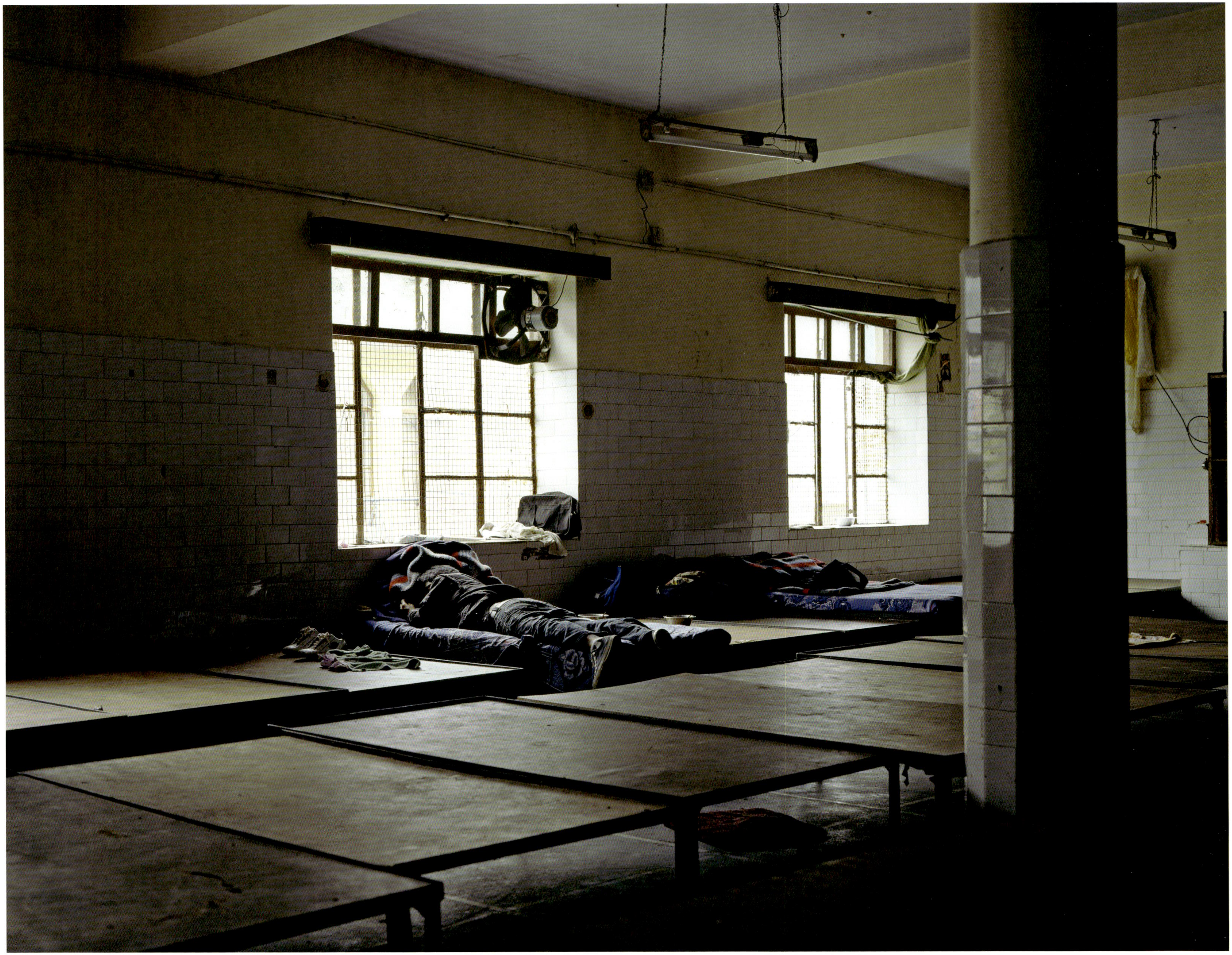

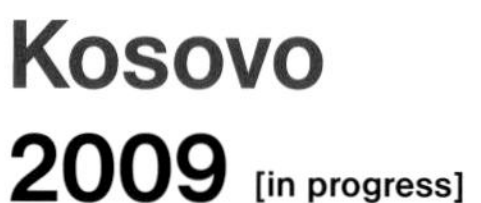

Kosovo
2009 [in progress]

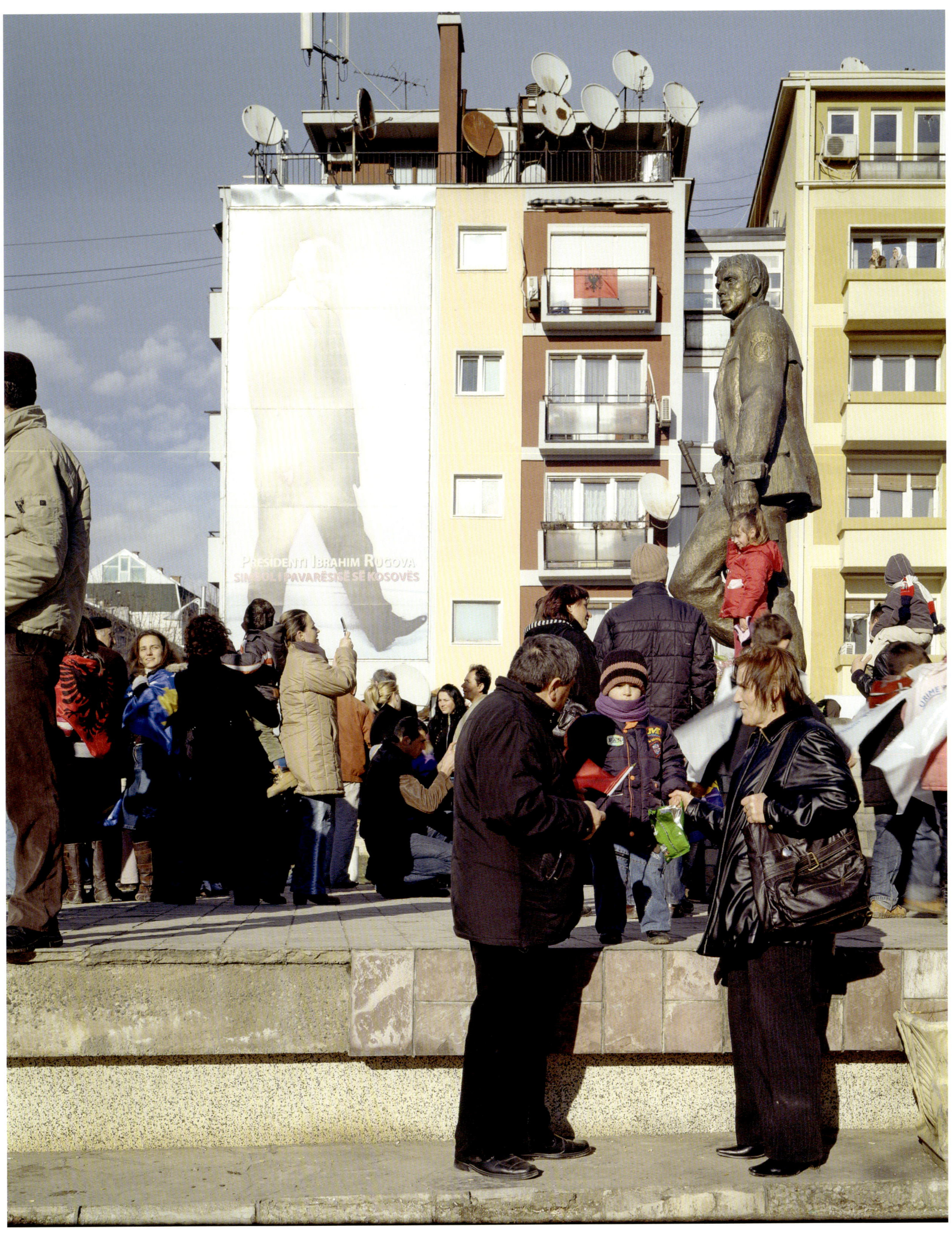
PRESIDENTI IBRAHIM RUGOVA

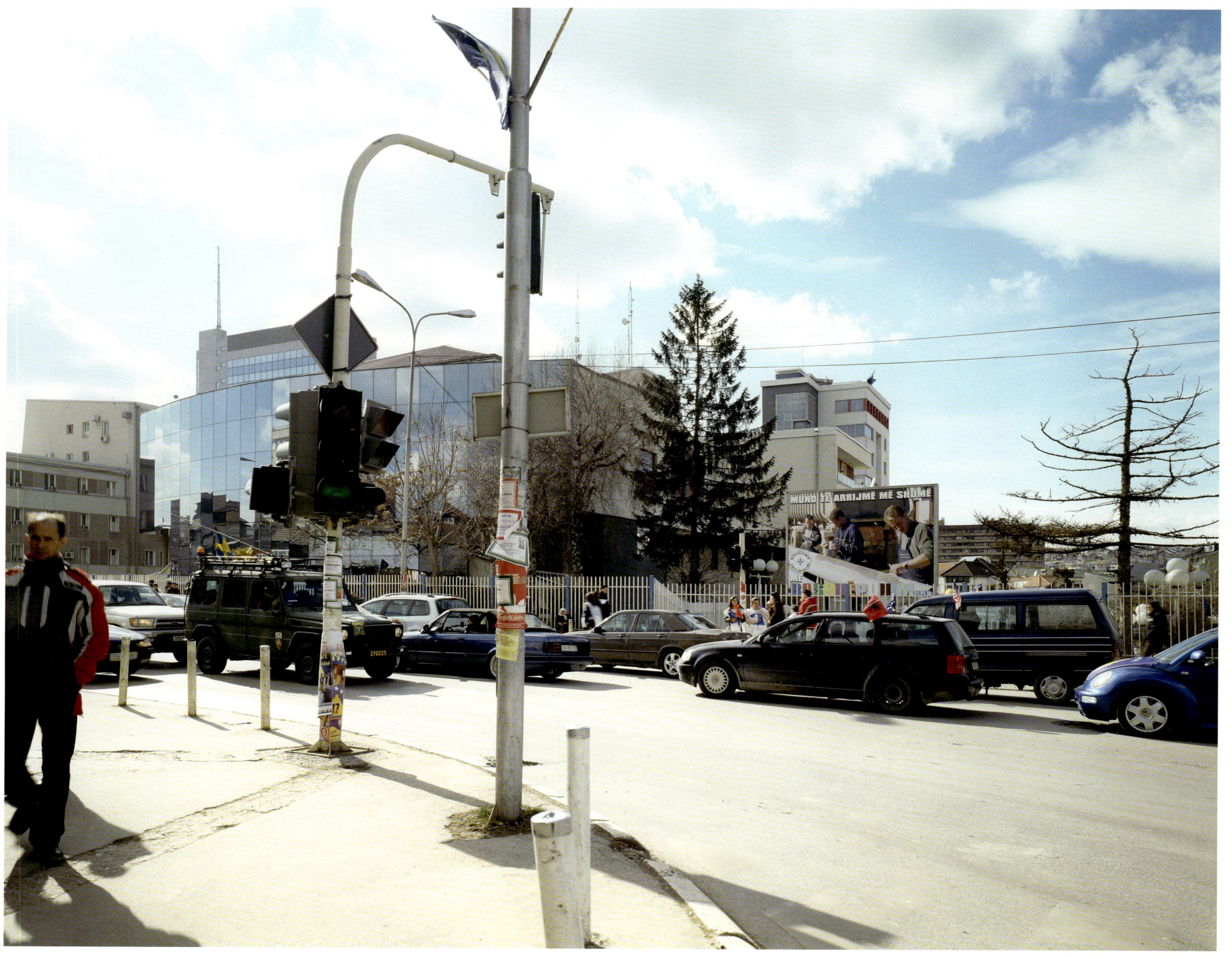
MUND TË ARRIJMË MË SHUMË

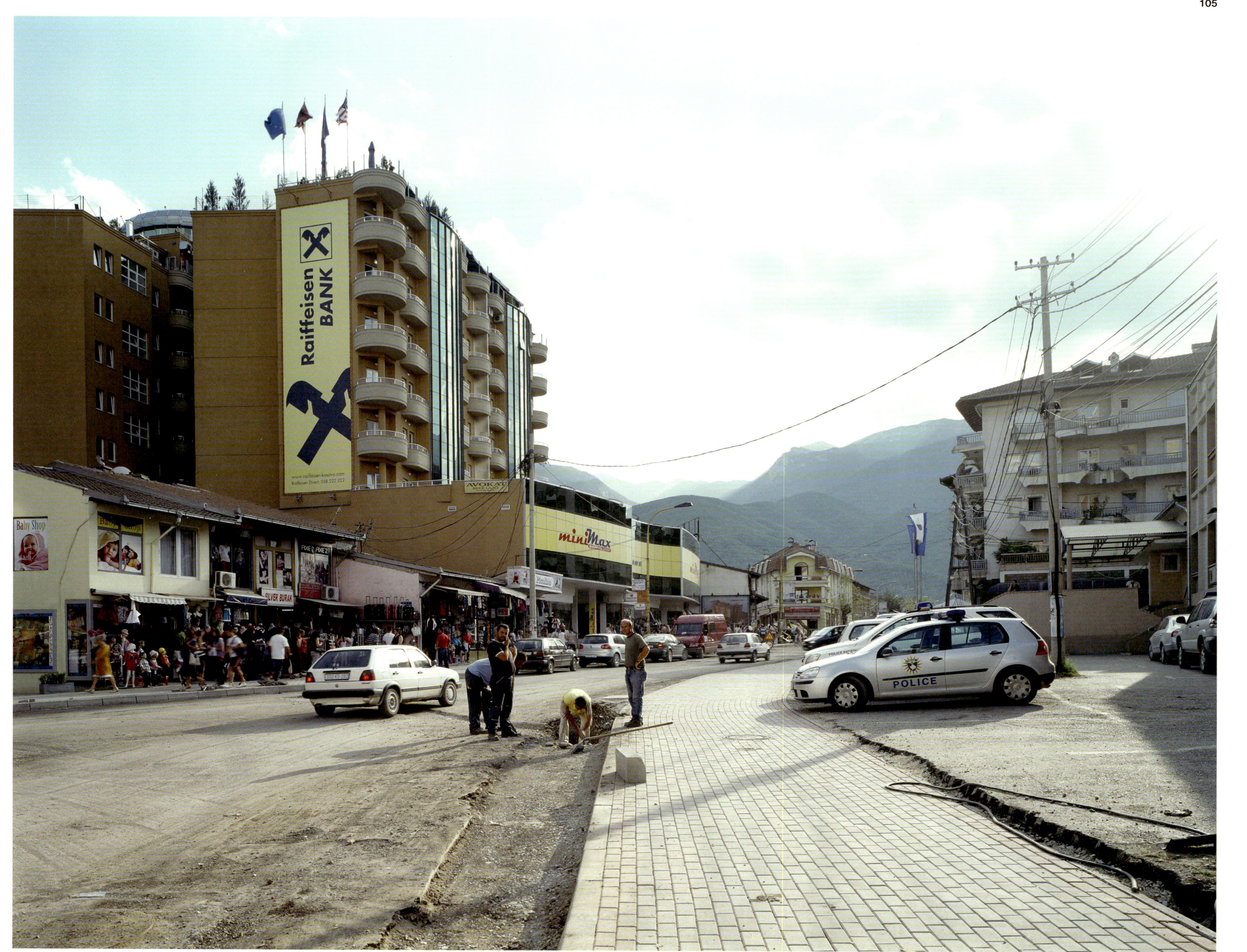
Raiffeisen BANK
www.raiffeisen-kosovo.com
Raiffeisen Direct 038 222 222
AVOKAT
miniMax
Baby Shop
SILVER BURAK
POLICE

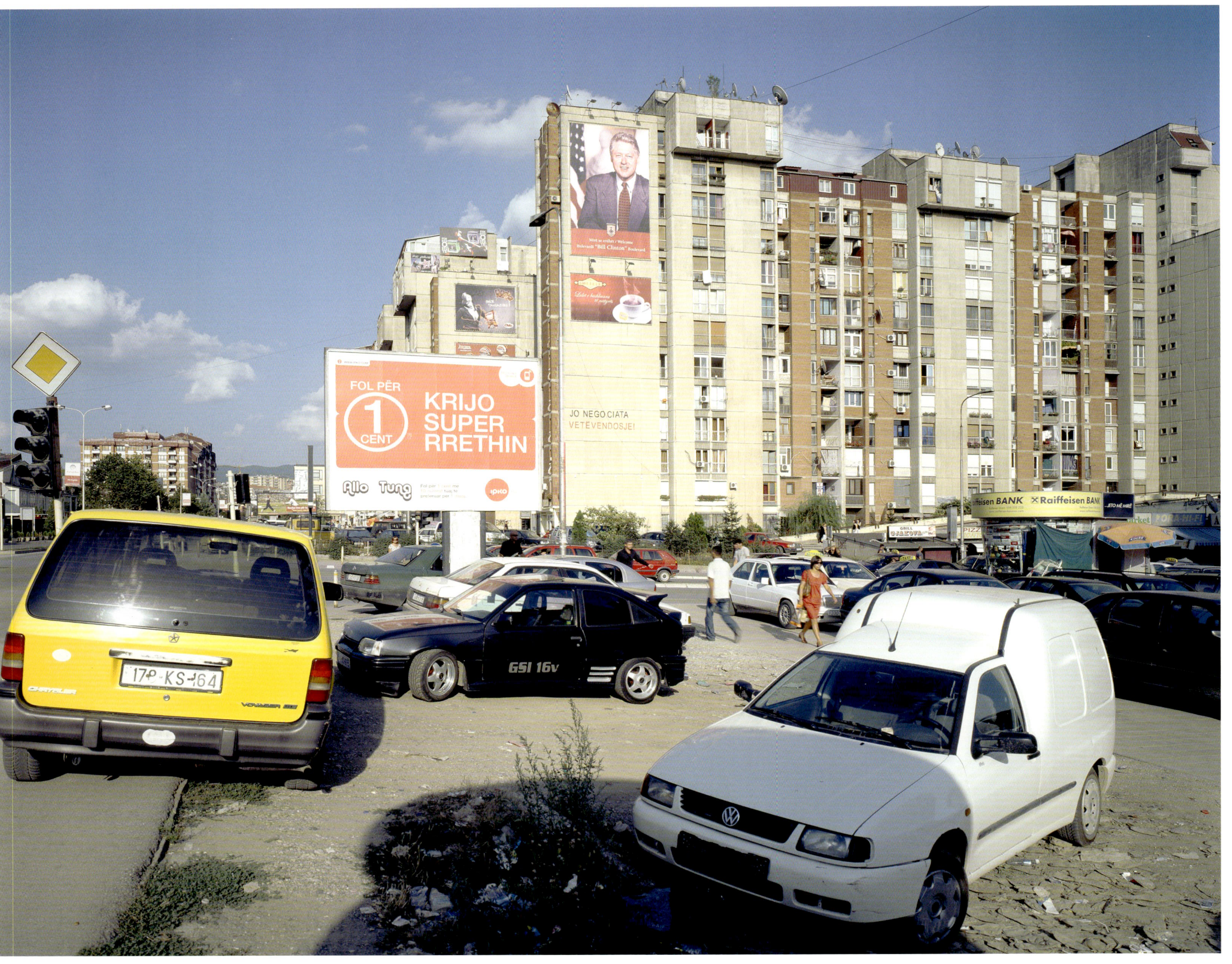
FOL PËR
1
CENT
KRIJO
SUPER
RRETHIN
Allo
Tung
ipko
JO NEGOCIATA
VETËVENDOSJE!
GSI 16v
17P-KS-464
Raiffeisen BANK

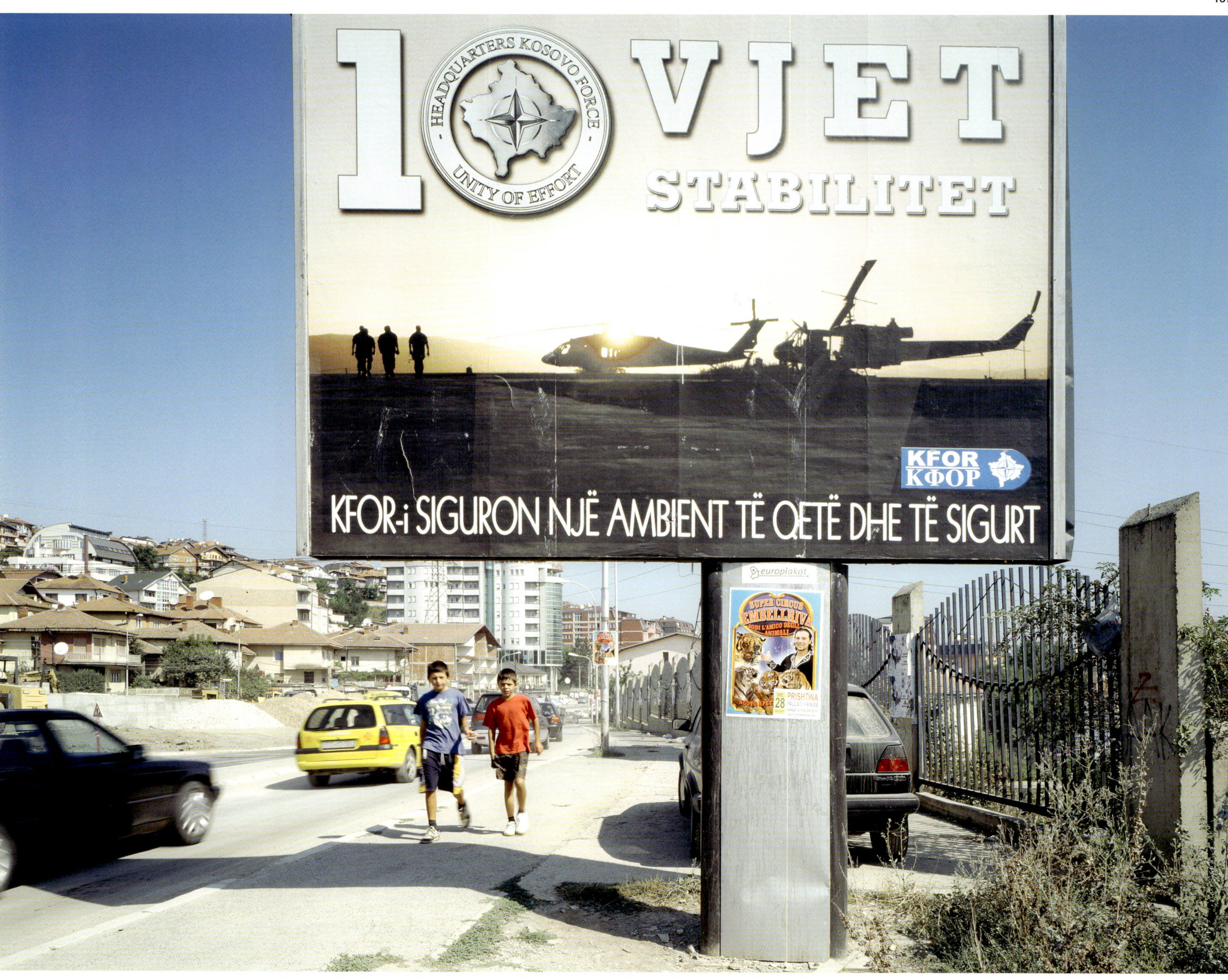
10 VJET
HEADQUARTERS KOSOVO FORCE
UNITY OF EFFORT
STABILITET
KFOR
КФОР
KFOR-i SIGURON NJË AMBIENT TË QETË DHE TË SIGURT
europlakat
PRISHTINA
28

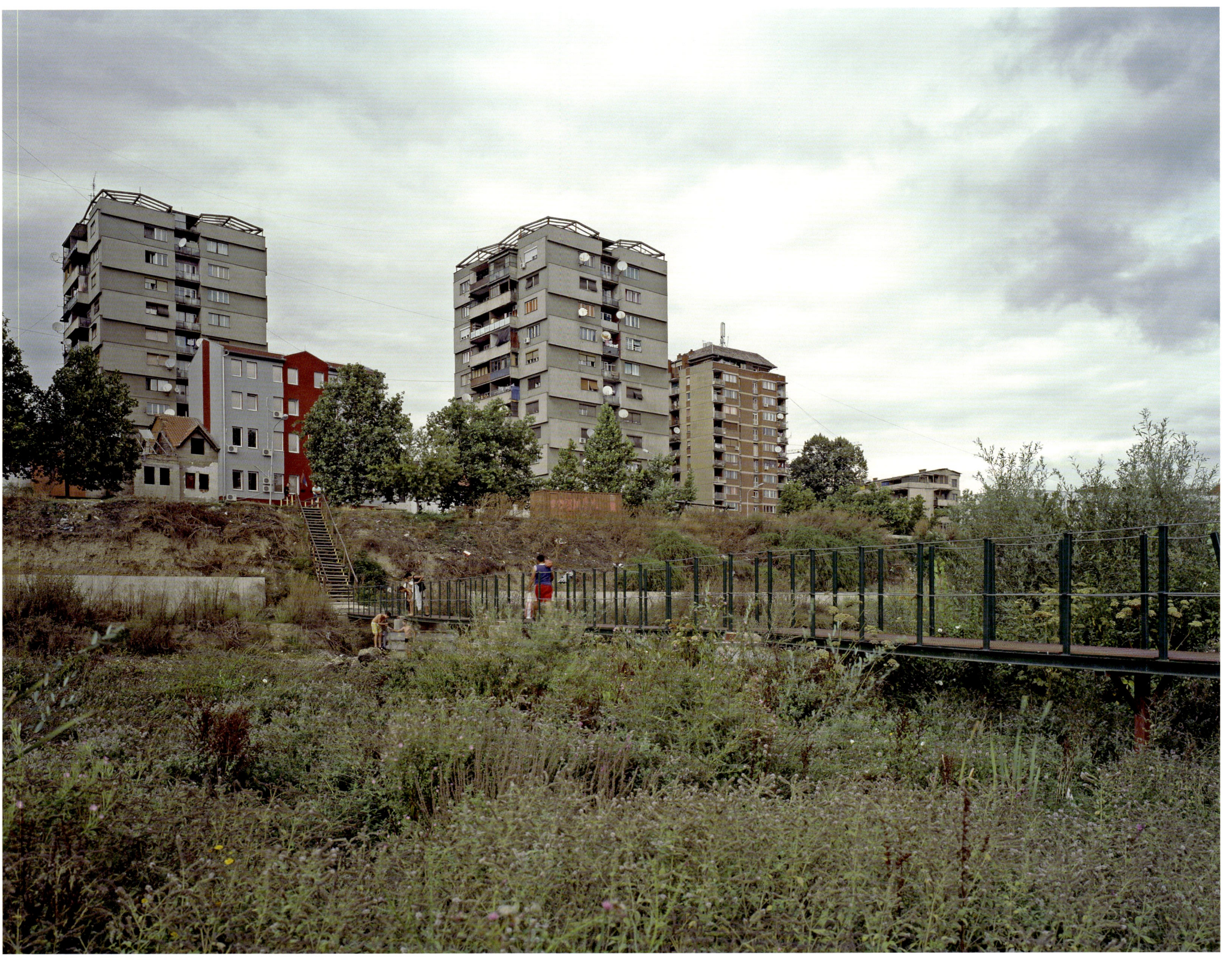

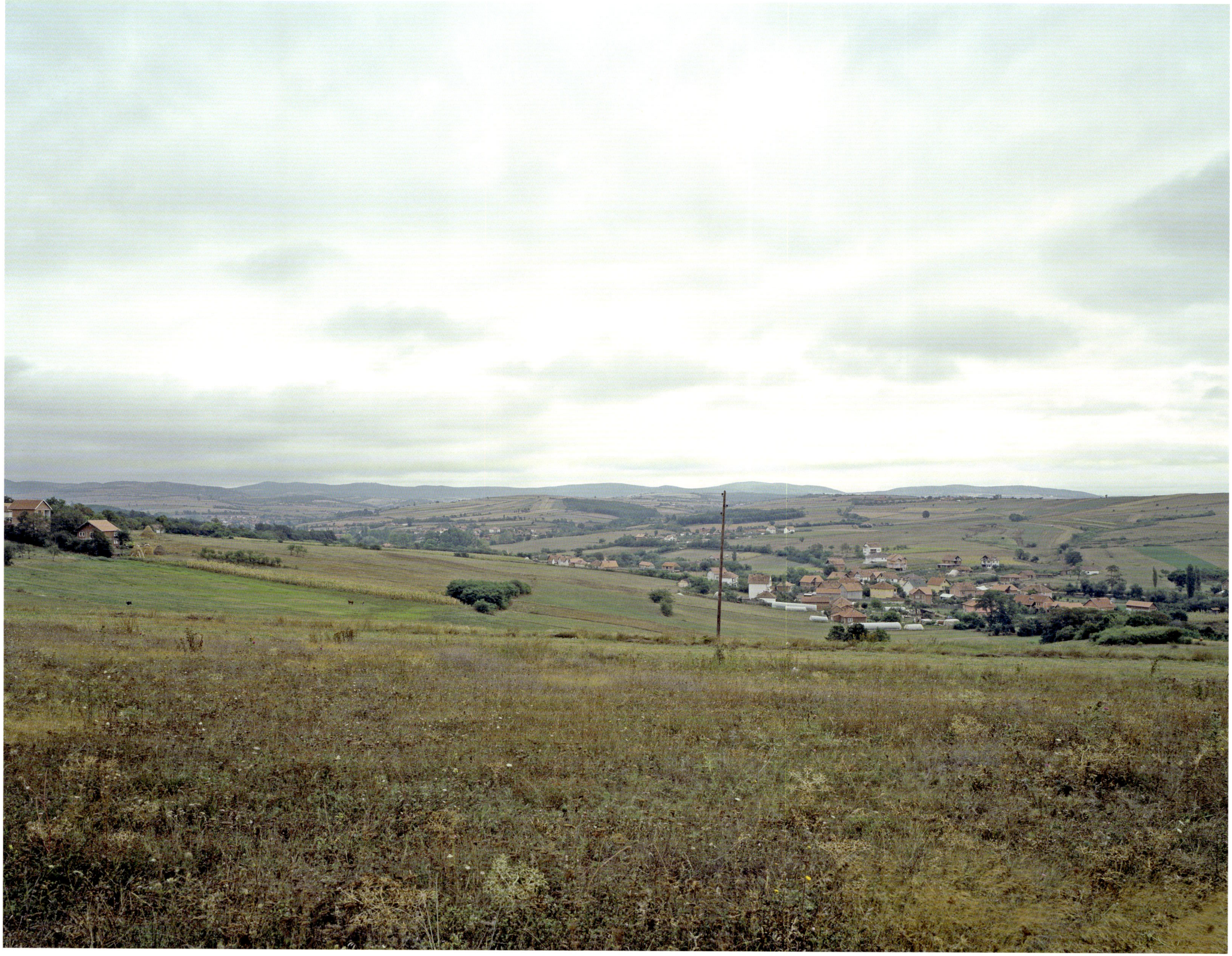

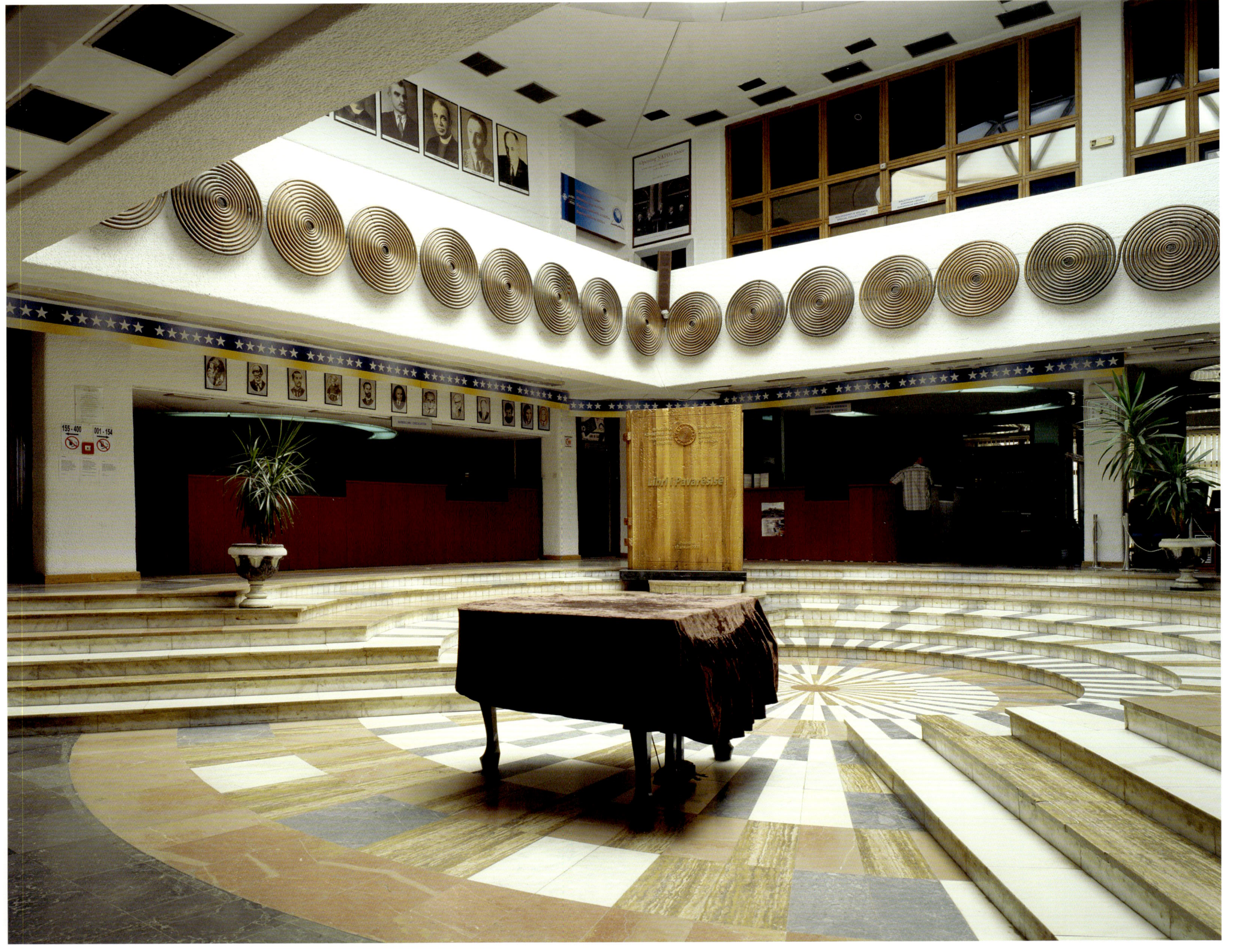
155 - 400
001 - 154
Libri i Pavarësisë

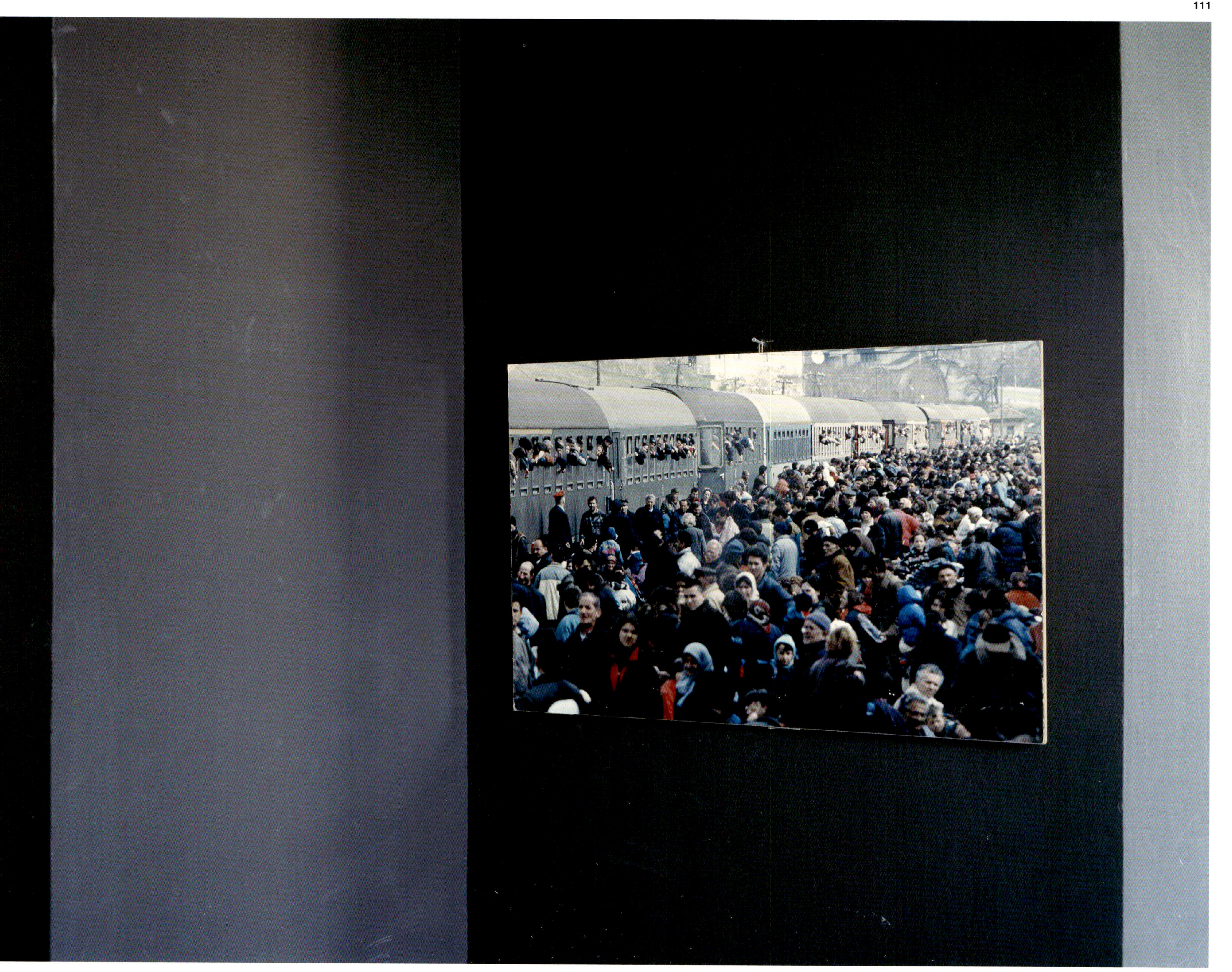

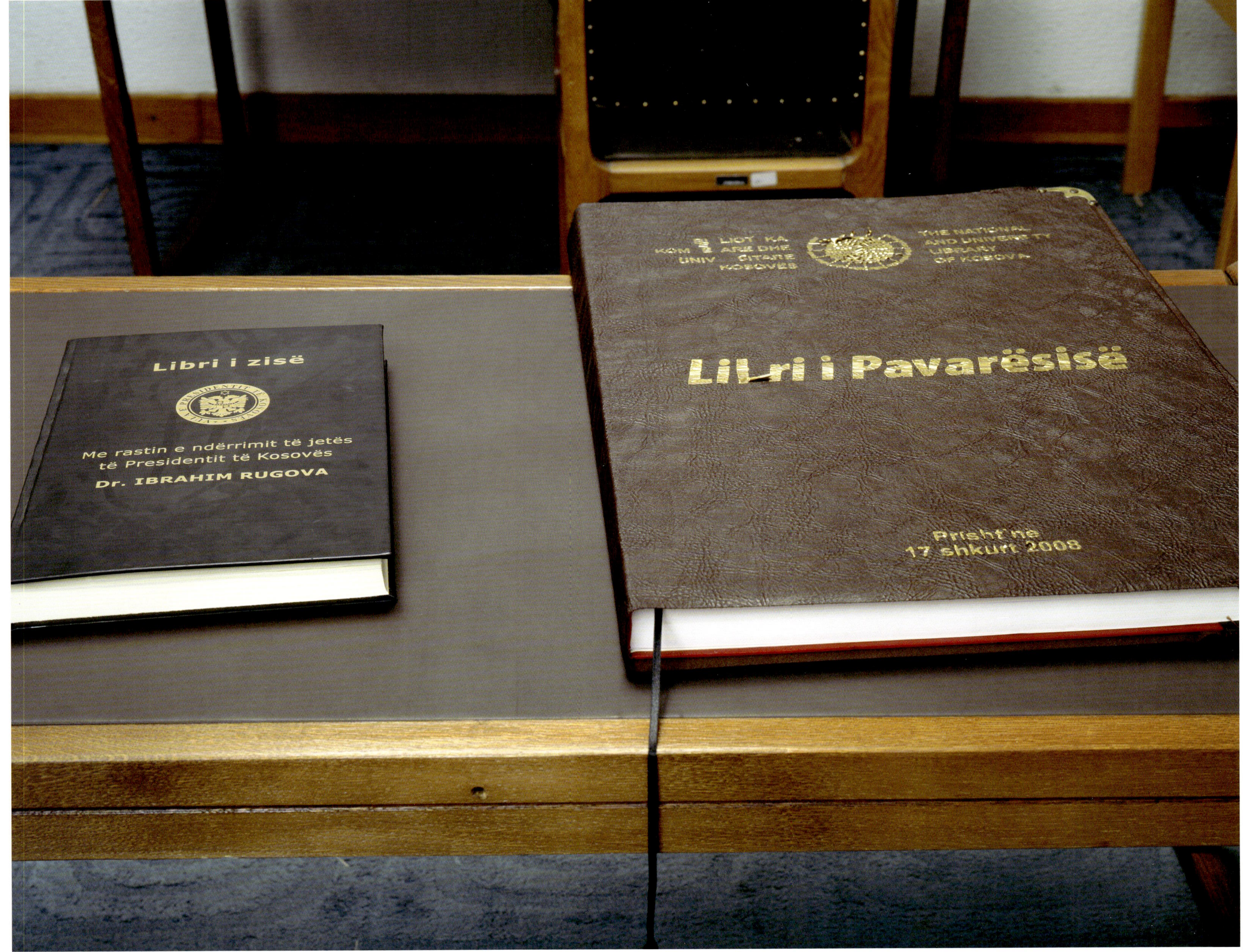
Libri i zisë
Me rastin e ndërrimit të jetës
të Presidentit të Kosovës
Dr. IBRAHIM RUGOVA
THE NATIONAL
AND UNIVERSITY
LIBRARY
OF KOSOVA
Prisht'në
17 shkurt 2008

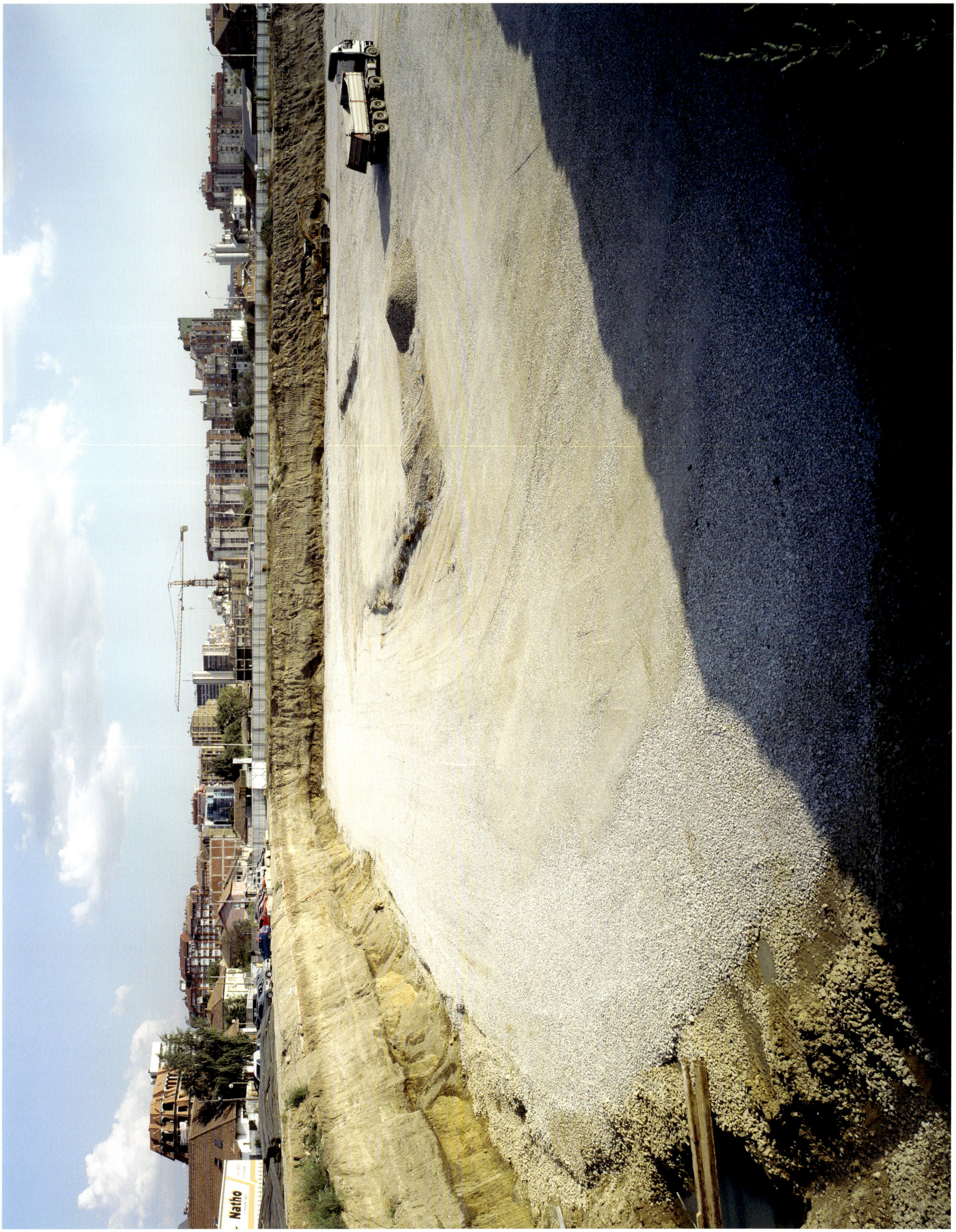

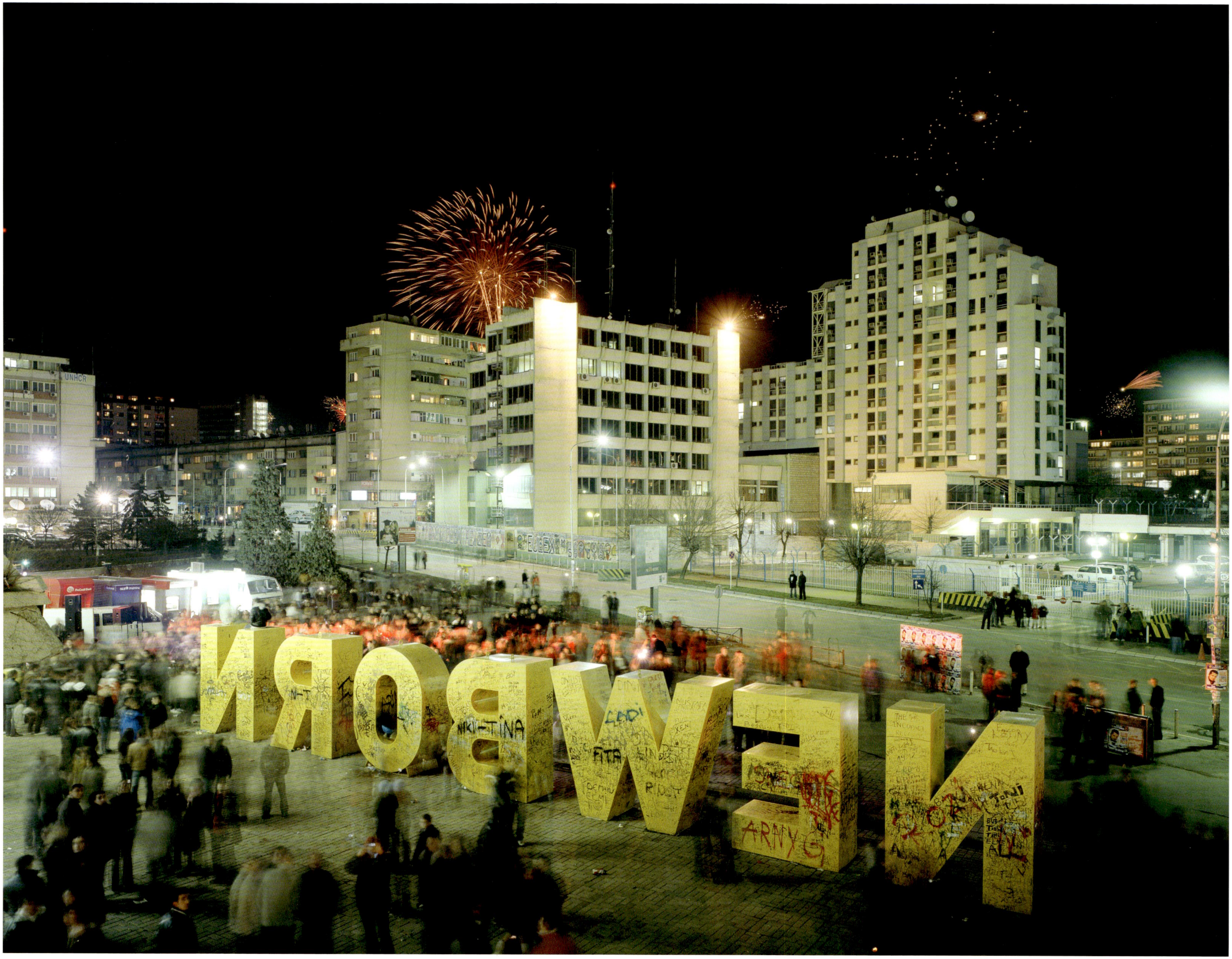

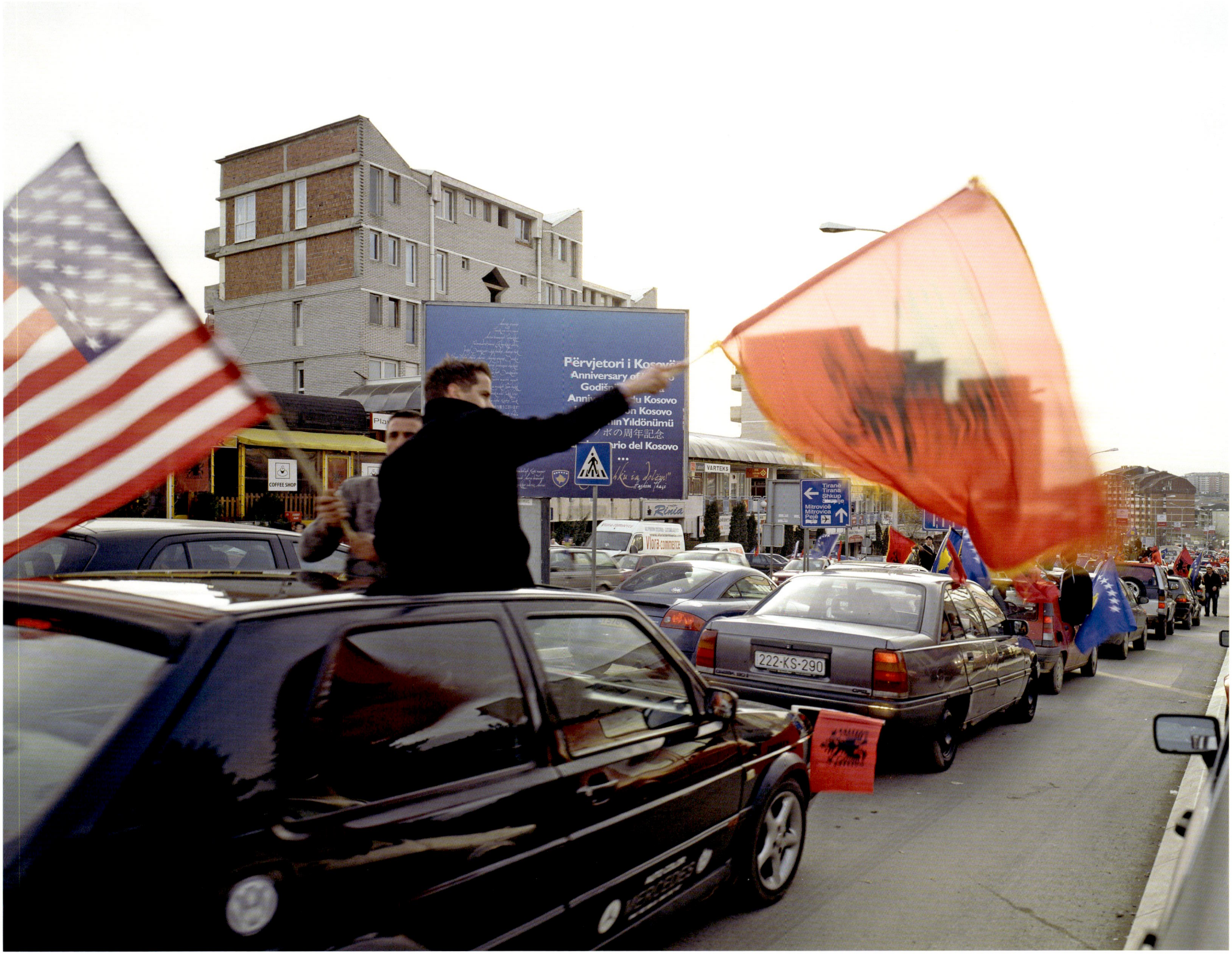
Përvjetori i
Anniversary of
du Kosovo
Kosovo
Yıldönümü
ボの周年記念
rio del Kosovo
COFFEE SHOP
VARTEKS
Rinia
Vlora commerce
Tiranë
Tirana
Shkup
Mitrovicë
Mitrovica
Pejë
222-KS-290

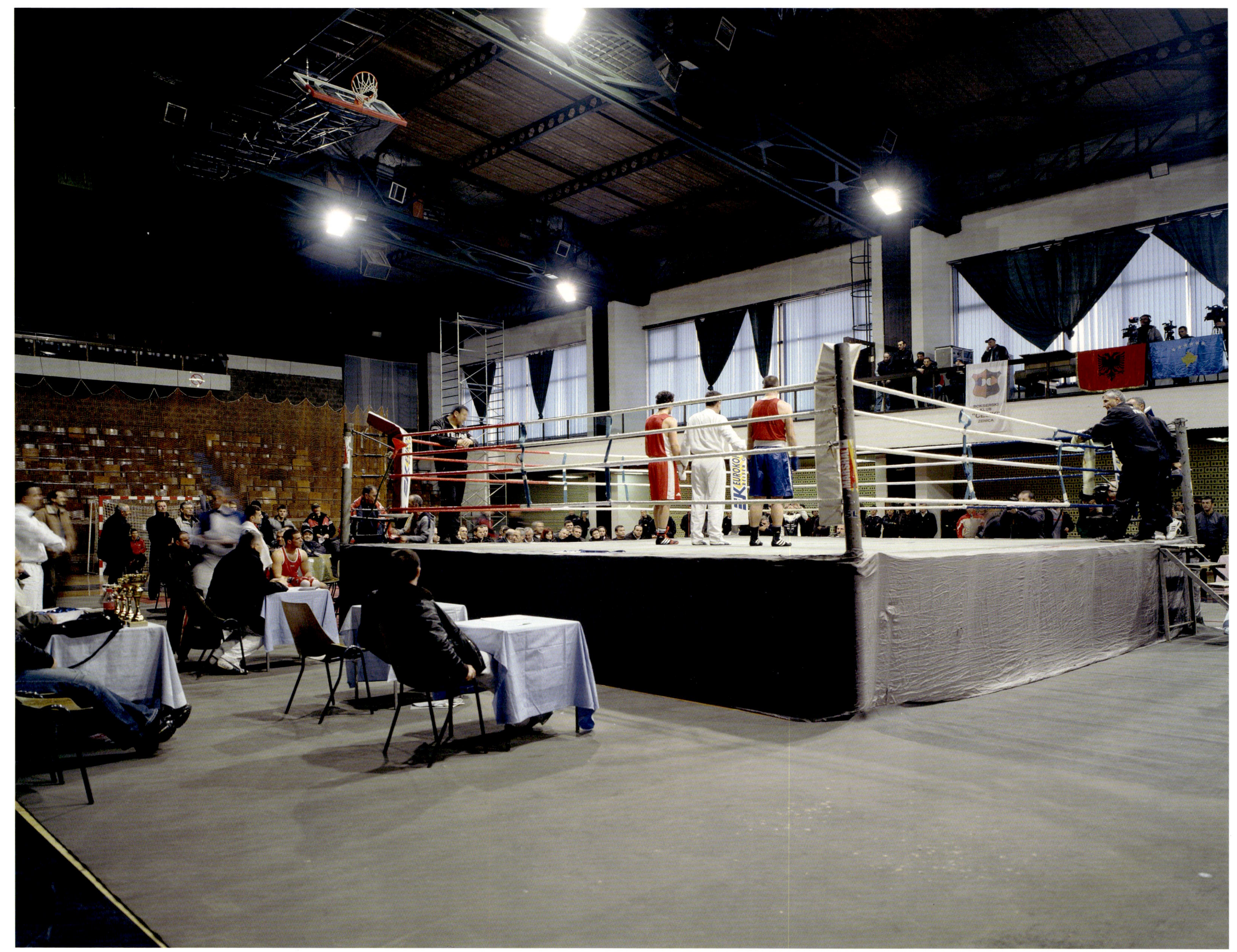

New Fabris, Châtellerault
2009

The summer of 2009 was marked in France by widespread strikes and factory sit-ins, all sparked by the same trend of management teams to delocalize production facilities to countries offering cheaper labor. The workers refused to be "discarded like used Kleenex"—a comparison heard time and time again in televised interviews—deciding instead to turn to increasingly radical forms of action in order to obtain a decent severance deal, if nothing else. The workers turned to new tactics such as boss-napping (the practice of detaining management on company premises), destroying equipment, and even threatening to raze the factory to the ground, thereby creating a shift in the balance of power between management and workforce. The conflict between workers and management at the New Fabris factory in Châtellerault drew a great deal of media attention. The factory sit-in began on June 15 with an ultimatum set for July 31. If no financial agreement was reached by then, the factory would be destroyed. The workers showed their determination by setting up gas canisters, which they claimed were linked to a detonator, in a highly visible spot on the roof of one of the factory buildings.

The ultimatum—particularly the way it was staged—not only shaped the negotiations, but also created an attention-grabbing event for the media, and thus indirectly for the government, in the person of Christian Estrosi, the French Minister for Industry. Estrosi was forced to act as a go-between, offering to set up a job protection scheme in the Châtellerault region.

The use of ever more radical tactics—such as the ransack of the administrative headquarters in Compiègne by workers from the Continental factory—as a means of forcing the government, the media, and public opinion to focus on an issue, reflects the breakdown of worker-management relations in a globalized economy.

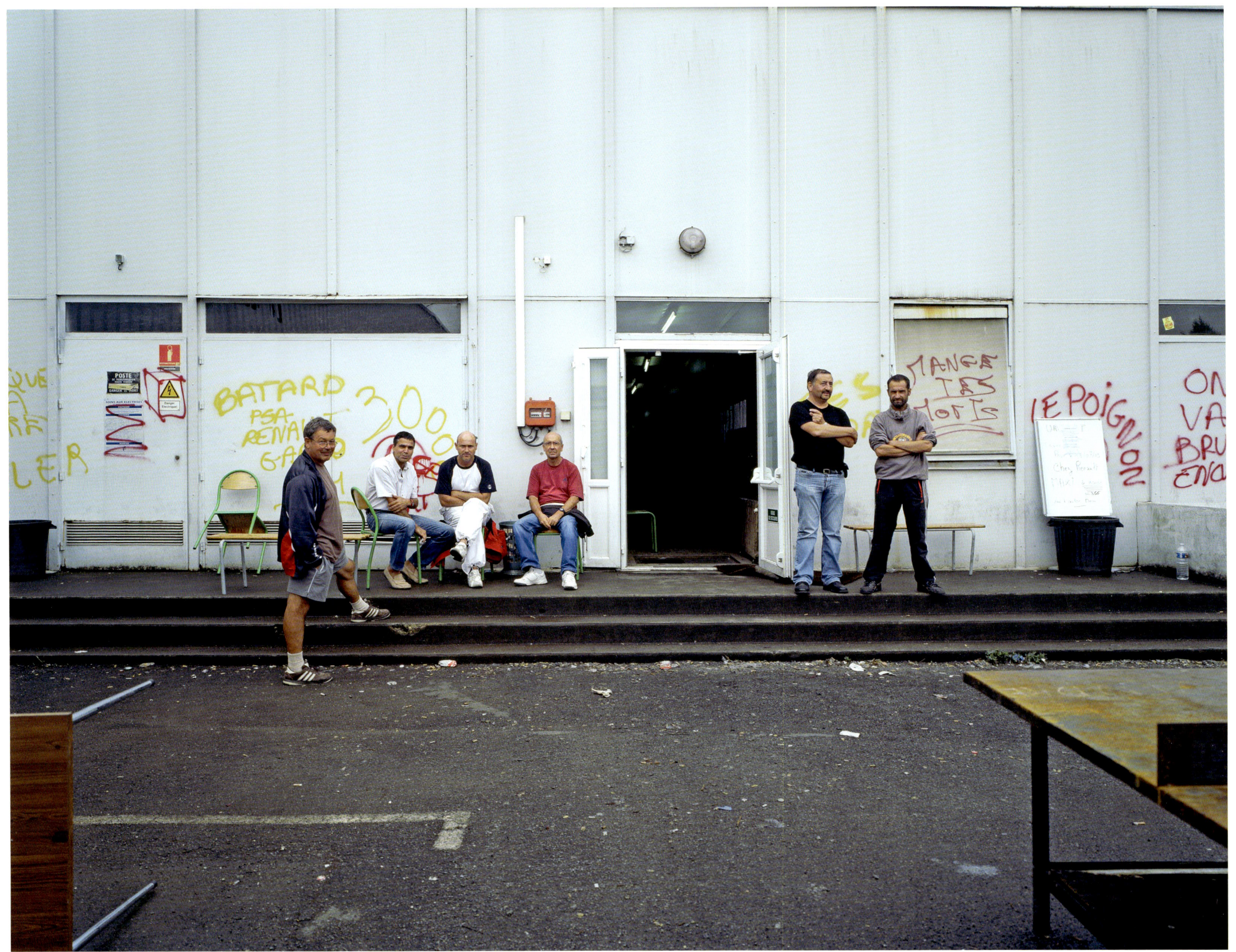
BATARD
PSA
LE POIGNON
MANGE

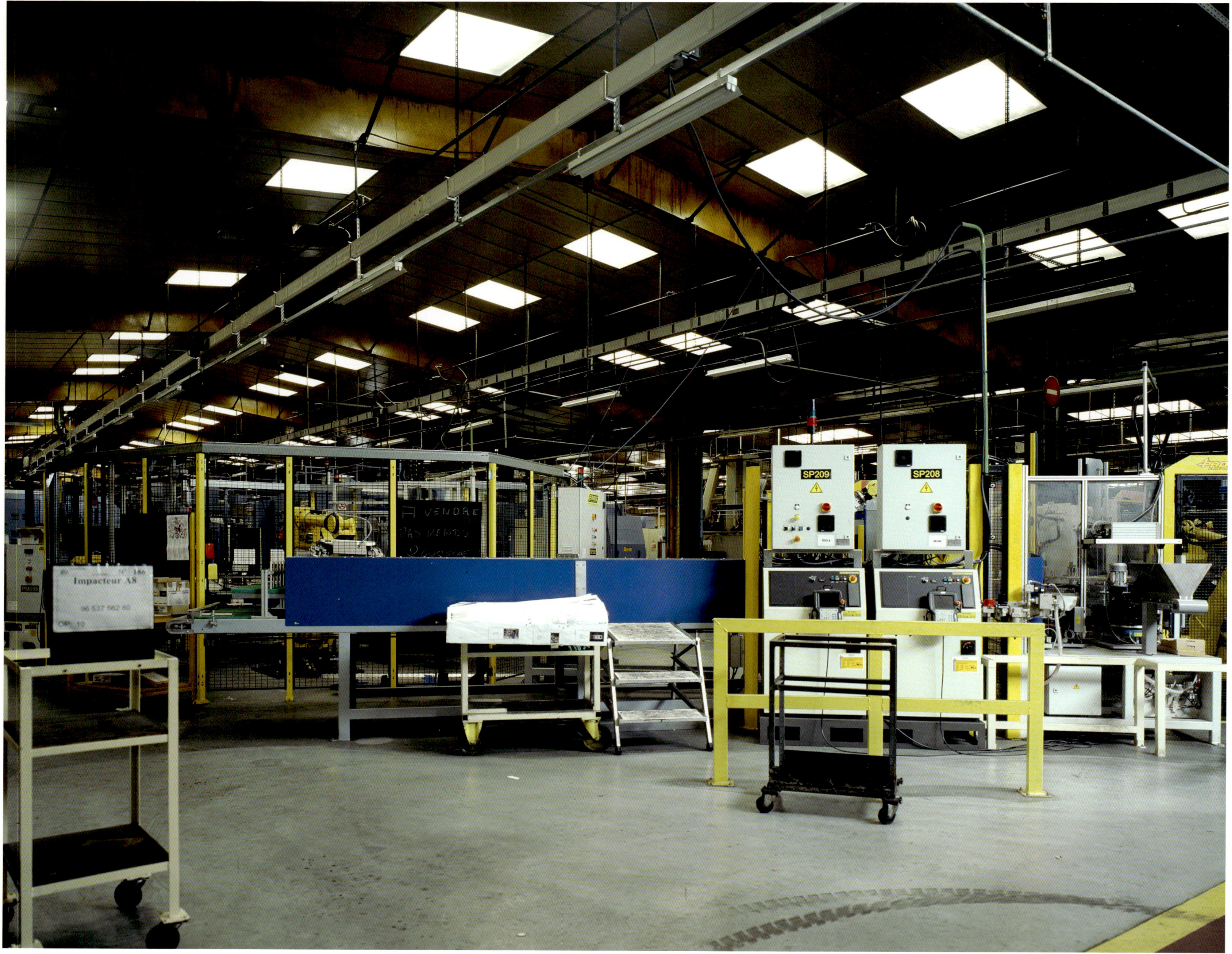
Impacteur A8
96 537 562 80
SP209
SP208
A VENDRE

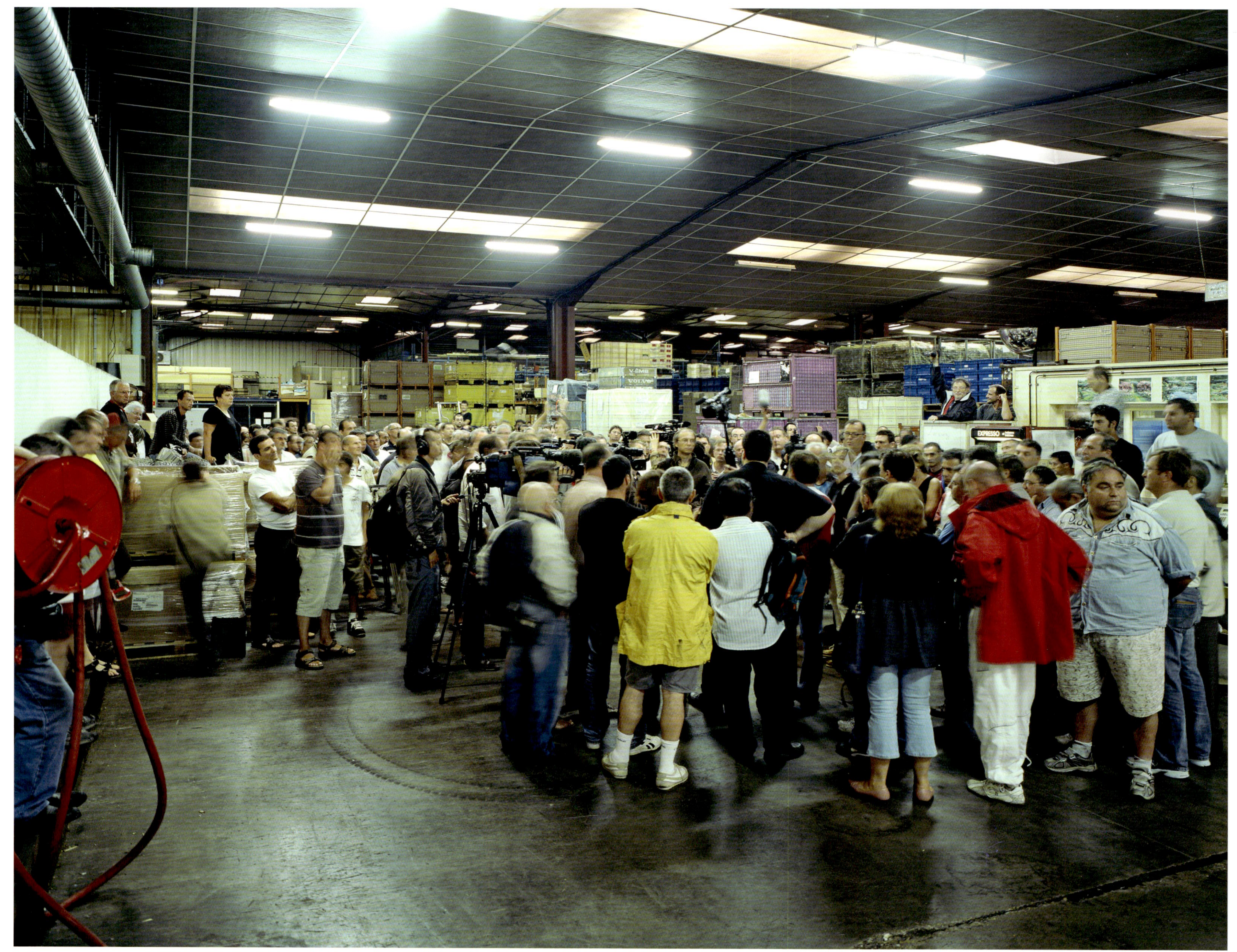

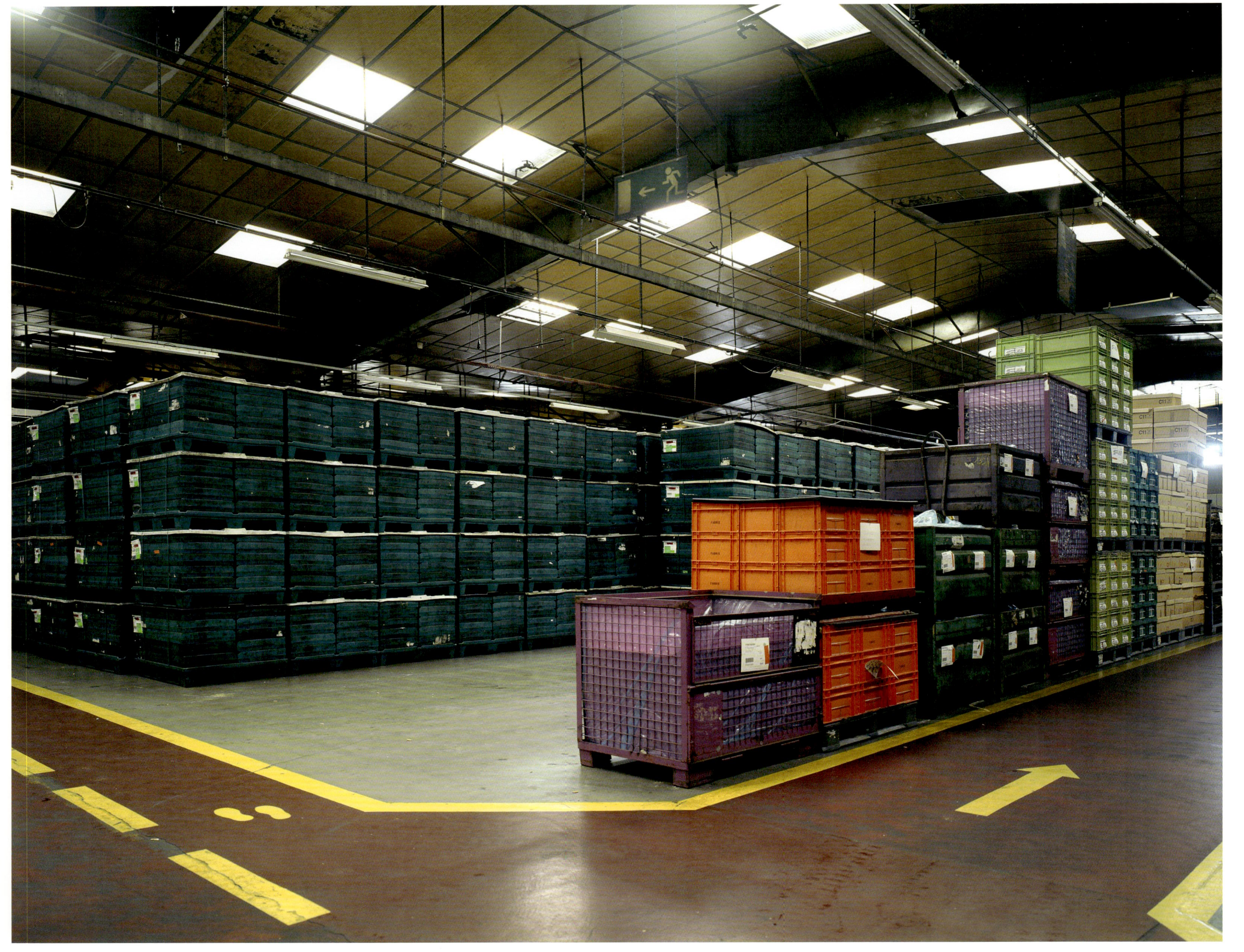

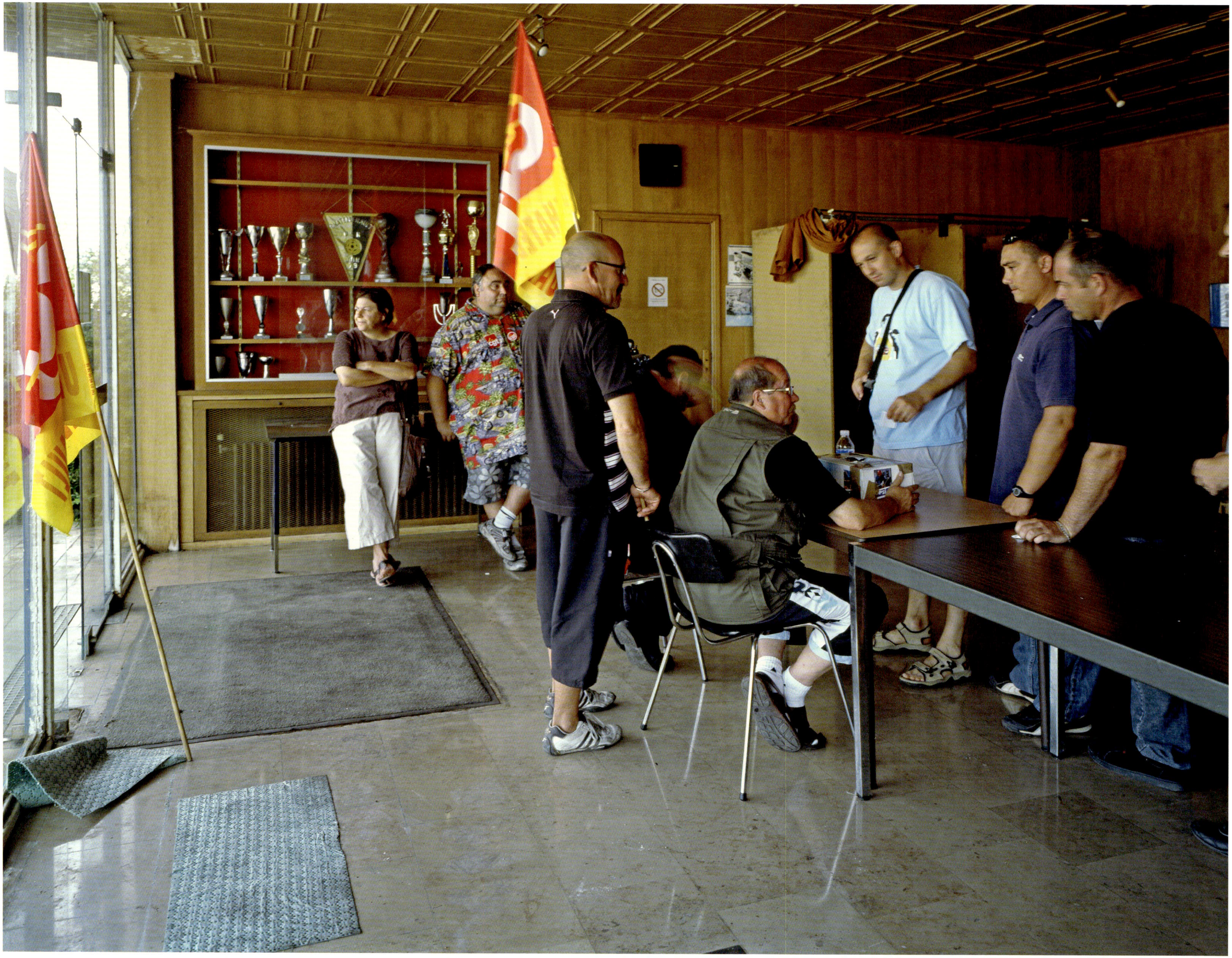

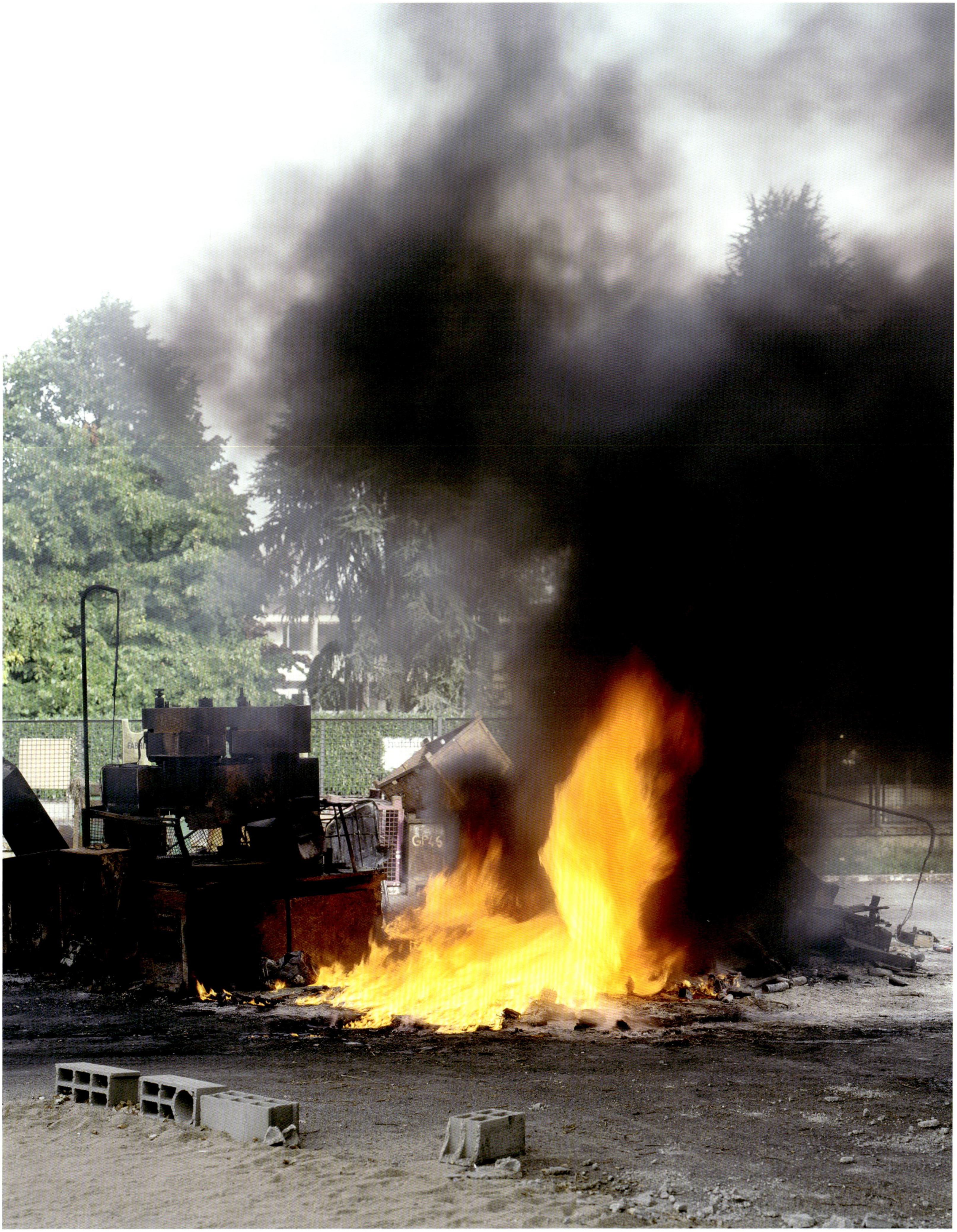

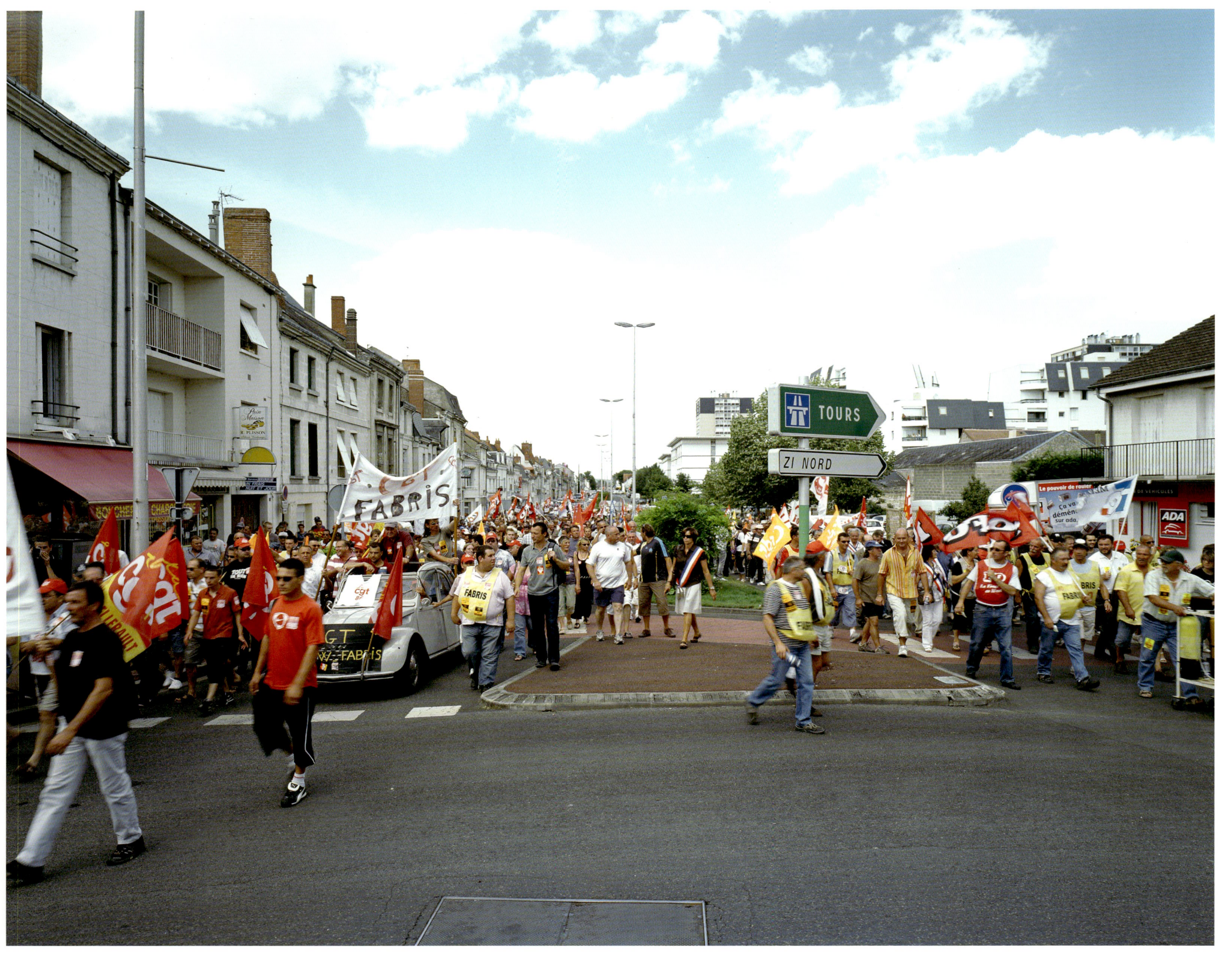
TOURS
ZI NORD
FABRIS
CGT
FABRIS
ADA

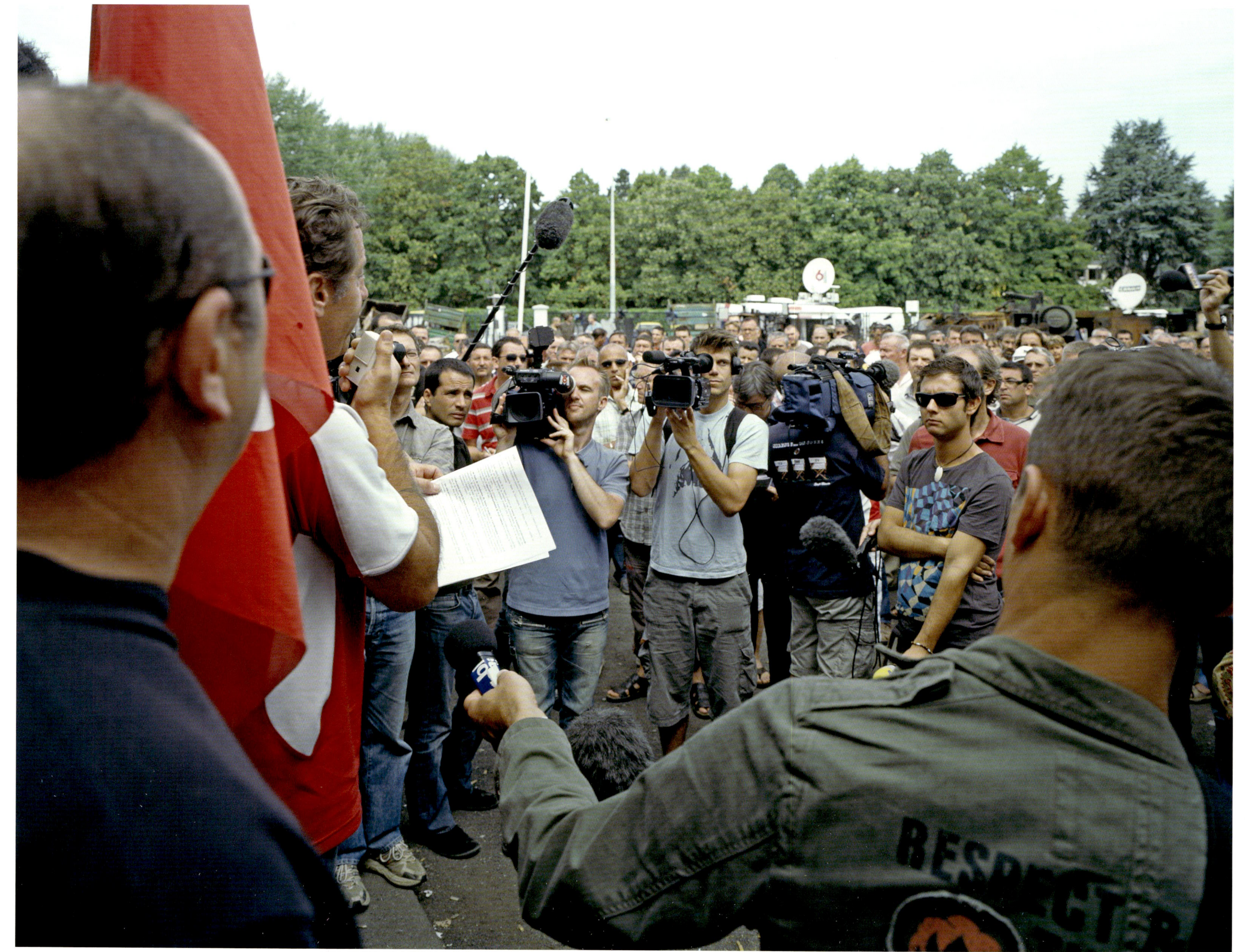
RESPECTER

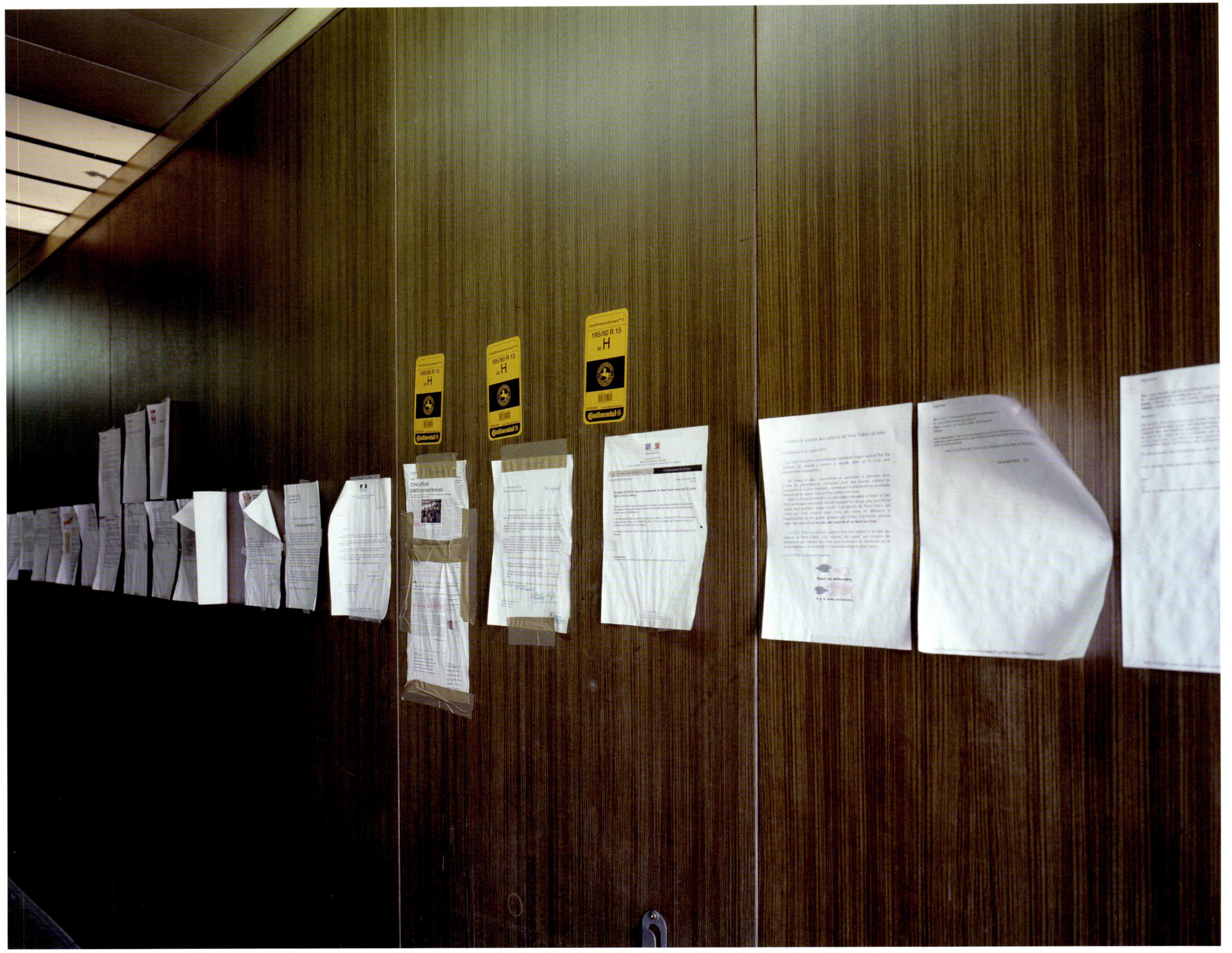

195/60 R 15
H
Continental
195/60 R 15
H
Continental
195/60 R 15
H
Continental
C'est officiel

The Newspaper Reader

Carles Guerra

On November 14, 2005, a few days before the opening of the World Summit on the Information Society (WSIS) in Tunis, the newspaper Libération announced on its front page that its correspondent had suffered a brutal attack. The news story clearly laid out the existing state of censorship in the Tunisian Republic, the host nation that had been delegated by the UN to organize the meeting of 50 heads of state. On the next page, the journalist Christophe Boltanski explained what had happened to him in first person. A group of men had attacked and beaten him. Apparently, this was a common way of intimidating journalists under the regime of Zine Ben Ali: "They ripped off my bag, and continued to hit me, until one of them cried out in French, and not Arabic: That's enough." On the next page, the then-Secretary General of Reporters without Borders, Robert Ménard, could not help but comment ironically on the case: "Organizing an Internet and information society summit in Tunisia is like what it would have been to give the presidency of the UN Commission on Human Rights to Libya a few years ago." The result was that censorship and intimidating behavior toward journalists clouded the summit's objectives, leading many to wonder why a debate on access to information and the North-South digital gap had been entrusted to a country like Tunisia. In spite of this, the photographs taken by Bruno Serralongue during the sessions that took place in the Kram Palexpo facilities, the summit headquarters from November 16 to 18, do not show any clear signs of violence. They give us no information about any sort of explicit protest. The images, taken with the large-format camera that he always takes to the place of the event he is covering, set out a sequence whose style is almost corporate, like a dry, neutral company report. Wide-angle shots allowing him to reveal the hierarchy of the participants in the meetings, axonometric perspectives giving shape to convention-hall architecture, and a few half-body portraits, like the one dedicated to Mr Joe Shirley Jr, president of the Navajo nation, round out the limited number of images that make up the series "World Summit on the Information Society, Tunis" (2005). The results seem to fulfill the requirements of a commission. Thus the images do not appear to correspond to the freedom of an artist who has attended the sessions without official press accreditation, as was the case. Bruno Serralongue refuses to accept authorization or special conditions reserved for members of the professional media. He arranges his access to such events in the same way as any other average citizen who handles his own travel and stay, in much the same way as he would organize a personal holiday.

Still, some of the photographs taken in Geneva two years earlier, during the first stage of the information society summit, did show a demonstration against the event. In other photos from the series entitled "World Summit on the Information Society, Geneva" (2003) we also see messages from opposition activists and protestors. The slogan "L'information ne se vend pas, elle se partage" (Information is not sold, it is shared) hangs on a banner in an informal-looking interior full of computers. The photograph's title attributes the phrase to Polymedia Lab, an alternative organization. On the other hand, "Unlimited Potential, ICT4 Development" is the title of an image of the Microsoft stand. The same approach is used for hegemonic and critical positions. Both of them receive the same documentary treatment.

We could say that Bruno Serralongue's photographic practice—which bears no personal relation to the artist—rarely lets itself be carried away by moral or ideological empathy. It takes on a necessarily cool perception of the world, filtered by distance. Thus his images cannot be judged by what he allows into the frame, but by the specific conditions of their production, even though here, to be sure, the exuberant visual quality of the photographic medium tends to conceal them. This exuberance fetishizes them to such a degree that the spectator can simply miss them. The reproduction quality of the large-format camera ends up being deceptive, as the rich and profuse visual detailing is but a mere distraction when faced with the photographic procedure being put into place.

Bruno Serralongue's photographs are those of a reader who chooses to go to the event site so as to check out the news story with his own eyes. From the series produced at the end of the 1990s to the most recent work, the photographer's trips have always been guided by the goal of illustrating a journalistic text. From early on, the procedure of "News Items" (1993–1995) set out a production sequence where a news story published in the press (Internet, radio, newspaper, or television news) worked as a starting point. At that time the artist sought to corroborate minor local dramas that he had read for himself in newspapers such as Nice-Matin. When he arrived at the site of the events published the day before, there would hardly be a trace of them left. Everything that he was able to shoot using this method was little more than the scene of a story read a few hours earlier, or at most a few days before. Of the 51 photographs that make up the series, only four actually showed details related to the story itself. For this reason, his photographs do not in general contribute any special sort of knowledge. They simply support the news item with an empirical, after-the-fact experience. This is the case above all because Bruno Serralongue uses his photography to verify and interpret what the press has already published. As a result, his encounter with the event is like a return voyage to the story, a second empirical contact that occurs with a relative delay in relation to the first one. This contact is then complicated a posteriori by the fact that his works are made to move in an art context, which is distinguished as we know by demands that are different from those of the rest of the world. This does not mean, however, that time is wasted.

In little over a decade Bruno Serralongue has accumulated a wide array of events. Parties, concerts, fairs, summits, forums, encounters, debates, and demonstrations have replaced the exercise of empirical proof that would move within local limits until taking on a global dimension. In series such as "Encuentro" (1996), "Homenaje" (1997), "Free Tibet" (1998), "Korea" (2001), "World Social Forum, Mumbai" (2004), "La Otra" (2006), or in other more recent ones such as those on the Tibetan diaspora ("Tibet in Exile (Dharamsala)," 2008) and the independence of Kosovo ("Kosovo," 2009–in progress), long-lasting geopolitical conflicts are visualized, even though their complexity has stretched out so widely that it is impossible for them to fit into the strict frame of photography. Even though Bruno Serralongue's typical shots continue to provide us with sparse views, the gestalt that is generated by means of the accumulation of series gives shape to a global cartography. It is a gestalt that moves well away from the modern idea of photographic representation as a cut of reality sliced off from the rest of the world. If we sift through the history of photography we will end up referring to the photography books of Ernst Jünger (1895–1998), published in the 1930s, in order to find something similar. Ernst Jünger (a prominent right-wing German writer who belonged to a generation that fought in the First World War) composed the pages of Der gefährliche Augenblick [The Dangerous Moment] (1931) and Die veränderte Welt [The Transformed

World] (1933) with press photographs acquired in agencies of the time, and his peculiar way of observing the world gave rise to something like a monstrous, totalizing vision, unperturbed by the most jolting of images, where "shock, catastrophe, and terror constitute a frenetic celebration of perception."[1] In spite of everything, this procedure is what has triumphed in the communicative regime that pertains to our globalized world. Consequently, the illusion of an immediate access to past and remote events could not be separated from this ideological link to Ernst Jünger's protofascism. Here, Bruno Serralongue's commentary on that way of representing the present allows for the fact that the contemporary individual constitutes in themself an information agency, bringing together and managing a great diversity of images. As he affirmed in a recent interview with Marta Gili and Dirk Snauwert, "I have my very own AFP—all the news formats available to readers/viewers. So I don't have access to the raw information in the form of news wires, but rather to information sorted and selected by news desks."

Thus, instead of defining itself as a photographic essay, Bruno Serralongue's work seeks out ways of articulating visual alternatives, quite apart from the narrative models of the news report. An exhibition of Serralongue's work in Geneva's Centre de la Photographie in 2007 gave rise to the creation of new groups of photographs, with the result resting on the premise of combining photographs related to each other, even though the images belonged to different series.[2] With these temporary groups, pseudo-genres are perceived, such as portraits, general views of stadiums, auditoriums, television crews, the odd street level snapshot, flags and other symbols related to activist identity, group photographs, and posters featuring a great diversity of texts. The loss of "adherence,"[3] the term used by Michael Fried in commenting on Roland Barthes' <u>Camera Lucida</u> (1981), means that the referent is detached from the photograph. The photographic image becomes an autonomous sign and allows us to compare (to give an example not found in the Geneva show) a view of two indigenous huts in the series "Encuentro" (1996) with a modern meeting room in the Kram Palexpo during the Tunis summit. Both of the images document ephemeral constructions, or, depending on how you look at them, both have a certain tribal character. What would Ernst Jünger think of this pair of photos? In any case, this apparent narrative disorder restores a level of perception that could be lacking when only one photograph is presented. <u>Backdraft</u>, the title of the

Bruno Serralongue exhibition we have referred to previously, alludes to a situation in which a slow burning fire does not seem to be alive, but which can end up having devastating consequences. Thus it is possible that Bruno Serralongue's photographs, taken one by one, suffer from a certain ideological uncertainty (as we have already suggested), though this is not the case when they are taken as a whole. His work tests out the possibility of a global militancy, forced (assuming the idea is to act in this hyper-connected world) to cross distances at a pace that cannot keep up with media coverage nor comprehend empirically unfathomable processes.

In this way, slowly but surely, Bruno Serralongue's method and its repetition have expunged from his work the fascination of the scoop so central to photojournalism. The difference with this photographic genre—to which Bruno Serralongue's work is not considered an alternative[4]—is the idea that direct contact with reality is not what brings information to life. If anything, as Judith Butler has suggested in her comments on the images of Abu Ghraib, from now on photography will be contained within the news story.[5] She reveals that in Iraq, the taking of photographs during torture was part of the event. The traditional distinction between what happens in front of the lens, its capture on film, at its subsequent dissemination in the form of an image has been dissolved. These three separate moments today all exist in the single click. Post-media era photographers, such as Bruno Serralongue, must therefore interrogate themselves about the significance of this persistent desire to be in actual contact with the event. This desire could only compensate a deficient scheme by way of correction. Any diagnosis of what this hypothesis would be grounded upon supposes that the technological progress of our communicative regime places us in a teleological framework. Rather than bringing us closer to the event, technological sophistication further alienates us from it, so that in spite of the strict code of ethics that is supposed to envelop contemporary journalism, we, the readers of newspapers, are only able to believe what we are told. The speed of data transmission and the ephemeral nature of the event make it impossible for us to correspondingly take on the role of information receivers set apart from the facts, and the perspective of the observers (those able to give witness to the story), who are able to see it without any sort of mediation. The images that end up coming to us can only be believed in function of the trust we have in the source, yet they do not at all allow for rational acceptance. In this sense, the enthusiasm that active participation of citizens arouses in the development of news items, the growing importance of amateur journalism, and the rise of crowdsourcing end up being little more than a smokescreen, alibis of a false democratization. Behind it all there lurks a flaw in our public sphere that points to the fact that without an image, opinion does not exist, meaning that the image has frequently played a key role as a mere certification, losing value with every repetition to which the procedure is submitted. This is what the photographic practice of Bruno Serralongue sets out: to repeat the text—never mind interpret it—by means of the fabrication of an image that pulls back until its function is limited to an illustrative, simply denotative modality. In this sense, his photographs are cleared of any informational responsibility. The performative value of his photographic series will end up being much more eloquent than their iconic content.

The series "Korea" (2001) would exemplify a way of coming to the subject of the news item where the reader's passivity is inverted. Accustomed to receiving information, the reader who incarnates Bruno Serralongue's photographic practice is in search of the character at the center of the news story. In a succinct description of the "Korea" series, the photographer explains how he made the portrait of three South Korean workers who had previously gone to Paris with the goal of extraditing Kim Woo-choong, a Daewoo board member who fled after leaving the company in a state of bankruptcy. The text that accompanies the series reads as follows: "Park Jun Kyu and Hwang Yi Min are union men. Yu Man Hyeong was an assembly line worker at a Daewoo Motors plant. They came to France in February 2001 in order to extradite Kim Woo-choong, the former boss of Daewoo, who had been on the run since the group went bankrupt. When I went to Seoul in November 2001 to do a new piece of work, I met up with the three of them and they agreed to pose for a photograph. Their portrait forms the central element in this new series." In reality, though, the series could also be described as a heroic act on the part of these three workers, who had traveled around the world of financial capital in search of the fugitive. The heroism of South Korean workers (a subject Bruno Serralongue has dealt with more deeply in <u>Rapport de forces</u>, 2004,[6] with a series of pictures of tombs honoring the memory of self-immolated workers who were protesting against unemployment) could not be represented by means of visual resources, not even by what we know as the documentary style. If the heroism of these union reps consisted in defying the distance financial capitalism establishes through its mobility, carrying out a more difficult action than what would commonly be expected, Bruno Serralongue responds with a personal movement that inverts the trip the South Korean workers had made. In this way, the idea that photography should continue to be the ally of a false universalism that makes it possible to see and comprehend everything by means of its technique, is rejected. In 1981 photographer Allan Sekula warned that, "The worldliness of photography is the outcome, not of any immanent universality of meaning, but of a project of global domination."[7] In a more intensely globalized world, Bruno Serralongue's photographic methods are an example of what anyone could do, when in general the idea is that there is nothing at all that can be done. Yet the limitations experienced when trying something that exceeds the expectations of our time (to use an expression from Alain Badiou), are also accepted.[8]

When seeking to explain how a reader becomes an author—or expressed in another way, how resistance against the limits imposed by representation's division of labor leads to a reorganization of the assigned roles of writers, critics, the public, and readers—we might recall the famous Walter Benjamin article written in 1937, at a time of rising fascism. In "The Author as Producer," the German philosopher cited the newspaper as the ideal place for this transformation to happen: "The showplace of this literary confusion is the newspaper. Its content is 'material' which refuses any form of organization other than that imposed by the reader's impatience. This impatience is not only that of the politician who expects a piece of news, or of a speculator who awaits a tip: behind them hovers the impatience of whoever feels himself excluded, whoever thinks he has a right to express his own interests himself. For a long time, the fact that nothing binds the reader to his paper as much as this avid impatience for fresh nourishment every day, has been used by editors, who are always starting new columns open to his questions, opinions, protestations. So the indiscriminate assimilation of facts goes hand in hand with the similar indiscriminate assimilation of readers, who see themselves instantly raised to the level of co-workers."[9] If this is not enough of an argument to justify reclassifying Bruno Serralongue's photography as photography done by a reader, just observe how Walter Benjamin concludes the paragraph we have just quoted. It is not only a leap to action—or a way of providing agency to the consumer of information—but an alteration of the abilities that readers are supposed to have: "The reader is indeed always ready to become a writer," says the German philosopher, "that is to say, someone who describes or even who prescribes."[10] All we have to do is take a look at the Bruno Serralongue website or the habitual presentations of his photographic series, which are always accompanied by a text written by the artist himself. The sources of these paragraphs are journalistic articles that fuel a discreet arrangement of news stories. In Rapport de forces, for example, the texts have been written using references to South Korea drawn from Le Monde diplomatique between 1982 and 2003, while in Spillovers (2004),[11] another book published by the artist, we find heterogeneous sources cited at the end of each section.

This would open up the possibility of describing Serralongue's photographic practice as an advanced montage, where texts and images are managed. Yet we must remember that this management takes place from a position limited by the economy of the reader. In the early 1970s, John Baldessari cleverly revealed what the position of this reader meant, and what were—and what continue to be, depending how you look at the question—its limitations. In the short video The Meaning of Various Newsphotos to Ed Henderson (1973), the artist shows photographs clipped out from a newspaper. Behind the camera there is someone trying to decipher them. The interpreter can only try to speculate about how, where, and when each snapshot shown to him was made. By taking the photographs out of the context of the page, their accessory character is more intensely dramatized. Yet here we also see how difficult it is for the interpreter to retrieve the original meaning of each image appearing in the press. Instead of this information, the commentaries based on suppositions highlight the creativity of the newspaper reader. The question we thus have to ask is this: is there such a big difference between interpreting these press clippings with the photographs' original captions and without them? To a certain degree, the processes we have looked at in the Baldessari video are not that different from those carried out by Bruno Serralongue. With his photographic series he too is seeking to erase the captions from beneath the images appearing in the press. This would be useful as a way of finding a place for other meanings derived from the experience of a reader who accepts his limitations, and even his different capacity when compared with a professional journalist. The series "Calais," 2006–2008, could be considered an attempt to undo the meaning of images associated with illegal immigration. If, as Giorgio Agamben claims, our laws deprive the immigrant of his humanity, the definition of this complex subject that is the immigrant is complemented by a profile that identifies him as a natural object, confused, mixed, and hybridized with a forested space. Since 1999, the area of Sangatte in the north of France has been a crossing point for people attempting to traverse the English Channel. Bruno Serralongue's project, which included some 20 images and a slideshow called "Risky Lines" (2007), was conceived as just another representation that would add itself to the images seen in different media on the subject. We could make an effort to define their internal qualities and explore the photographs Bruno Serralongue has made until now hermeneutically, but the fact is that we will only be able to conclude that this project is a mere quantitative supplement of the images already circulating in the media sphere, including those taken by support groups, avid photojournalists, and supposedly neutral and objective media, only that with his contribution we would be able to define the essential policy of this documentary work. To paraphrase Susan Buck-Morss, an excess of images protects us from the temptation to choose one of them as the one true one.[12] In any case, all this will lead us to the conclusion that Bruno Serralongue's photographic practice does not intervene exclusively in the local and particular meaning of each photograph he produces. His field of action situates him beyond a visuality whose purpose is to exhaust the event with the gaze. Perhaps Serralongue proposes a general demobilization, which would render ineffective the mechanisms of a daily press obsessed with reporting everything. Serralongue's photographs connect us with events of different kinds and, simultaneously, create a distance from them. For this reason it is not at all unusual to discover that in many of his photographs what we are looking at are dialogues, conversations, and debates, discursive situations in comparison to which the photographic medium falls short.

1 Karl-Heinz Bohrer, Die Aesthetik des Schreckens. Die pessimistiche Romantik und Ernst Jünger Frühwerk, Ullstein, Frankfurt 1983, p. 360.
2 The exhibition Feux de camp, held at the Jeu de Paume (2010), was conceived following the same principle of thematic groups of photographs.
3 Michael Fried, "Barthes' Punctum," Critical Inquiry, vol. 31, no. 3, March 2005.
4 "In the face of media reality, I produce a subjectivity, rather than an alternative. This is because I believe that the alternative quickly bounces back, while subjectivity resists. It is not the images that resist ... " Interview by Thomas Seelig with Bruno Serralongue, in infra-mince, no. 5, 2009, p. 48.
5 See Judith Butler, Frames of War: When Is Life Grievable, Verso, London 2009.
6 Bruno Serralongue, Rapport de forces, One Star Press, Paris 2004.
7 Allan Sekula. "Traffic in Photographs," in Photography Against the Grain: Essays and Photo Works 1973–1983, Nova Scotia College of Art and Design, Halifax 1984, p. 96.
8 As Alain Badiou says quite precisely: "In any period of time, in any sequence of history, we have to maintain a relationship with what exceeds our possibilities." http://sloght.org/content/11385.
9 Walter Benjamin, "The Author as Producer," in Reflections: Essays, Aphorisms, Autobiographical Writings, Schocken Books, New York 1978, p. 224.
10 Ibid.
11 Bruno Serralongue, Spillovers, Cneai/Air de Paris, Chatou/Paris, 2004.
12 See Susan Buck-Morss, Thinking Past Terror: Islamism and Critical Theory on the Left, Verso, London 2003.

"A Repertoire of Collective Action"
Bruno Serralongue, Marta Gili, and Dirk Snauwaert in Conversation

Marta Gili

I think that we ought to start this conversation with a discussion of your particular working method. It's a significant part of your discourse and the starting point for your artistic practice. Can you explain it?

Bruno Serralongue

My method consists of drawing on information published and broadcast in the news, whether in the newspapers, on the internet, on TV, or on the radio. You could compare it to press agencies like AFP (Agence France Presse), which receive information and transmit it to news desks on a daily basis. I have my very own AFP—all the news formats available to readers/viewers. So I don't have access to the raw information in the form of news wires, but rather to information sorted and selected by news desks. I then make my own selection in turn, and if the information refers to a forthcoming event, anywhere in the world, that I find of interest, I try to get there by my own means to take photographs.

Dirk Snauwaert

When you take photographs, is it fair to say that the insistence and precision of your "analogue" method of framing—the viewpoint, de-centered subject, composition, and off-screen space—have come about as a result of the advent of digital photography and its capacity for producing images in large quantities and the potential for fully manipulating and "fictionalizing" the images? Is your "documentary" use of the medium, in which the author becomes invisible, part of the tendency to take over outdated technologies as a form of archaeology exploring that which belongs to the past, but not yet to history?

Bruno Serralongue

No. Don't forget that I began my photographic work in 1993, before digital photography existed. Analogue photography was all there was back then. I'm not denying the differences between analogue and digital, but the uses and functions of photography in society haven't changed. People still believe in what it shows as much as they ever did. The same goes for documents.

Marta Gili

It seems as if you are trying to maintain a certain degree of critical independence by developing such a precise procedure. But independence

vis-à-vis whom or what? The agencies, the media, photographers, or the event itself?

Bruno Serralongue

Back in 1936, Walter Benjamin pointed out in "The Work of Art in the Age of Mechanical Reproduction" that, "with the increasing extension of the press, which kept placing new political, religious, scientific, professional, and local organs before the readers, an increasing number of readers became writers—at first, occasional ones [...] And today there is hardly a gainfully employed European who could not, in principle, find an opportunity to publish somewhere or other comments on his work, grievances, documentary reports, or that sort of thing ... Thus, the distinction between author and public is about to lose its basic character. The difference becomes merely functional; it may vary from case to case."[1] Benjamin underlines the fact that there are no longer any fixed identities, but rather roles to be taken on from time to time. The headline in the newspaper Libération on August 20, 2005, was, "Are we all journalists now?" alongside a photograph of the audience at a Beyoncé concert, all taking photos of her. Photojournalism is undergoing an identity crisis more than an economic one. What does being a professional mean when amateur pictures make the cover of magazines, as was the case with the London bombings in 2005? Clearly, what destabilizes professionals is the fact that such photographs circulate and are given access to the specialist press. Does privileged, "staff only" access still really exist?

That is a long-winded prelude to saying that the question I have always been interested in asking is, "Who produces the image?" The method I have established allows me to ask it, because it doesn't address the subject of an image—which is often the same for amateurs and professionals alike—but rather its production, which is always unique and is the photographer's real signature. The point is not to maintain critical independence, then, but to construct it.

Marta Gili

Photo agencies have been in decline for a number of years now, and the situation is getting progressively worse; they are undergoing a real economic crisis which started out as an identity crisis, I quite agree. Apart from the fundamental question that you have raised about the production of the image, can't the concepts "information" and "event" be said to be undergoing a similar decline?

Bruno Serralongue

One of the French President's advisers stated in an interview printed in Le Monde on January 8, 2008, that media coverage of presidential events had risen by 450% since Nicolas Sarkozy's election! Is that a good thing? It appears that media presence is what counts. Your time on air is time that is not available to your opponents. So if the concepts of information and event are in decline, it's because everything is now a media event. As Jean-Charles Massera said, "the information society organizes time, true to its mediatized experience of history treated as the present, on a model of time reduced to eventful moments."[2] Everything is an event, because that's how we live in the information society. You have to be in the event. We are told that there is no choice. As the philosopher Jean Baudrillard said, "We are in the world screen"—in other words, we are susceptible to emit and/or receive events/information. But the risk is then failing to spot which events could have long-term historical significance.

Marta Gili

What stance does your work take in relation to the event? Why did you go to Chiapas in 1996 and Calais between 2006 and 2008, for instance? To be at the heart of the event?

Bruno Serralongue

Since 1995, my work has been guided by the notion of community. What I found interesting was placing the photographic site at the heart of a community rather than at the instant of the event. Then I very quickly realized that the two things were, in fact, the same. That is how I ended up in southeastern Mexico photographing the Intergalactic Encounter for Humanity and against neoliberalism, organized at the behest of the Chiapas guerrillas (the "Encuentro" series, 1996).

I only produce a few series every year—two, sometimes just the one, with a small handful of photographs per series, from five for "Destination Vegas" (1996) to 22 for "Calais" (2006–2008). There are links between the events, which echo each other, even if they are several years apart—for instance, "Free Tibet" (1998) and "Tibet in Exile (Dharamsala)" (2008). Since they are chosen with reference to specific criteria, they represent both a point of view on some key social issues and conflicts of the late 20th and early 21st centuries, given a planetary audience and echo by the media, and a highly individual cartography of my own interests.

A network of references and "figures" is created from series to series, to the point of forming a “repertoire of collective action.” I’ve taken this expression from the American historian and sociologist Charles Tilly (1929–2008). While I was planning the exhibition at the Jeu de Paume, I was thinking about the significant repetitions that eventually built up a repertoire. It was only recently that I became aware of the repertoire’s existence. First of all it had to build up gradually, in the shadow of the series. But still, I believe that it was present as a project from the outset, even if I’m only expressing it clearly today. That is what pushed me to produce photographs at the heart of collective events.

Another reason for my approach is linked to my interest for the history of art in general and photography in particular. I came to photography through my university studies. I can sum it up in the words of Christian Boltanski—“Photography is photojournalism, the rest is painting”—quoted by Michel Nuridsany in the catalogue for the group exhibition Ils se disent peintres, ils se disent photographes that he curated at the ARC Paris in the late 1980s. What I find interesting in this quote is really the affirmation of a field of action proper to photography. Nuridsany begins his text with this quote and concludes by modifying it slightly, replacing “photojournalism” with “reportage.” Photography’s field of action is indeed reportage: photojournalism refers to a profession, while reportage refers to photography’s own specific regimen.

Dirk Snauwaert

Is the creation of this “repertoire” driven by the desire to describe or identify phenomena of “collective action”—a descriptive quality that is the core principle behind photography—or can it rather be seen as a desire to redefine the notion of the “historical moment,” in the sense of a shift from the “moment” toward a sequence and repetition of events and actions? What then becomes of the notions of bearing witness and proof associated therewith?

Bruno Serralongue

Bearing witness, proof, historical documents, archives, and description are all contained within the technological system—a skilful combination of optics, chemistry, and electronics—which has been in constant use since the first half of the 19th century and which is known as photography.

The artist makes choices which sort through this common heritage to bring out certain notions at the expense of others. They may all remain constantly present, but they may be dormant, like sleeper cells of terrorists or spies. Which means that the work resides not solely in what is shown, but also in the potentialities of meaning that arise from the conditions in which the picture is taken—thanks to which a new work can emerge from a very narrow set of possibilities. Which means that two photographs can be taken at the same instant at the same event, maybe even of the same person or the same scene, but if one is taken by a journalist and the other by myself, the former will be information, the latter counter-information. I'm not fascinated by the event. Can you be fascinated by a press conference? I'm not obsessed with being at the heart of events, which is something that certainly drives a lot of photojournalists. They put themselves into situations where they can create photographs that can have a historical impact and bear witness to History. Some photographs have achieved that. In my case, the conditions are not there for that to happen to me. On the other hand, my photographs are historical documents. In other words, they are relative and ambiguous.

Marta Gili

With reference to the "repertoire of collective action," do all the images that you "wrested" from their series to give them a shared theme for the exhibition, like a flip book, take on a new political or aesthetic status when they are reorganized?

Bruno Serralongue

I don't think so. They are the same photographs, after all! Still, it is a possible effect that could be due to the shift in attention. The aim is indeed to shift the gaze that the viewer brings to the work. To shift the gaze of viewers who are already familiar with my work, but also my own gaze at the same time. The viewer might feel an impression of disorder on discovering the way the works are hung, since it is neither chronological nor linear. No picture rail has been installed, so no order of visit is imposed. Visitors can cast their gaze round and take in the whole exhibition. I've noticed seven sets in my series that can be included in the "repertoire of collective action": press conferences, meetings, demonstrations, fireworks, fires, portraits, scenography/show, and works to read.

The initial hypothesis for the Jeu de Paume exhibition was to juxtapose photographs taken at different events which were not necessarily connected, but which reveal resemblances and constants.

The question thrown up by these montages is the nature of the proximity between these series, for example between the machines set on fire by striking workers at the New Fabris factory ("New Fabris, Châtellerault," 2009) and a dying camp fire where huddled migrants try to keep warm in the depths of a Calais winter ("Calais," 2006–2008). Is it the fire? I'm tempted to say that's not much to be going on! Actually, I think that such juxtapositions refer to a political structuring of the world and power relationships as expressed through the media. I think that the necessity of being on the world screen causes a rarefaction of forms of struggle, to the advantage of visual figures, which are compulsory but nonetheless effective in their own way. The New Fabris workers' gas canisters were empty and were not connected to any detonator; they were visually effective but had no destructive power. Yet the bluff still worked. At least in part.

My plans for exhibitions are influenced by whatever I'm reading at the time. An interview with Jean Baudrillard published in Le Monde on May 28, 2005, served to formulate the hypothesis for this exhibition (and so what if Baudrillard's emphatic style is open to mockery): "We are no longer critical TV viewers, which presupposes the continued existence of a space of intelligence and of distance. We are no longer in the society of the spectacle, in staging, in alienation by screens, etc. We are no longer in front of a stage; we are in a network, we are the network. The current hegemony of media power is such that there is no more domination by the spectacle, but rather a form of tentacular homogeneity that is not even imperialist. And we are immersed in it. We are in the world screen. Our present merges with the flux of images and signs; our minds dissolve in a surfeit of information and the accumulation of permanent topicality which digests the present itself."

1 Walter Benjamin, "The Work of Art in the Age of Mechanical Reproduction," in Illuminations, trans. Harry Zohn, Schocken, New York 1969, p. 232.

2 Jean-Charles Massera, "The Lesson of Stains (Towards an Aesthetics of Reconstitution)," in Pierre Huyghe, The Third Memory, trans. Brian Holmes, Centre Pompidou, Paris 2000, p. 124.

Fires

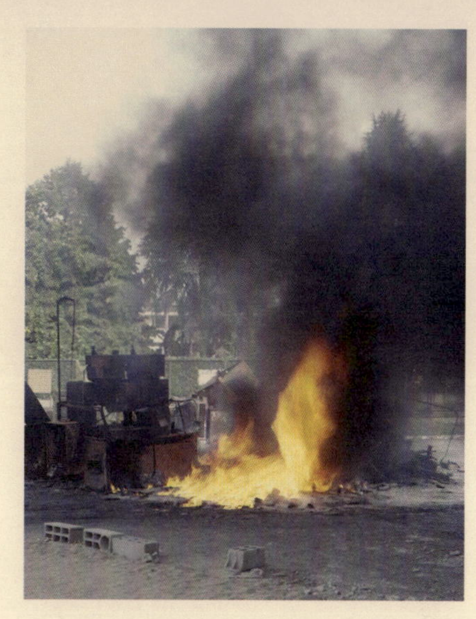

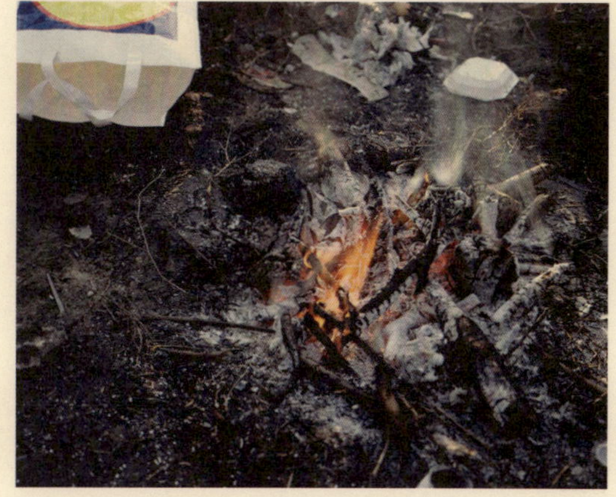

To Read

MAS
KULTURAL

EARTH SUMMIT
2002
should Ensure
Earth

LE DEVELOPPEMENT N'EST PAS LE DEVOIR DE L'ETAT
SEUL LE CITOYEN EST L'ARTISAN ET LA FINALITE DU
DEVELOPPEMENT AUSSI LUI APPARTIENT-IL DE PARTICIPER
A L'ESSOR DE LA SOCIETE OU IL VIT.

STEEL METAL & ENGINEERING
WORKERS FEDRATION OF INDIA
MAHARASHTRA STATE
World Social Forum
नार्दन रेलवे मैंस यूनियन
PUBLIC SERVICES INTERNATIONAL
ANOTHER WORLD IS POSSIBLE WITH EQUALITY
Lets Build Strong Global Solidarity!
Protect Workers' Right!!
Success of IVth WSF!
Winning of Workers' Dignity!!
NEPAL FILM WORKERS UNION
PSI COORDINATION COMMITTEE NEPAL

10 VJET
STABILITET
KFOR
KFOR: SIGURON NJË AMBIENT TË QETË DHE TË SIGURT

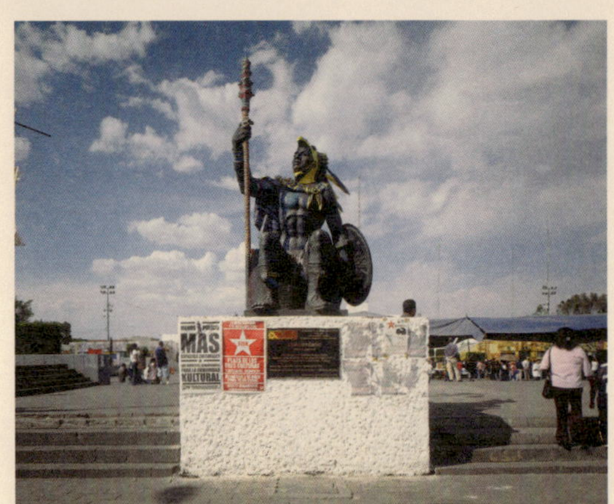

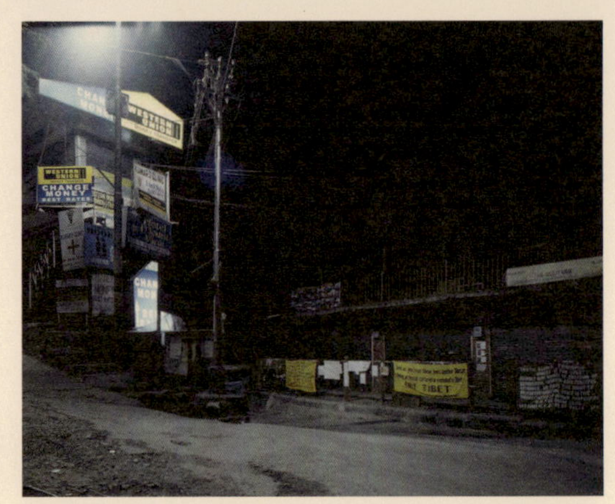

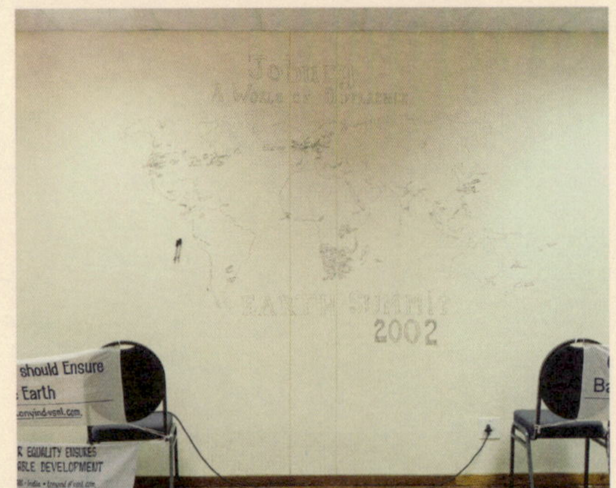

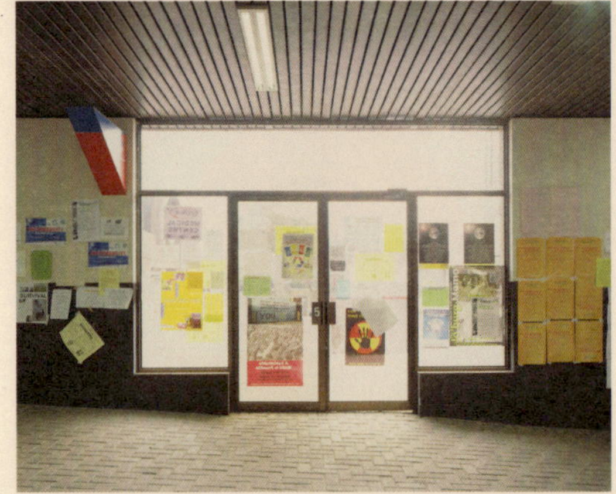

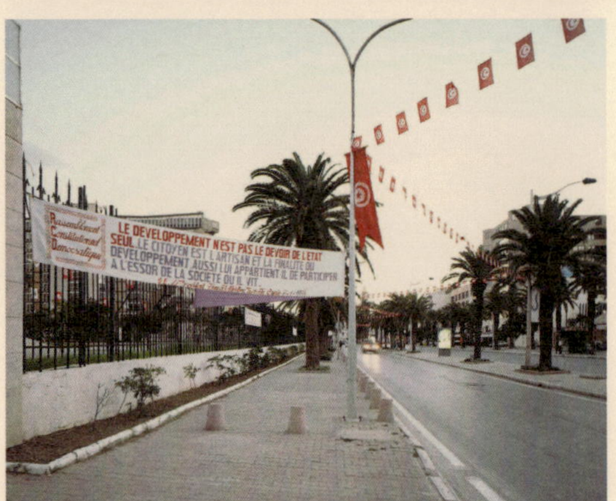

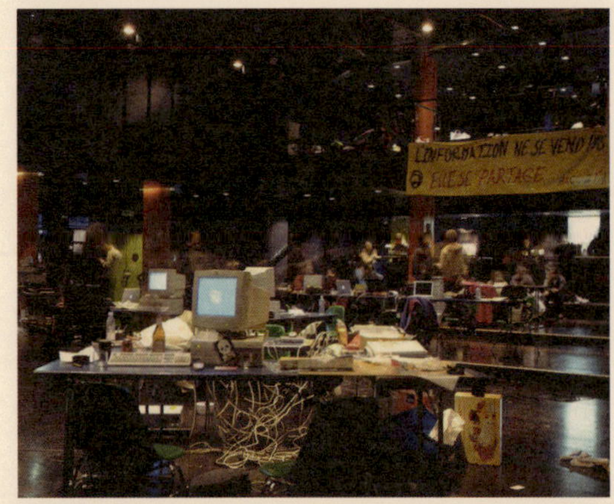

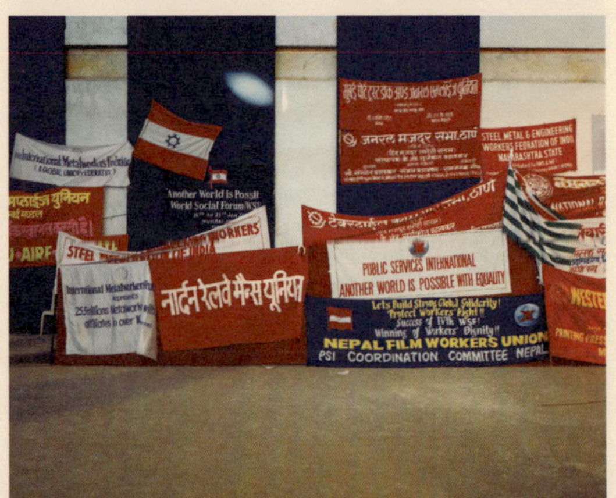

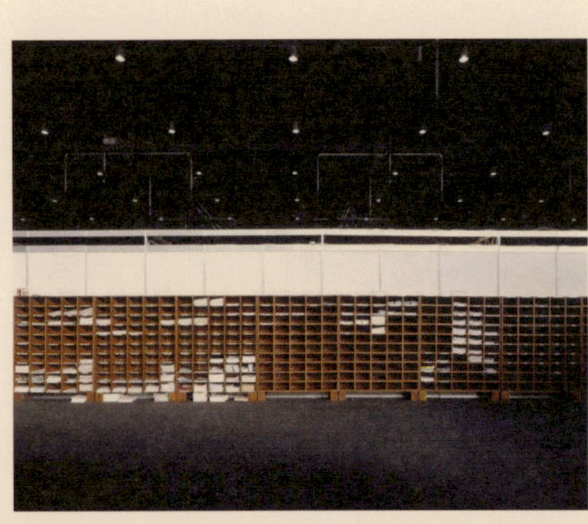

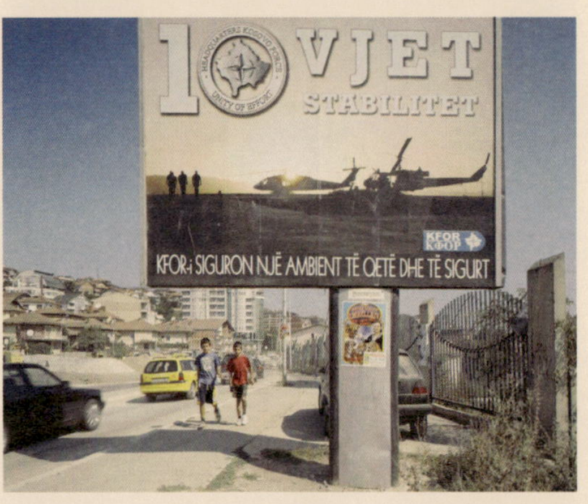

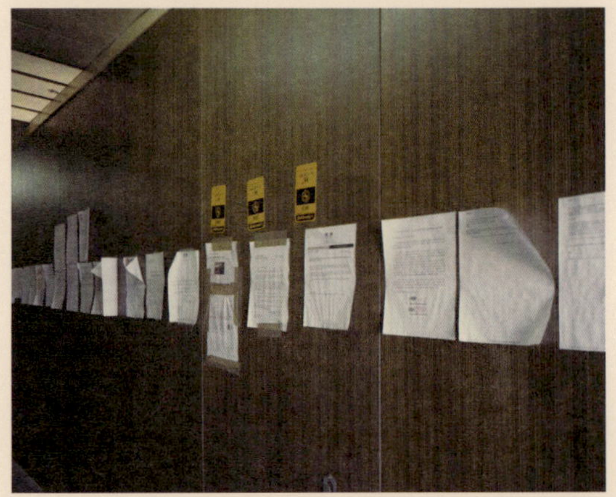

Press Conferences

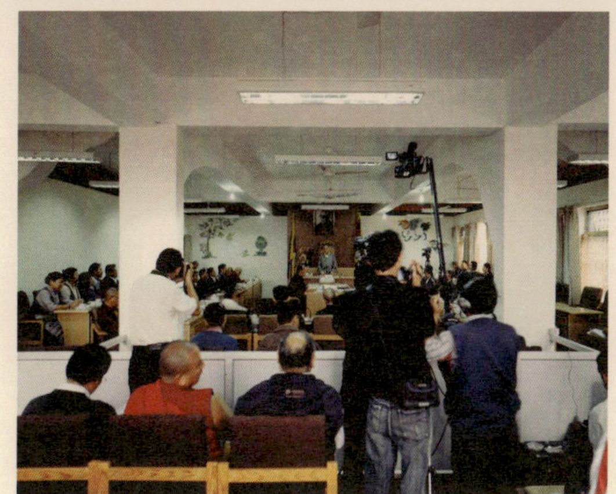

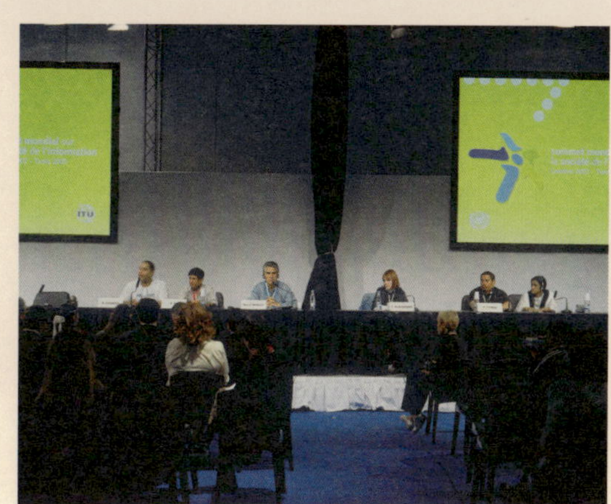

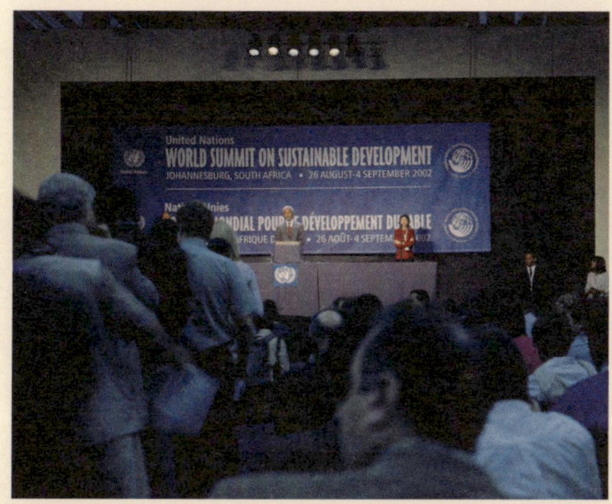

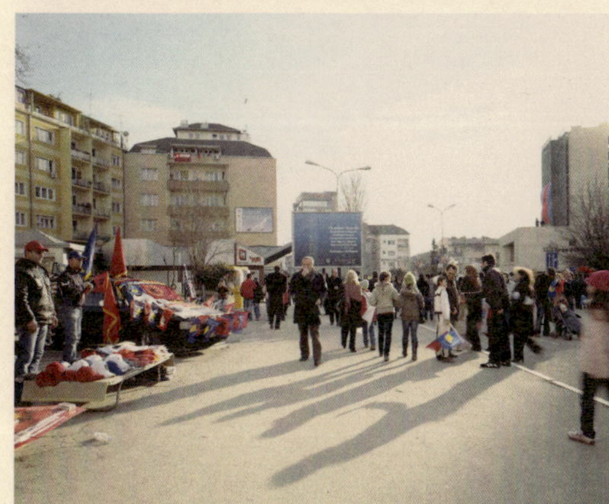

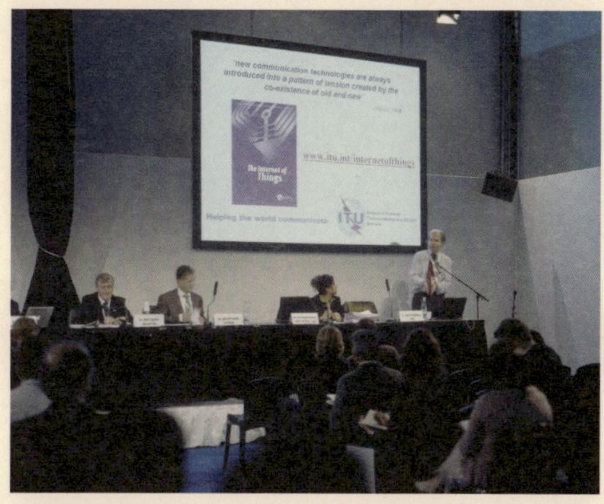

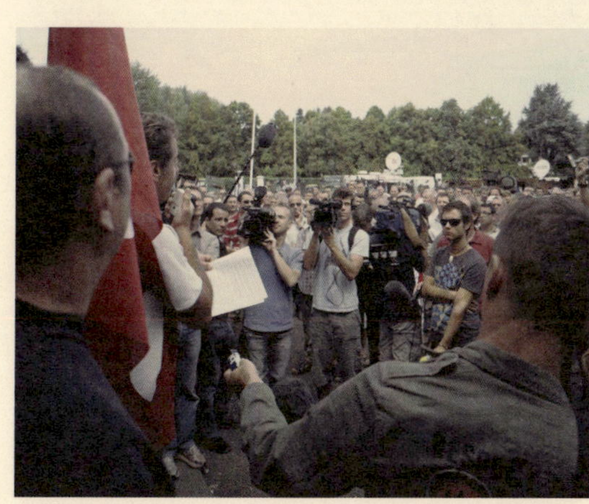

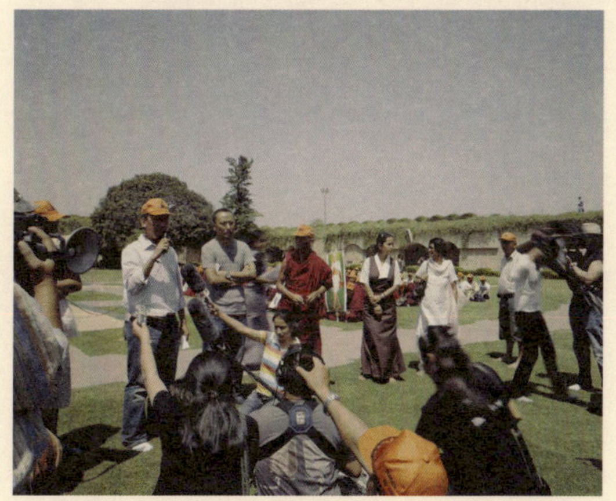

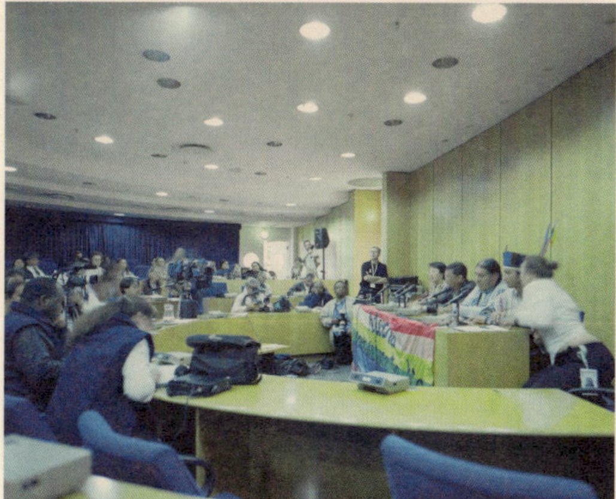

Fireworks

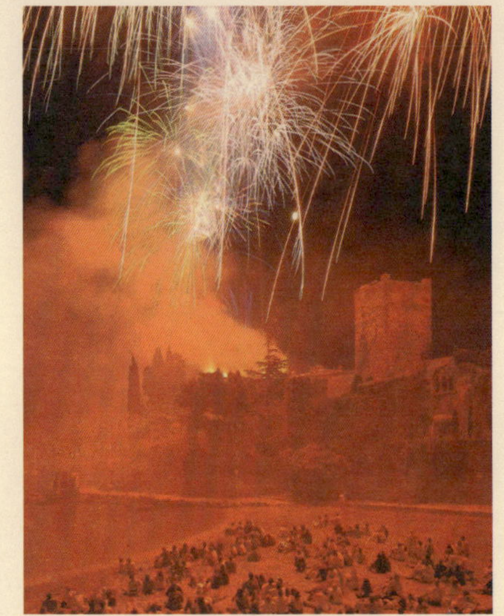

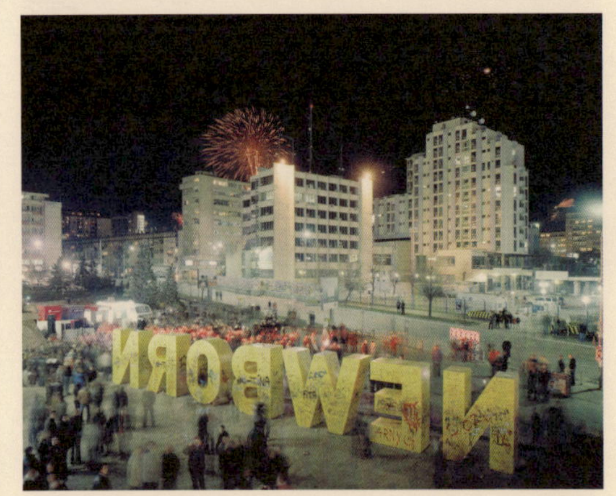

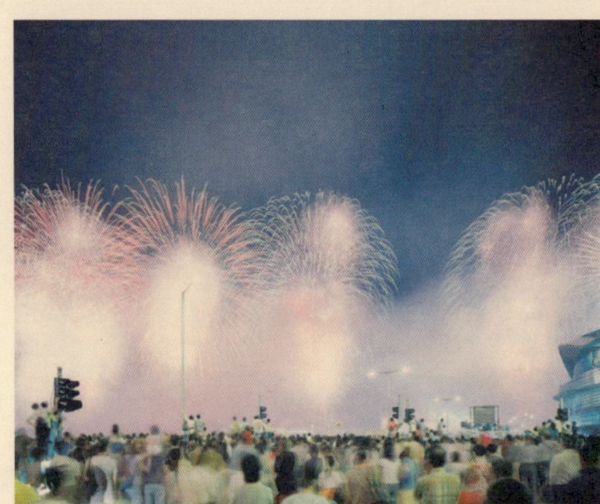

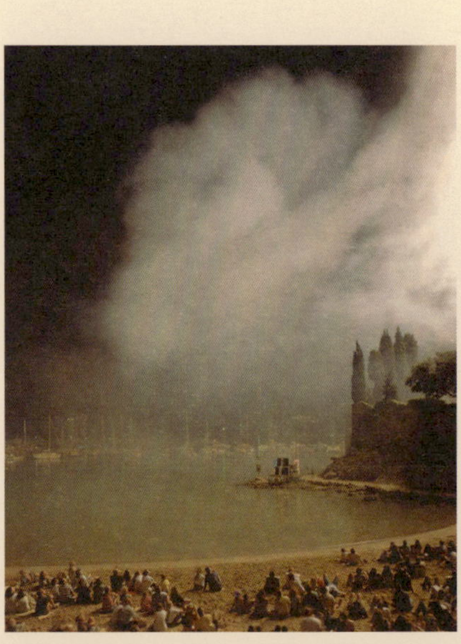

Demonstrations

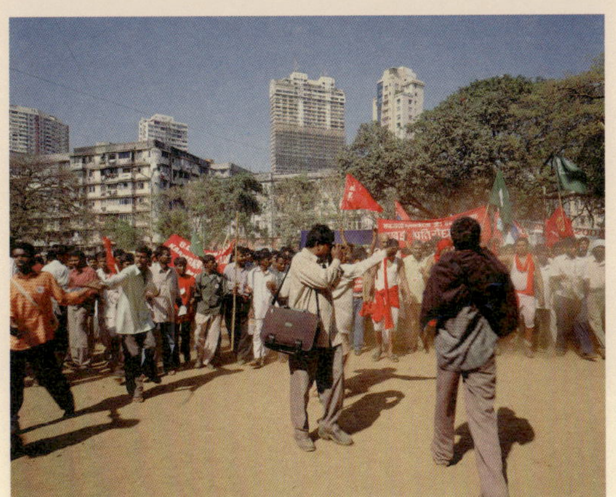

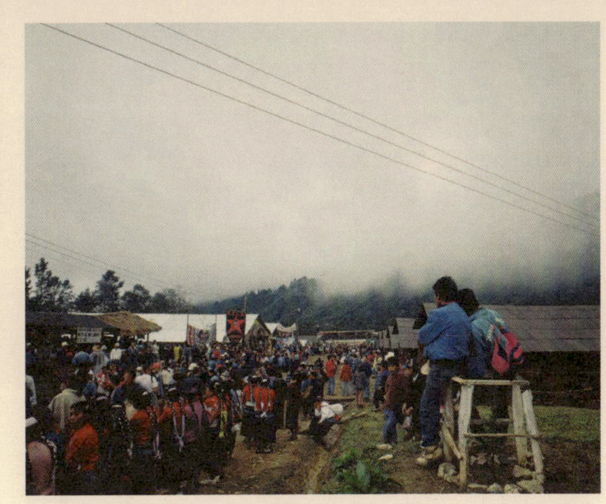

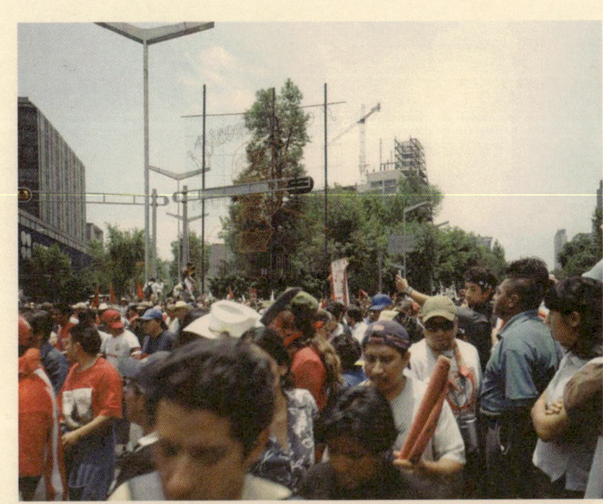

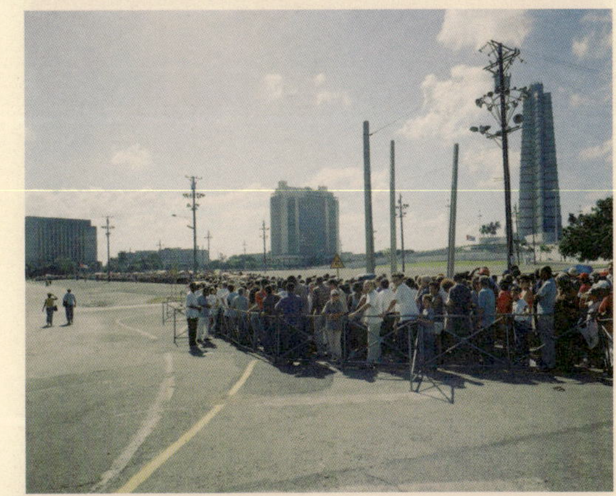

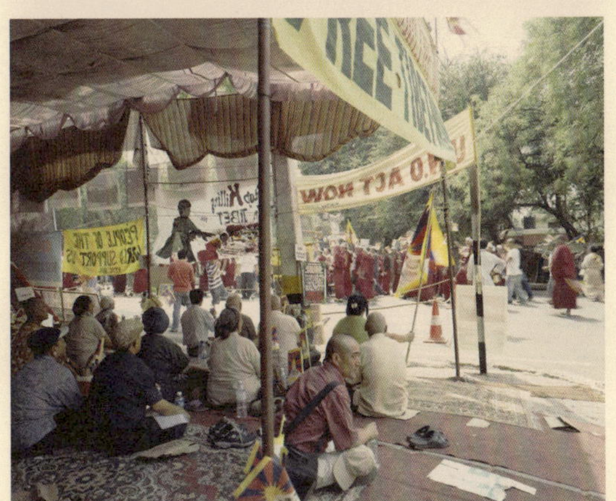

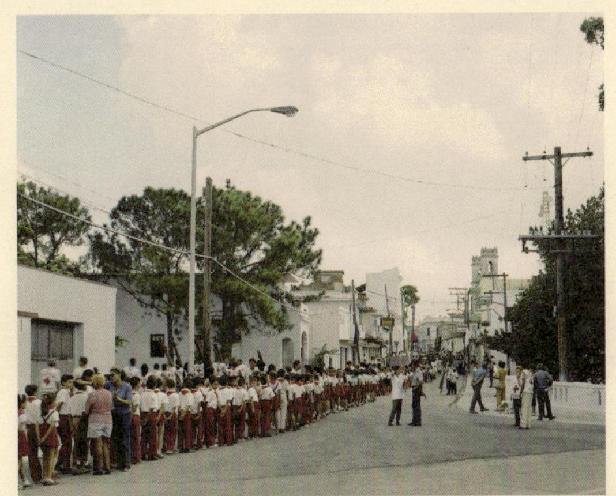

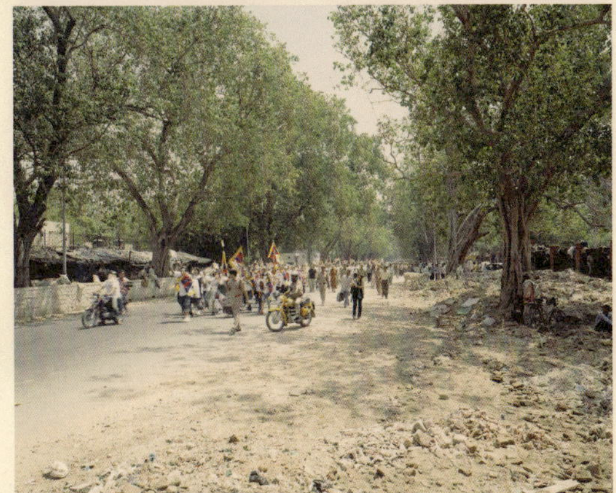

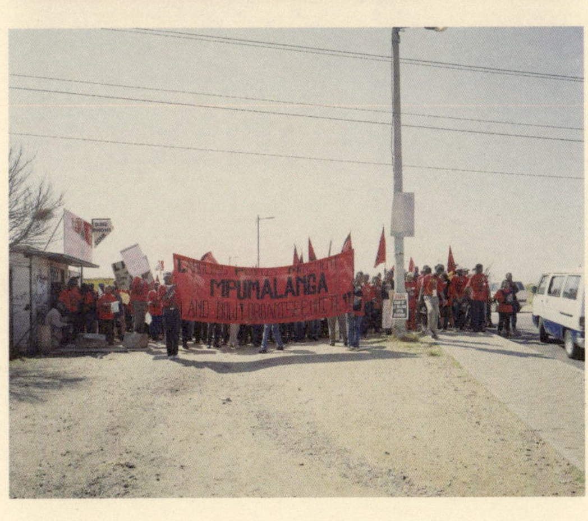

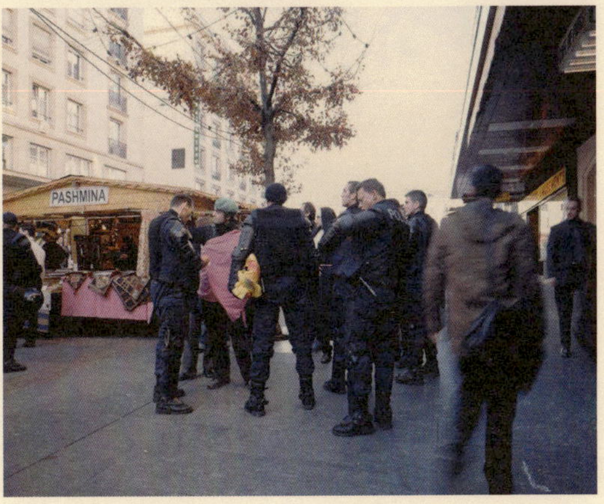

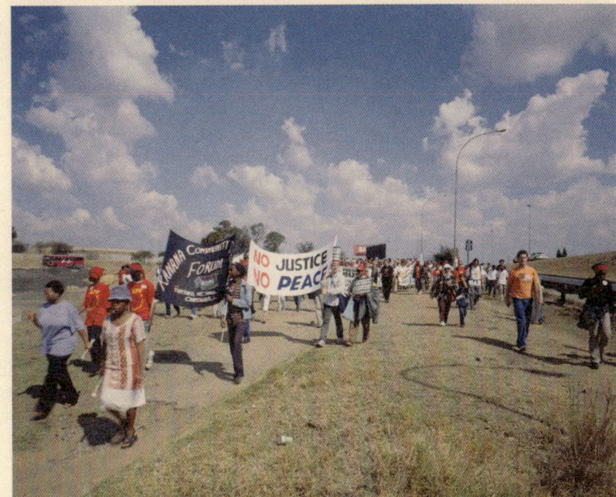

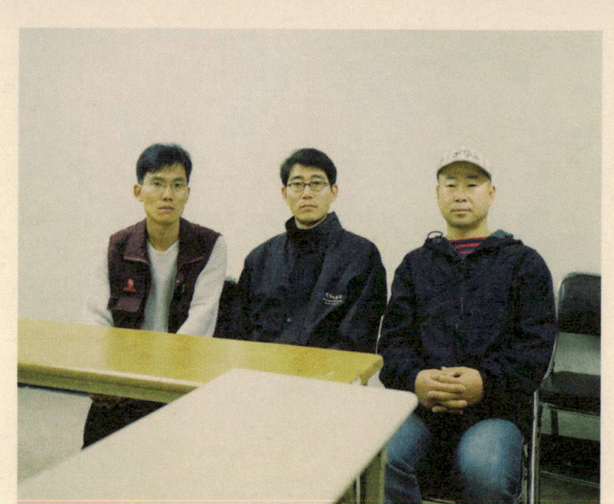

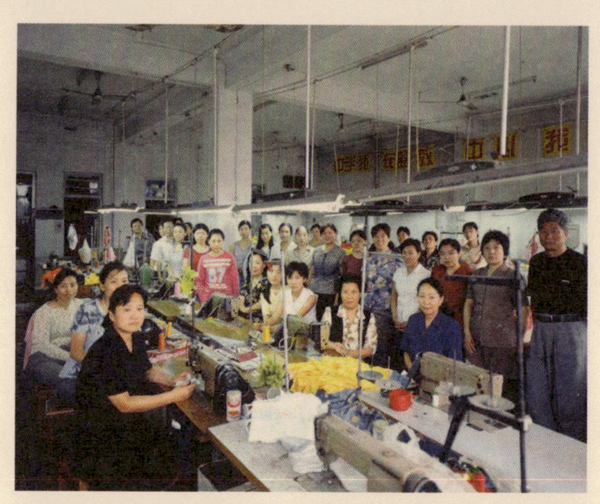

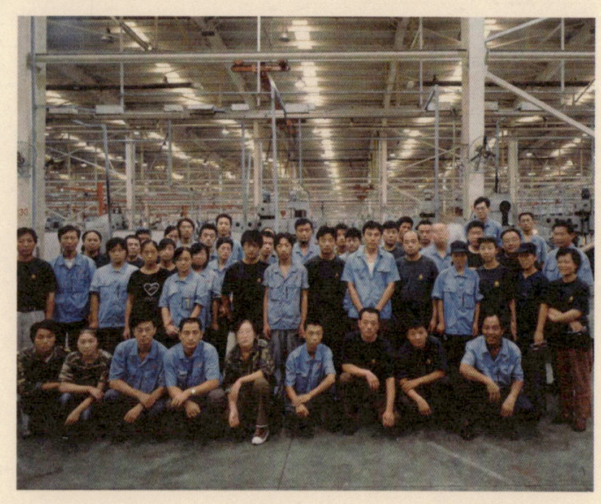

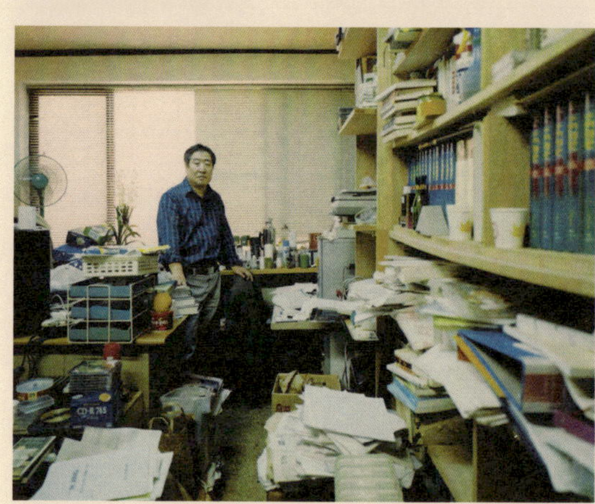

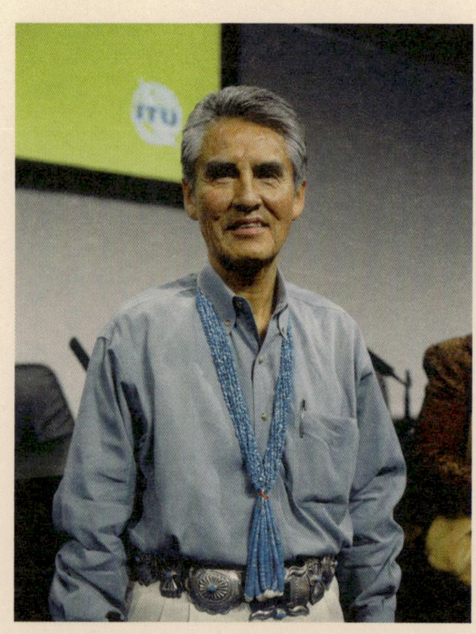
ITU

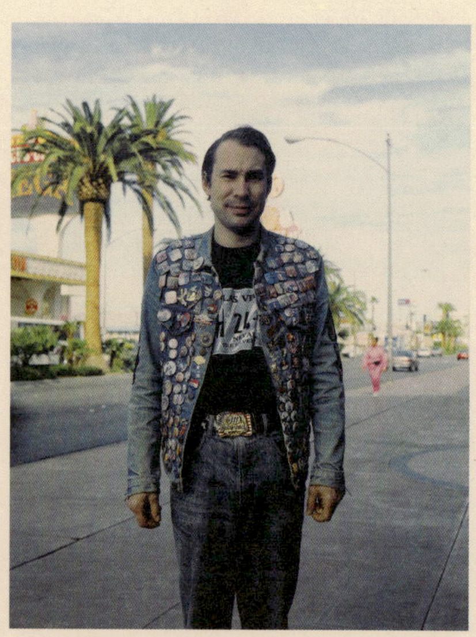

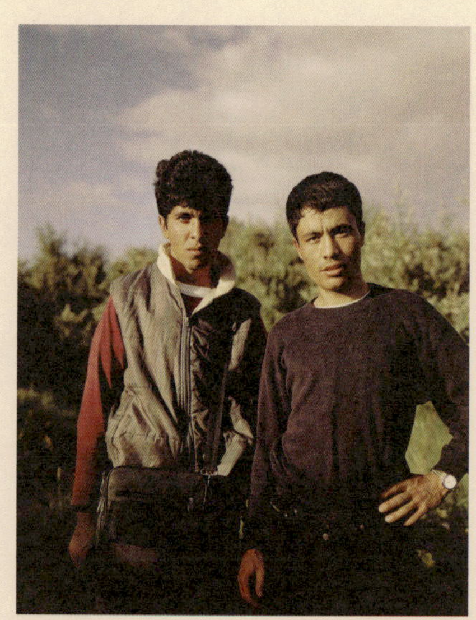

Meetings

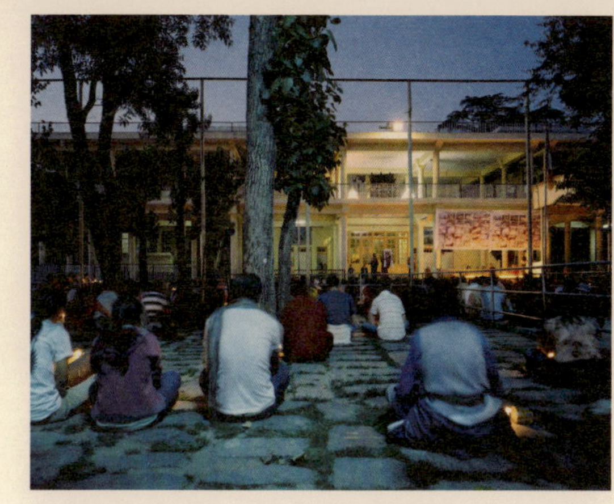

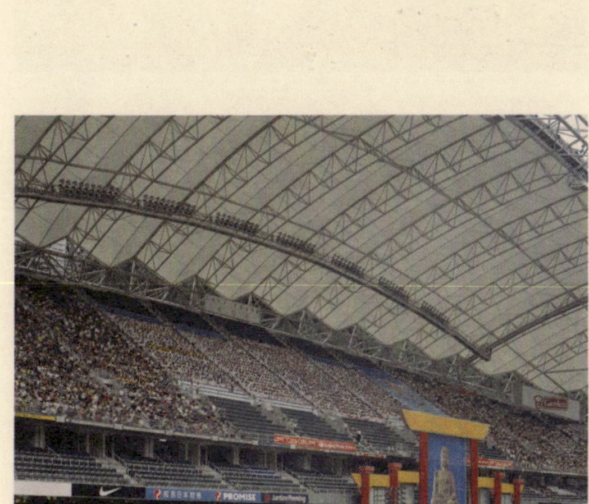

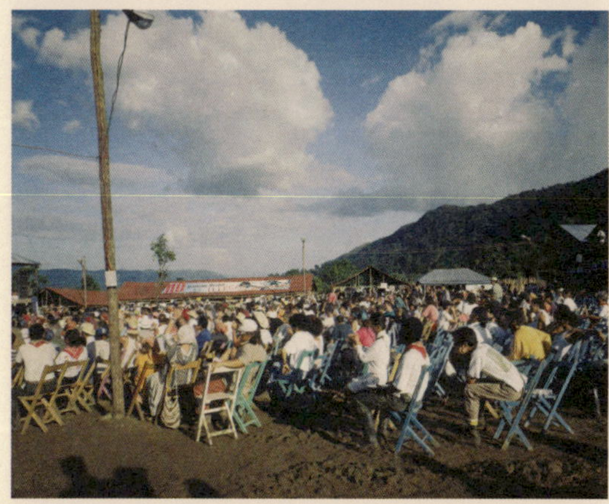

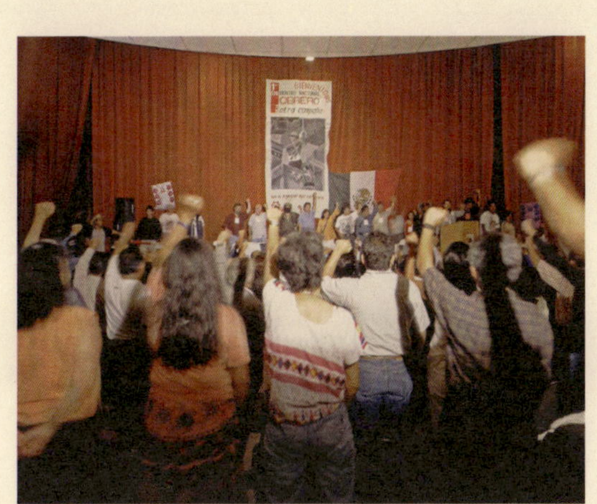

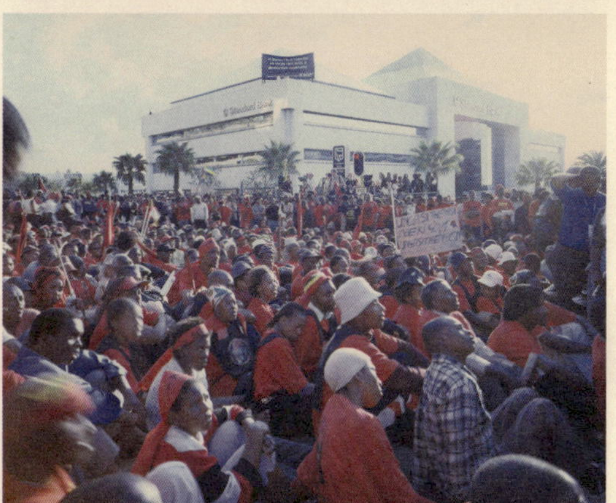

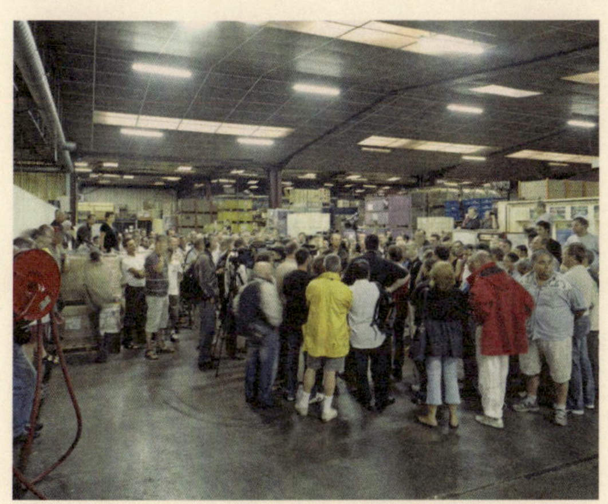

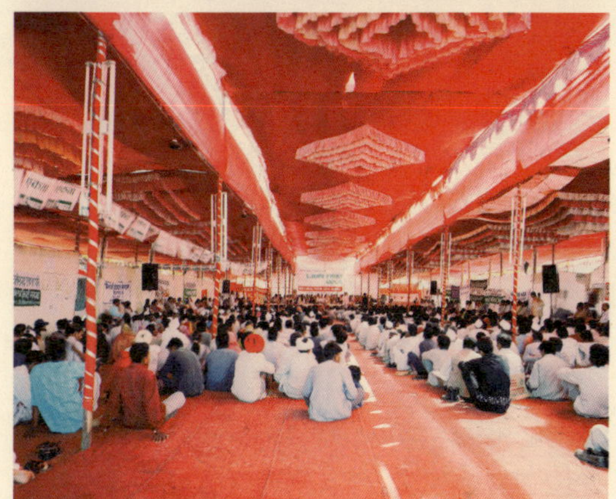

Scenography
Shows

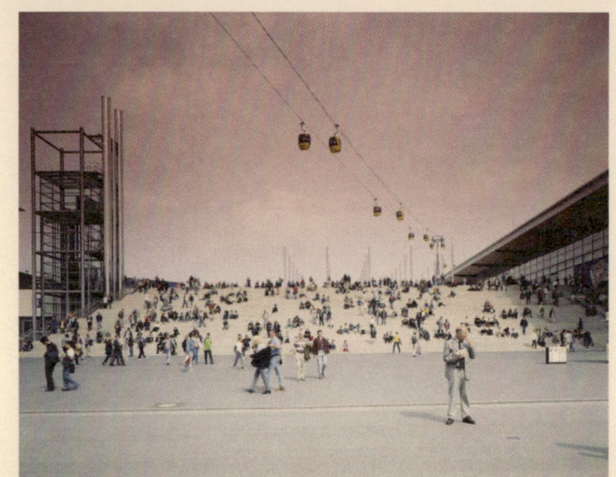

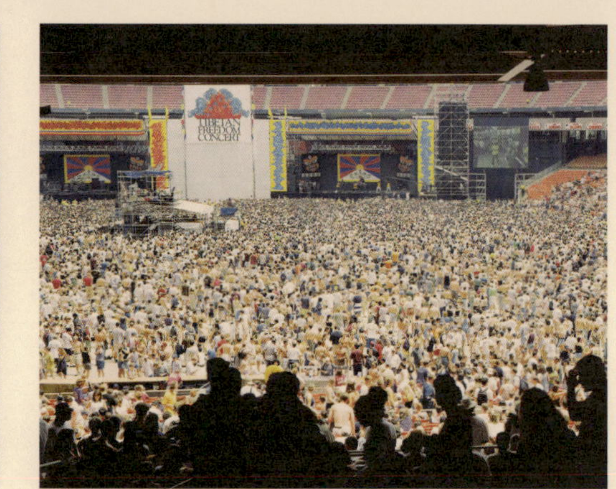

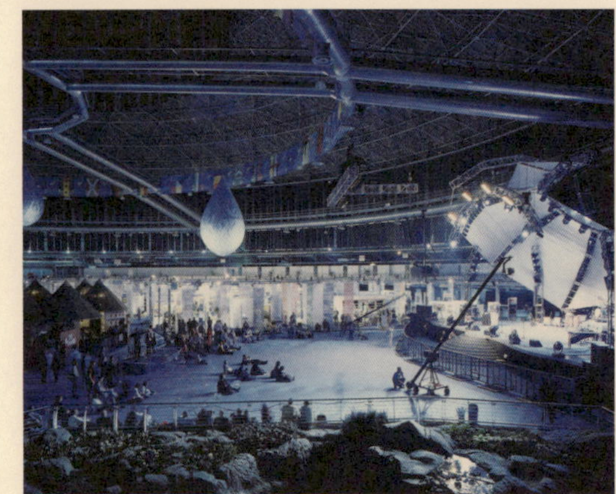

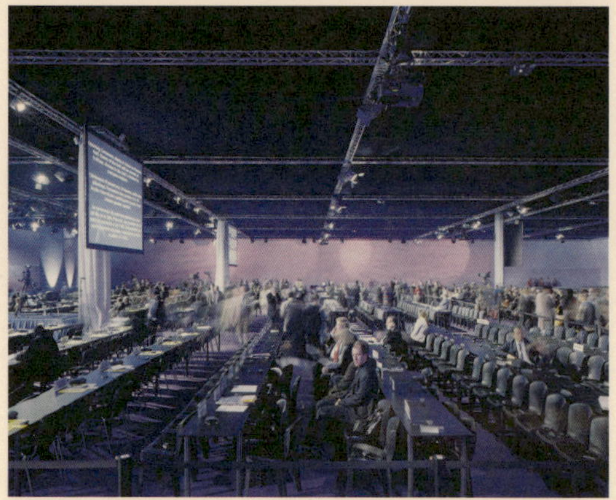

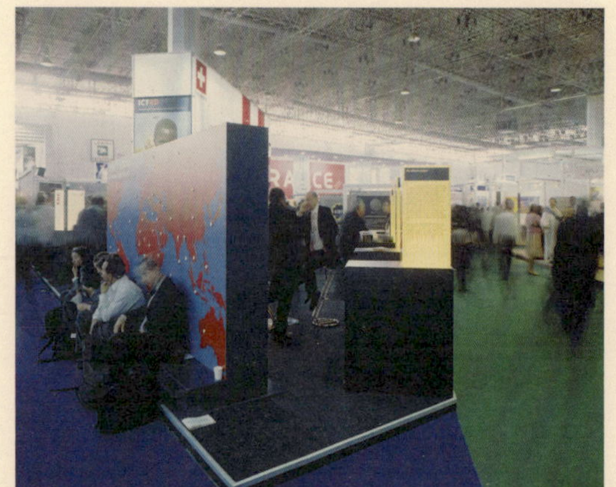

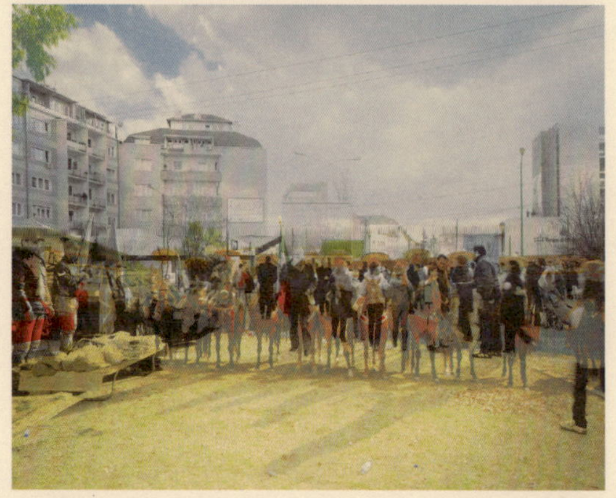

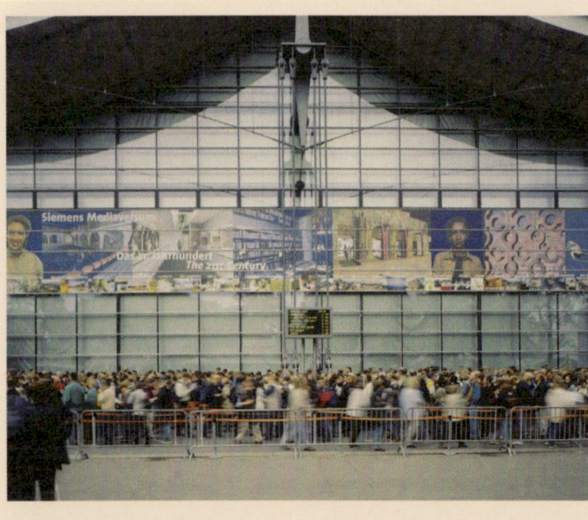

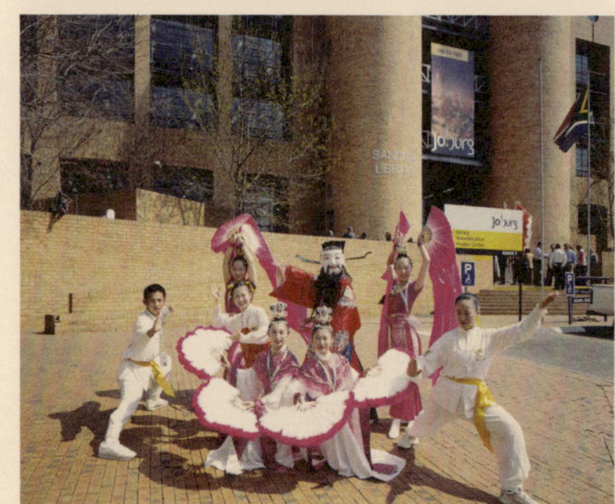

List of Works

The photographs reproduced in this publication are indicated by a folio number preceding the title of the photograph.

For certain series, the different printing formats are explained by the edition numbers. In the case of an edition of three, the third print (3/3) is a smaller format. In the case of edition of five, the fourth and fifth prints (4/5 and 5/5) are a smaller format.

★ Work exhibited at Wiels
● Work exhibited at the Jeu de Paume
■ Work exhibited at La Virreina
▲ Work exhibited at the Jeu de Paume and at La Virreina

"Les Faits divers" [News Items], 1993–1995

From October 1993 to April 1995 I systematically read through the "human interest" section in the daily newspaper Nice-Matin. Using information in the article I selected, I would find my way to the scene of the event and take a photograph. A summary of the published article is silkscreened onto the white reserve under the print.

51 photographs; Ilfochrome prints with silkscreen mounted on aluminum, frame and glass,
102 × 85 cm each
Edition of 3 + 2 AP

– n°1, samedi 9 octobre 1993
– n°2, mercredi 10 novembre 1993
– n°3, jeudi 18 novembre 1993
– n°4, vendredi 19 novembre 1993
– n°5a, vendredi 19 novembre 1993
– n°5b, vendredi 19 novembre 1993
– n°6, samedi 4 décembre 1993
– n°7, lundi 6 décembre 1993
– n°8, vendredi 10 décembre 1993
– n°9, mardi 4 janvier 1994
● – n°10, mercredi 5 janvier 1994
– n°11, samedi 8 janvier 1994
– n°12, dimanche 9 janvier 1994
– n°13, jeudi 13 janvier 1994
– n°14, mercredi 2 mars 1994
– n°15, mercredi 2 mars 1994
– n°16, vendredi 4 mars 1994
– n°17, vendredi 4 mars 1994
– n°18, lundi 7 mars 1994
– n°19, lundi 28 mars 1994
– n°20, mardi 29 mars 1994
– n°21, mardi 29 mars 1994
– n°22, mercredi 30 mars 1994
– n°23, dimanche 10 avril 1994
– n°24, vendredi 22 avril 1994
● – n°25, mardi 26 avril 1994
– n°26, mercredi 27 avril 1994
– n°27, lundi 9 mai 1994
– n°28, samedi 14 mai 1994
– n°29, lundi 16 mai 1994
– n°30, dimanche 22 mai 1994
– n°31, mardi 24 mai 1994
– n°32, mercredi 25 mai 1994
– n°33, vendredi 24 juin1994
– n°34, jeudi 7 juillet 1994
– n°35, vendredi 29 juillet 1994
– n°36, mardi 2 août 1994
– n°37, samedi 20 août 1994
– n°38, lundi 19 septembre 1994
– n°39, vendredi 14 octobre 1994
– n°40, jeudi 17 novembre 1994
– n°41, samedi 26 novembre 1994
– n°42, samedi 17 décembre 1994
– n°43, dimanche 18 décembre 1994
– n°44, lundi 19 décembre 1994
– n°45, lundi 9 janvier 1995
– n°46, dimanche 22 janvier 1995
– n°47, mercredi 8 février 1995
– n°48, mercredi 1er mars 1995
– n°49, samedi 4 mars 1995
– n°50, jeudi 23 mars 1995
– n°51, mercredi 5 avril 1995

"Les Fêtes" [Fetes], 1994

In 1994 I spent four months of summer traveling around Alpes-Maritimes following the seasonal celebrations organized in the towns and villages of this French region. These were a mixture of traditional events and tourist attractions.

31 photographs; Ilfochrome prints mounted on aluminum, frame and glass, 30 × 25 cm each
Edition of 3 + 2 A

– Fête de la musique, 21 juin 1994
– Rassemblement US (Voiture), 25 juin 1994
– Rassemblement US (Harley Davidson), 25 juin 1994
– Défilé de voitures anciennes, 26 juin 1994
– Fête tahitienne, 26 juin 1994
– Gala de danse, 1er juillet 1994
– Les nuits du Brusc, 7 juillet 1994
– Courses de karts, 10 juillet 1994
– 2e festival de l'élevage, 10 juillet 1994
– Fête du cheval, 10 juillet 1994
– Bal de Bacchus, 29 juillet 1994
– 4e concours d'élégance de voitures, 30 juillet 1994
– Danses provençales, 30 juillet 1994
– Courses de carrioles, 1er août 1994
– Fête du Château, 1er août 1994
– Courses de VTT, 6 août 1994
– Spectacle de ski nautique, 6 août 1994
● – Fête vénitienne, 6 août 1994
– Fête des moissons (Char), 6 août 1994
– Fête des moissons (Fontaine), 6 août 1994
– Fête du blé et de la lavande, 7 août 1994
– Miss Hippodrome, 10 août 1994
– Election de Miss Hippodrome, 10 août 1994
148–1 ● – Feu d'artifice pyromélodique (Rouge), 16 août 1994
148–5 ● – Feu d'artifice pyromélodique (Blanc), 16 août 1994
– Election Miss Côte-d'Azur, 19 août 1994
– Concours de bûcherons, 4 septembre 1994
– Fête du palmier, 10 septembre 1994
– Fête du sport, 11 septembre 1994
– Meeting aérien (Présentation), 17 septembre 1994
– Meeting aérien (Alpha Jet), 17 septembre 1994

"Les Manifestations" [Demonstrations], 1995 ★

France was paralyzed by a wave of strikes and demonstrations in November and December 1995, the likes of which had not been seen since 1968. The movement began on November 24 in response to proposals for a far-reaching reform of the French social security system and civil service pensions, known as the Plan Juppé, taking its name from the then Prime Minister, Alain Juppé. The movement swiftly spread to students and was widely supported by private-sector workers.

Six major countrywide demonstrations were held, with millions of workers and students marching through cities across France to demand the withdrawal of the Plan Juppé. December 12 saw the largest demonstration, with 2.3 million protestors in over 250 towns and cities. The slogan "All united" became the rallying cry for the movement, which enjoyed widespread popular support.

I photographed the demonstrations in Paris. A slideshow of 691 photographs presents the marchers. Each slide is only shown once over the course of the exhibition. The extremely long transition time between slides—around 32 minutes—means that each slide is subjected to a powerful heat, gradually distorting its colors and contrast.

Since the slideshow was first shown in 2000, the descriptive power of the images has diminished, just as the memories of the event commemorated by the images have faded. The same entropic movement is in play. However, our interest in the images can then shift to demonstrations as the last remaining possible means of insurrection.

Slideshow, 691 slides
Edition of 3 + 1 AP
The projection time of each image is adjusted to the duration of the exhibition so that the image is only projected once.

"Encuentro," 1996

From July 27 to August 3, 1996, the mountain region in southeastern Mexico was home to the "Intergalactical Meeting Against Neoliberalism and for Humanity." Summoned by the Zapatista Indians through the voice of Subcomandante Marcos, some four to five thousand people from all over the world headed toward the Chiapas Mountains. Forums were held in the five specially-built villages (Oventic, La Garrucha, Morelia, Francisco Gomez, La Realidad), followed by a full closing assembly in La Realidad, the Zapatista army base camp. A year later, a second, less headline-grabbing event took place in Spain. Many commentators now agree that these rallies are where the modern Global Justice movement, including the World Social Forum, began.

15 photographs; Ilfochrome prints mounted on aluminum, frame and glass,
125 × 156 cm or 40 × 51 cm each
Edition of 3 + 2 AP

– Indiens, Chiapas
– Commandants zapatistes I, Chiapas
– Commandants zapatistes II, Chiapas
– Le sous-commandant Marcos et sa garde, Chiapas
– Arrivée des participants à la Rencontre, Chiapas
– Policiers zapatistes à La Realidad, Chiapas
– Village indien I, Chiapas
– Village indien II, Chiapas
– Surveillance de l'Aguascalientes, Oventic, Chiapas
149–2 ▲ – Départ des participants, Oventic, Chiapas
– L'Aguascalientes Francisco Gomez I, Chiapas
– L'Aguascalientes Francisco Gomez II, Chiapas
151–3 ● – Assemblée plénière à La Realidad, Chiapas
– Les tribunes de l'Aguascalientes d'Oventic, Chiapas
– Arrivée de Super Barrio, Chiapas

"Destination Vegas," 1996

On November 24, 1996, veteran French rocker Johnny Hallyday gave a unique performance at the Aladdin Hotel and Casino in Las Vegas. What made it unusual was that the audience was comprised of French fans who had traveled all the way to the US to hear their idol. Five thousand of them took the specially chartered planes for a three-day lightning trip to the capital of Nevada.

5 photographs; Ilfochrome prints mounted on aluminum, frame and glass,
127 × 102.5 cm or 40 × 51 cm each
Edition of 3 + 2 AP

▲ – Inconnu, Las Vegas
– Richard, Las Vegas
– Pierre, Las Vegas
150–6 – Dominique, Las Vegas
– Albert, Las Vegas

"Corse-Matin," 1997

From May 15 to June 15, 1997, I worked as a photojournalist for the daily newspaper Corse-Matin. Twenty of my photographs were published.

20 photographs; 6 chromogenic prints and 14 gelatin silver prints, variable dimensions
Edition of 1 + 1 AP

– Pièce de théâtre A Pesta, photographie publiée dans Corse-Matin le 22 mai 1997 (45.5 × 61.7 cm)
– Concert Pierre Brozman, photographie publiée dans Corse-Matin le 22 mai 1997 (45.5 × 62.5 cm)
– Remise de Prix à RCFM, photographie publiée Rdans Corse-Matin le 22 mai 1997 (45.5 × 59 cm)
– Présentation d'une vidéo retraçant l'opération "Parler, lire, écrire" I, photographie publiée dans Corse-Matin le 22 mai 1997 (45.5 × 60 cm)
– Présentation d'une vidéo retraçant l'opération "Parler, lire, écrire" II, photographie publiée dans Corse-Matin le 22 mai 1997 (45.5 × 48.7 cm)
– Le nouveau coupé 406 Peugeot, photographie publiée dans Corse-Matin le 23 mai 1997 (45.5 × 60.7 cm)
– Meeting de l'UPC lors des élections législatives, photographie publiée dans Corse-Matin le 23 mai 1997 (45.5 × 61.8 cm)
– Meeting du PC lors des élections législatives, photographie publiée dans Corse-Matin le 23 mai 1997 (45.5 × 61.8 cm)
– Concert donné par l'orchestre de l'école de musique de la ville d'Erding I, photographie publiée dans Corse-Matin le 24 mai 1997 (45.5 × 62.8 cm)
– Concert donné par l'orchestre de l'école de musique de la ville d'Erding II, photographie publiée dans Corse-Matin le 24 mai 1997 (45.5 × 56.2 cm)
– La directrice de la Maison des Arts de Furiani, photographie publiée dans Corse-Matin le 30 mai 1997 (45.5 × 64.5 cm)
– Les membres du conseil d'administration de la Maison des Arts, photographie publiée dans Corse-Matin le 30 mai 1997 (45.5 × 60 cm)
– Les lauréats du concours de "La plus belle lettre", photographie publiée dans Corse-Matin le 2 juin 1997 (45.5 × 60 cm)
– Les bénévoles des œuvres hospitalières de l'Ordre de Malte triant des médicaments, photographie publiée dans Corse-Matin le 4 juin 1997 (45.5 × 57.6 cm)
– Des bénévoles des œuvres hospitalières de l'Ordre de Malte, photographie publiée dans Corse-Matin le 4 juin 1997 (45.5 × 48.8 cm)
– Séance de dédicaces du Père Gaston Pietri, photographie publiée dans Corse-Matin le 5 juin 1997 (45.5 × 61.4 cm)
– Séance de dédicaces du groupe A Filetta, photographie publiée dans Corse-Matin le 6 juin 1997 (45.5 × 64.5 cm)
– Des éducateurs du centre d'accueil Villa Fleur de Mai, photographie publiée dans Corse-Matin le 7 juin 1997 (45.5 × 60.6 cm)

- Gilles Angelini, membre de l'association Coiffeurs sans Frontière, photographie publiée dans Corse-Matin le 11 juin 1997 (45.5 × 48.2 cm)
- Guy-Paul Chauder lors du vernissage de son exposition, photographie publiée dans Corse-Matin le 11 juin 1997 (45.5 × 46.2 cm)

"Handover," 1997

On July 1, 1997, Hong Kong was retroceded to China. To accompany this occasion, and in addition to the official celebrations involving the English and Chinese delegations, festive events were held for the population all over the territory, climaxing in the firework displays of June 30 and July 1. The retrocession celebrations lasted six days, from June 28 to July 3.

14 photographs; Ilfochrome prints mounted on aluminum, frame and glass,
125 × 156 cm or 40 × 51 cm each
Edition of 3 + 2 AP

- Concert, Fun Fair, Hong Kong, 29 juin 1997
- Puzzle de la Chine, Fun Fair, Hong Kong, 29 juin 1997
- Fun Fair, Hong Kong, 29 juin 1997
- Asian Extravaganza, Hong Kong, 29 juin 1997
- Sea Scouts, Carnival of Unity, Hong Kong, 30 juin 1997
- Derniers souvenirs, Carnival of Unity, Hong Kong, 30 juin 1997
- Carnival of Unity, Hong Kong, 30 juin 1997
- Fun Fair, Hong Kong, 30 juin 1997
- Fireworks Display (Blanc), Hong Kong, 30 juin 1997

148–4 – Fireworks Display (Violet), Hong Kong, 30 juin 1997
- Fireworks Display (Rouge), Hong Kong, 30 juin 1997

151–2 – Rassemblement bouddhiste, Celebration of the Unification, Hong Kong, 1er juillet 1997

148–3 ● – Fireworks Display (Rouge et vert), Hong Kong, 1er juillet 1997
- Laser, Hong Kong, 1er juillet 1997

"Homenaje," 1997

The 30th anniversary of the death of Ernesto Guevara was marked by his official burial in Cuba. From October 12 to 17, his remains, along with those of six other guerrilleros who died with him in Bolivia, were presented to the Cuban people for a final homage. The coffins were placed in the José Martí mausoleum, in Havana. The Cubans were able to watch over them for two days and two nights before the funeral procession made its way along the road to Santa Clara, the first town to be freed by Castro and his troops, for a final popular homage and a military ceremony. That is where they lie today.

6 photographs; Ilfochrome prints mounted on aluminum, frame and glass,
125 × 156 cm or 40 × 51 cm each
Edition of 3 + 2 AP

- Portrait d'Ernesto Guevara, La Havane, 13 octobre 1997

149–4 ● – Hommage du peuple aux sept guérilleros, La Havane, 13 octobre 1997
- Le départ du convoi mortuaire, La Havane, 14 octobre 1997
- Arrivée du convoi mortuaire, Santa Clara, 14 octobre 1997

149–6 – Hommage du peuple aux sept guérilleros, Santa Clara, 15 octobre 1997
- Portrait d'Ernesto Guevara, Santa Clara, 16 octobre 1997

"Free Tibet," 1998

The Tibetan Freedom Concert was held on Saturday and Sunday June 14, 1998, in the Robert F. Kennedy Stadium, Washington, with 120 000 spectators and 50 of the most famous bands in the USA. This was the third concert organized by Adam Yauch (member of the Beastie Boys) and the Milarepa Fund in support of the people of Tibet, and the most important protest concert since Live Aid in 1985. Monday June 15, 1998, was decreed a National Day of Action and there was a demonstration with members of the Senate and Congress, showbiz personalities, and representatives of the Tibetan government in exile occupying the lawn outside the Capitol.

7 photographs; Ilfochrome prints mounted on aluminum, frame and glass,
125 × 156 cm or 40 × 51 cm each
Edition of 3 + 2 AP

152–2 ▲ – KRS ONE on Stage, Washington DC
- Tibetan Monk, Washington DC
- On Capitol Lawn I, Washington DC
- On Capitol Lawn II, Washington DC
- Free Tibet, Washington DC
- Missing in Action, Washington DC
- Entrance of RFK Stadium, Washington DC

"Parc de Sceaux," 1998

Unique group of 10 photographs, chromogenic prints mounted on aluminum, 48.5 × 39.5 cm
Commissioned by the Fonds national d'art contemporain, through the CAUE 92 (Conseil d'architecture, d'urbanisme et de l'environnement des Hauts-de-Seine)

- Plus de 19
- Je t'aime
- Joggers
- Buts
- Jeunes mariés
- Cerfs-volants
- Roulades
- Modèles réduits
- Etirements
- Karaté Kid

"Soft Dreams (Arco 99)," 1999

8 photographs; Ilfochrome prints mounted beneath a passe-partout, frame and glass, 32 × 37 cm each (without frame: 18 × 23 cm)
Edition of 3 + 2 AP

- Soft Dream A to H, Arco 99, Madrid

"Jornal do Brasil," 1999

As for the series Corse-Matin (1997), I worked as a photojournalist for the Brazilian national daily Jornal do Brasil. Nine photographs were published between November 9 and 24.

Group I of 19 photographs; unframed digital C-print, dimensions variable
Edition of 3 + 2 AP

- Aliments toxiques, photographie pour le Jornal do Brasil, 24 novembre 1999 (52 × 104 cm)
- Hugo Cabo Filho, entraîneur de l'équipe de natation de Vasco, photographie pour le Jornal do Brasil, 18 novembre 1999 (52 × 40 cm)
- Plateforme de travaux sous-marins, photographie pour le Jornal do Brasil, 12 novembre 1999 (52 × 116 cm)
- Assassinat d'une touriste française, photographie pour le Jornal do Brasil, 8 novembre 1999 (52 × 40 cm)
- Bus incendiés dans la favela de Cajuiero, photographie pour le Jornal do Brasil, 22 novembre 1999 (52 × 116 cm)
- La réalisatrice Katia Lund et les acteurs dans la favela Morro do Vidical, photographie pour le Jornal do Brasil, 25 novembre 1999 (52 × 84 cm)
- Le ministre de la culture Francisco Weffort assiste à un concert à Candelaria, photographie pour le Jornal do Brasil, 8 novembre 1999 (52 × 40 cm)
- Coupure de gaz dans le quartier de Leblon, photographie pour le Jornal do Brasil, 23 novembre 1999 (96 × 104 cm)
- José Carlos Martin, président du Syndicat des taxis de la ville de Rio, photographie pour le Jornal do Brasil, 10 novembre 1999 (52 × 40 cm)
- Entraînement de l'équipe de football de Flamengo, photographie pour le Jornal do Brasil, 15 novembre 1999 (52 × 116 cm)
- Entraînement de l'équipe de football de Fluminense, photographie pour le Jornal do Brasil, 5 novembre 1999 (52 × 72 cm)
- Footballeurs français de l'équipe "Foot du Monde", photographie pour le Jornal do Brasil, 17 novembre 1999 (52 × 116 cm)
- Patrick Garnier et Roberto Dickman, commissaires d'une exposition sur les voitures, photographie pour le Jornal do Brasil, 24 novembre 1999 (52 × 116 cm)
- Inflation galopante, photographie pour le Jornal do Brasil, 19 novembre 1999 (52 × 84 cm)
- Vidéo-surveillance du pont entre Rio et Niteroi, photographie pour le Jornal do Brasil, 11 novembre 1999 (96 × 104 cm)
- Derniers opposants à un projet d'aménagement urbain, photographie pour le Jornal do Brasil, 22 novembre 1999 (52 × 72 cm)
- Préparation de la fête du Nouvel An au sommet du Pain de Sucre, photographie pour le Jornal do Brasil, 18 novembre 1999 (96 × 104 cm)
- Programme éducatif pour les femmes, photographie pour le Jornal do Brasil, 18 novembre 1999 (52 × 40 cm)
- La chambre du conseil municipal de la ville de Rio, photographie pour le Jornal do Brasil, 10 novembre 1999 (52 × 72 cm)

Group II of 19 photographs; 2 chromogenic prints and 7 sliver gelatin prints, dimensions variable
Edition of 1 + 1 AP

- Bus incendié dans la favela de Cujuiero, photographie publiée dans le Jornal do Brasil le 23 novembre 1999 (32 × 30.5 cm)
- Hugo Cabo Filho, entraîneur de l'équipe de natation de Vasco, photographie publiée dans le Jornal do Brasil le 19 novembre 1999 (32 × 38.5 cm)
- Le ministre de la culture Francisco Weffort assiste à un concert à Candelaria, photographie publiée dans le Jornal do Brasil le 9 novembre 1999 (32 × 39 cm)
- Inflation galopante, photographie publiée dans le Jornal do Brasil le 21 novembre 1999 (32 × 38.5 cm)
- Agriculture biologique, photographie publiée dans le Jornal do Brasil le 25 novembre 1999 (32 × 41 cm)
- La réalisatrice Katia Lund et les acteurs dans la favela Morro do Vidical, photographie publiée dans le Jornal do Brasil le 26 novembre 1999 (32 × 59.5 cm)
- La favela Morro do Vidical, photographie publiée dans le Jornal do Brasil le 26 novembre 1999 (32 × 81.5 cm)
- Coupure de gaz dans le quartier de Leblon, photographie publiée dans le Jornal do Brasil le 24 novembre 1999 (32 × 44.5 cm)
- Préparation de la fête du Nouvel An au sommet du Pain de Sucre, photographie publiée dans le Jornal do Brasil le 21 novembre 1999 (32 × 62.5 cm)

"Sunday Afternoon," 1999

In the busy parks and thoroughfares of Rio you see street photographers who offer to take photographs of passers-by. Some of them have Polaroids but most still work with cameras and tripods. On Sunday November 28, I took up position in Quinta da Boa Vista park and, with the help of my friend Helmut Batista, I offered my services as a photographer. Since I was using a Polaroid back, the sitters were able to take their portraits away with them. I used the negatives to reconstitute the series.

57 photographs numbered from 1 to 57; silver gelatin prints, frame and glass, 32 × 25 cm each
Edition of 3 + 2AP

"Overseas Containers," 2000

5 photographs numbered from 1 to 5; chromogenic prints mounted on aluminum, frame and glass,
83 × 103 cm
Commisioned by the Fonds national d'art contemporain, via Arc en Rêve, Bordeaux
Edition of 3

"Soft Dreams (Biennale de Lyon 2000)," 2000

Commissioned by the Ecole des Beaux-Arts de Lyon for their website
http://www.enba-lyon.fr/webscene/webscene.php

"Expo 2000," 2000

In 2000, the German city of Hannover hosted the universal exhibition Expo 2000 on the theme "Man—Nature—Technology." The 190 countries and institutions who took part set out to encourage visitors to think about how lasting economic development could be reconciled with global biodiversity. Expo 2000 thus took a different approach to previous universal exhibitions, which, ever since the first was held in London in 1851, have been designed to glorify industrial progress.

A thematic area measuring one hundred thousand square meters was created alongside the esplanade of 47 country pavilions. Eleven themes were selected, covering major issues for the 21st century: nutrition, health, mobility, work, and so on. Whether it was the choice of theme or the host city that was to blame, the exhibition was a flop. Only 18 million of a projected 40 million visitors turned up at Expo 2000 between June 1 and October 31, 2000. The Frankfurter Allgemeine Zeitung wrote that the overall impression was of "a holiday destination in the off-season."

15 photographs; Ilfochrome prints mounted on aluminum, frame and glass, 125 × 156 cm or 51 × 40 cm each
Edition of 3 + 2AP

152–1 – Escalier Central, Hanovre
152–7 – Pavillon du XXIe siècle, Hanovre
– Asia Hall, Hanovre
– African Pavillon, Hanovre
– Belvédère, Hanovre
– Place Centrale, Hanovre
– Pavillon du Boutan, Hanovre
– Pavillon des Émirats Arabes Unis, Hanovre
– Pavillon de la Lituanie, Hanovre
– Pavillon de la Norvège, Hanovre
– Open air Cinema, Hanovre
– Painting Car, Hanovre
– Panama House, Hanovre
– Hall de l'Asie Centrale, Hanovre
– Concert, Hanovre

"14 juillet 2000" [Fireworks], 2000

Fireworks recur in a number of my series. Usually they mark the climax of a celebration or commemorative event, unless, that is, they are themselves the event. In any case, they always represent a privileged, ritual moment (July 14 in France) that brings together an ephemeral community.

10 photographs; matte Ilfochormes prints mounted on aluminum, frame and glass, 158 × 125 cm and 51 × 40 cm each
Edition of 3 + 2AP

– Feux d'artifice, Sérandon, 14 juillet 2000 1 to 10
● n° 10

"Korea," 2001

Park Jun Kyu and Hwang Yi Min are union men. Yu Man Hyeong was an assembly line worker at a Daewoo Motors plant. They came to France in February 2001 in order to extradite Kim Woo-choong, the former boss of Daewoo, who had been on the run since the Group went bankrupt. When I went to Seoul in November 2001 to do a new piece of work, I met up with the three of them and they agreed to pose for a photograph. Their portrait forms the central element in this new series.

Series composed of 3 groups

Group I
– 1er décembre 1982–5 décembre 2001 (Paris/Séoul), 2002

33 photographs and texts on paper, inkjet prints on archive paper, 61 × 730 cm
Edition of 3 + 2AP

Group II
150–1 ▲ – Park Jun Kyu, Hwang Yi Min, Yu Man Hyeong (dans une salle de réunion au siège du KCTU), Séoul, 2001
– Hwang Yi Min, Yu Man Hyeong, Park Jun Kyu (devant le bâtiment des syndicats), Séoul, 2001
– Park Kwang-su (dans une salle de montage à l'université), Séoul, 2001
150–4 ▲ – Kim Sung-ok (dans son bureau à l'université), Séoul, 2001

4 photographs; Ilfochrome prints mounted on aluminum, glass and frame, 125 × 156 cm
Edition of 3 + 2AP

Group III
– n°25, Seoul
– n°27, Seoul
– n°28 (Daewoo Tower), Seoul
– n°29, Seoul
– n°32, Seoul
– n°34, Seoul
– n°35, Seoul
– n°40, Seoul
– n°43, Seoul
– n°45, Seoul
– n°46, Seoul

11 photographs; silver gelatin prints mounted on aluminum, frame and glass, 125 × 156 cm each
Edition of 3 + 2AP

"Manifestations du collectif des sans-papiers de la Maison des Ensembles, place du Châtelet, Paris" [Demonstrations by the Maisons des Ensembles sans-papiers collective, place du Châtelet, Paris], 2001–2003 ●

45 photographs; Ilfochrome prints mounted on aluminum, frame and glass, 29.5 × 37.5 cm each
Edition of 3 + 2AP

5 – Manifestation du collectif des sans-papiers de la Maison des Ensembles, place du Châtelet, Paris, samedi 8 septembre 2001
– Manifestation du collectif des sans-papiers de la Maison des Ensembles, place du Châtelet, Paris, jeudi 20 septembre 2001
– Manifestation du collectif des sans-papiers de la Maison des Ensembles, place du Châtelet, Paris, samedi 22 septembre 2001
– Manifestation du collectif des sans-papiers de la Maison des Ensembles, place du Châtelet, Paris, jeudi 27 septembre 2001
6 – Manifestation du collectif des sans-papiers de la Maison des Ensembles, place du Châtelet, Paris, samedi 29 septembre 2001
– Manifestation du collectif des sans-papiers de la Maison des Ensembles, place du Châtelet, Paris, jeudi 4 octobre 2001
– Manifestation du collectif des sans-papiers de la Maison des Ensembles, place du Châtelet, Paris, samedi 6 octobre 2001
– Manifestation du collectif des sans-papiers de la Maison des Ensembles, place du Châtelet, Paris, jeudi 11 octobre 2001
– Manifestation du collectif des sans-papiers de la Maison des Ensembles, place du Châtelet, Paris, samedi 13 octobre 2001
– Manifestation du collectif des sans-papiers de la Maison des Ensembles, place du Châtelet, Paris, jeudi 18 octobre 2001
– Manifestation du collectif des sans-papiers de la Maison des Ensembles, place du Châtelet, Paris, samedi 20 octobre 2001
– Manifestation du collectif des sans-papiers de la Maison des Ensembles, place du Châtelet, Paris, jeudi 25 octobre 2001
– Manifestation du collectif des sans-papiers de la Maison des Ensembles, place du Châtelet, Paris, samedi 27 octobre 2001
– Manifestation du collectif des sans-papiers de la Maison des Ensembles, place du Châtelet, Paris, samedi 3 novembre 2001
– Manifestation du collectif des sans-papiers de la Maison des Ensembles, place du Châtelet, Paris, jeudi 13 décembre 2001
– Manifestation du collectif des sans-papiers de la Maison des Ensembles, place du Châtelet, Paris, jeudi 20 décembre 2001
– Manifestation du collectif des sans-papiers de la Maison des Ensembles, place du Châtelet, Paris, samedi 12 janvier 2002
– Manifestation du collectif des sans-papiers de la Maison des Ensembles, place du Châtelet, Paris, samedi 19 janvier 2002
– Manifestation du collectif des sans-papiers de la Maison des Ensembles, place du Châtelet, Paris, samedi 26 janvier 2002
– Manifestation du collectif des sans-papiers de la Maison des Ensembles, place du Châtelet, Paris, samedi 02 Février 2002
– Manifestation du collectif des sans-papiers de la Maison des Ensembles, place du Châtelet, Paris, samedi 16 Février 2002
– Manifestation du collectif des sans-papiers de la Maison des Ensembles, place du Châtelet, Paris, samedi 9 mars 2002
– Manifestation du collectif des sans-papiers de la Maison des Ensembles, place du Châtelet, Paris, samedi 23 Mars 2002
– Manifestation du collectif des sans-papiers de la Maison des Ensembles, place du Châtelet, Paris, samedi 30 Mars 2002
– Manifestation du collectif des sans-papiers de la Maison des Ensembles, place du Châtelet, Paris, samedi 6 Avril 2002
– Manifestation du collectif des sans-papiers de la Maison des Ensembles, place du Châtelet, Paris, samedi 4 Mai 2002
– Manifestation du collectif des sans-papiers de la Maison des Ensembles, place du Châtelet, Paris, samedi 11 Mai 2002
– Manifestation du collectif des sans-papiers de la Maison des Ensembles, place du Châtelet, Paris, samedi 01 Juin 2002
– Manifestation du collectif des sans-papiers de la Maison des Ensembles, place du Châtelet, Paris, samedi 15 Juin 2002
– Manifestation du collectif des sans-papiers de la Maison des Ensembles, place du Châtelet, Paris, samedi 22 Juin 2002
– Manifestation du collectif des sans-papiers de la Maison des Ensembles, place du Châtelet, Paris, samedi 29 Juin 2002
– Manifestation du collectif des sans-papiers de la Maison des Ensembles, place du Châtelet, Paris, samedi 13 Juillet 2002
– Manifestation du collectif des sans-papiers de la Maison des Ensembles, place du Châtelet, Paris, samedi 20 Juillet 2002
– Manifestation du collectif des sans-papiers de la Maison des Ensembles, place du Châtelet, Paris, samedi 27 Juillet 2002
– Manifestation du collectif des sans-papiers de la Maison des Ensembles, place du Châtelet, Paris, samedi 14 septembre 2002
– Manifestation du collectif des sans-papiers de la Maison des Ensembles, place du Châtelet, Paris, samedi 21 septembre 2002
– Manifestation du collectif des sans-papiers de la Maison des Ensembles, place du Châtelet, Paris, samedi 28 septembre 2002
– Manifestation du collectif des sans-papiers de la Maison des Ensembles, place du Châtelet, Paris, samedi 12 octobre 2002
– Manifestation du collectif des sans-papiers de la Maison des Ensembles, place du Châtelet, Paris, samedi 26 octobre 2002
– Manifestation du collectif des sans-papiers de la Maison des Ensembles, place du Châtelet, Paris, samedi 09 novembre 2002
– Manifestation du collectif des sans-papiers de la Maison des Ensembles, place du Châtelet, Paris, samedi 30 novembre 2002
– Manifestation du collectif des sans-papiers de la Maison des Ensembles, place du Châtelet, Paris, samedi 14 décembre 2002
– Manifestation du collectif des sans-papiers de la Maison des Ensembles, place du Châtelet, Paris, samedi 21 décembre 2002
– Manifestation du collectif des sans-papiers de la Maison des Ensembles, place du Châtelet, Paris, samedi 28 décembre 2002
7 – Manifestation du collectif des sans-papiers de la Maison des Ensembles, place du Châtelet, Paris, samedi 11 janvier 2003

"Earth Summit, Johannesburg," 2002

20 photographs; Ilfochrome prints mounted on aluminum, frame and glass, 125 × 156 cm or 51 × 40 cm each
Edition of 3 + 2AP

– Daily press briefing by the spokesman for the Host Government, with Mr Charles Nqakula, South African Minister of Safety and Security, Media Center, Sandton Convention Center, Johannesburg, 26 août 2002
14 – Federation of World Peace and Love, Sandton,
152–8 Johannesburg, 26 août 2002
– "Trade Unions at Johannesburg: 'Grounding Sustainability in Reality'" with John Evans, General Secretary of the Trade Union Advisory Committee to the OECD; Nilton Freitas, Central Unica do Trabalhadores; Anita Normark, General Secretary of the International Federation of Building and Wood; Vavi Zwelimzima, General Secretary of the Congress of South African Trade Unions; Lucien Royer, Health and Safety of Free Trade Unions, Media Center, Sandton Convention Center, Johannesburg, 27 août 2002
17 – "Indigenous Peoples and the WSSD: 'Have we
147–8 ▲ progressed in the last 10 years?'" with Cecil le Fleur, Indigenous Peoples of South Africa; Vicky Corpuz (Asia); Tom Goldtooth (North America); Pauline Tangiora (Pacific); Sebastiao Haji Manchineri (South America), Concil Chambers, Sandton Library, Johannesburg, 27 août 2002
16 – "WSSD Side Event: 'Energy & Sustainable Development in Africa.'" Speakers: Klaus Töpfer, Executive Director, UNEP; Abdoulie Janneh, Assistant Administrator and Regional Bureau Director for Africa, UNDP; Jayant Sathaye, Lawrence Berkeley National Laboratory; Ogunlade Davidson, Energy & Development Research Center, University of Cape Town; Njeri Wamukonya, UNEP Collaborating Center on Energy & Environment, Denmark; Youba Sokona, ENDA Tiers Monde, Senegal; Abeeku Brew-Hammond, KITE, Ballroom 3, Sandton Convention Center, Johannesburg, 28 août 2002
– ANC conference, Plenary Room, Civil Society Forum, NASREC, Johannesburg, 28 août 2002
13 – Street Hawkers and Farmers from Africa and Asia March to demand the Freedom to Trade, Speaker's Corner, Sandton, Johannesburg, 28 août 2002
146–4 ▲ – Posters, Civil Society Forum, NASREC, Johannesburg, 29 août 2002.
– "Challenging Type II Outcomes: 'How to Build Sound Partnerships for Water Security?'" with Bryan Pritchett, Chair, Board of Directors, National Wildlife Federation; Sasha Müller-Kraenner, Director, Henrich Böll Foundation North America; John Briscoe, Senior Water Advisory, Rural Development Department, World Bank; Karin Krchnak, Program Manager, National Wildlife Federation, Böll Forum, Hall 23, Civil Society

Forum, NASREC, Johannesburg, 29 août 2002
– “Day of Hunger,” People’s Earth Summit, Mears Hall, Saint Stithians College, Johannesburg, 30 août 2002
146–3 ▲ – “A World of Difference,” People’s Earth Summit, Saint Stithians College, Johannesburg, 30 août 2002
11 ▲ – “No Justice No Peace,” International United March
149–10 organized by Landless People’s Movement, Social Movement Indaba, NGOs, from Alexandra Far-East Bank to Sandton Convention Center, Johannesburg, 31 août 2002
149–8 – Landless People Movement, International United March, Alexandra Far-East Bank, Johannesburg, 31 août 2002
151–5 – Rally at Speaker’s Corner, International United
12 March, Sandton, Johannesburg, 31 août 2002
– The World Bank Press Briefing, with Ian Johnson, World Bank Vice President for Sustainable Development; Zephirin Diabré, Associate Administrator of the UNDP; Eduardo Doryan, World Bank UN Representative; James Bond, Director of Sustainable Development for the World Bank’s Africa Region, The Forum Building, Sandton, Johannesburg, 2 septembre 2002
15 – “International Oceans Community Present Type II
152–3 Initiatives” with Klaus Töpfer, Executive Director, United Nations Environment Program; Jean-Michel Cousteau, President, Oceans Future Society; Vice Admiral Conrad C. Lautenbacher Jr, Under Secretary of Commerce for Oceans and Atmosphere; James Mosley, Deputy Secretary, US Department of Agriculture; Dawn Martin, Executive Director, Oceana; Ellen Pikitch, Ph D, Director Marine Programs, Wildlife Conservation Society, Main Stage, Water Dome, Johannesburg, 2 septembre 2002
– “Basic Income Grant Human Chain,” starting from Speaker’s Corner, Sandton, Johannesburg, 3 septembre 2002
16 – Press briefing by Mr. Kofi Annan, United Nations
147–3 Secretary General, Media Center, Sandton Convention Center, Johannesburg, 4 septembre 2002
9 – US NGO’s Protest in front of the Export House, Sandton, Johannesburg, 4 septembre 2002
– “Earth: Either you’re with it, or you’re against it.” NGOs criticize the Johannesburg Summit with Jennifer Morgan, Climate Director, WWF; Martin Khor, Director, Third World Network; Fred Kalibwani, Vice Chair, PELUM (Kenya); Andrew Hewett, Executive Director, Oxfam International (Australia); Jocelyn Dow, President, Women’s Environment and Development Organistion, Michael Strauss, Earth Media, Media Center, Sandton Convention Center, Johannesburg, 4 septembre 2002

Risk Assessment Strategies, 2002

25 photographs reassembled in groups of 5; Ilfochrome prints mounted on aluminum, frame and glass, 25.5 × 38 cm each
Edition of 3 + 2AP

● – Group 1
21 Centurion Risk Assessment Services
Cocktail Molotov
Les armes à feu les plus utilisées (Du pistolet au bazooka)
19 Premiers secours (Blessure par arme blanche)
20 Scénario (Passage d’un check-point)

– Group 2
Premiers secours (Brûlures)
Mine bondissante
Camouflage (Homme)
Sans titre
Voiture piégée

– Group 3
Ballistic Danger Area
Ce qu’il faut toujours avoir dans son sac
La salle de cours de Centurion à Norton Manor
Premiers secours (Debriefing)
Un signe qui indique un piège

– Group 4
Body Armour
Booby Trap
Embuscade
Initiation au déminage
Scénario (Premiers secours dans un champ de mines)

– Group 5
Camouflage (Objets)
Course d’orientation
Danger Mines
Des mines de différents pays
Mise au point d’un scénario

“Cahiers (août-septembre 2003), Nantes” [Notebooks (August–September 2003), Nantes], 2003

Slideshow, 81 slides

“Cahiers (août-décembre 2003), Dervallières” [Notebooks (August–December 2003), Dervallières], 2003

Double slide projection, 160 slides

“Sommet mondial sur la Société de l’information, Genève” [World Summit on the Information Society, Geneva], 2003

15 photographs; Ilfachrome prints mounted on aluminum, frame and glass, 125 × 156 cm or 51 × 40 cm each
Edition of 3 + 2AP

23 – Documentation, Media Center, Palexpo, SMSI,
146–8 ▲ Genève, 10 décembre 2003
– “Media Liberties in the Information Society,” organized by Comedia, the Swiss media union and Amnesty International with Rita Freire, Brasilian journalist, vice-director of CIRANDA – Network ; Ignacio Ramonet, editor-in-chief Le Monde diplomatique; Tahar Abidi, Freelance journalist, member of the liberty Council in Tunisia, refugee in Paris, SMSI, Genève, 10 décembre 2003
– Tahar Abidi, journaliste tunisien indépendant, réfugié politique à Paris, SMSI, Genève, 10 décembre 2003
28 – “Internet Motoman or: ‘A Model for the world closing the Digital Divide: The first time that broadband Internet access for villages has been implemented for under $500,’” stand du Cambodge, ICT4 Development, SMSI, Genève, 11 décembre 2003
24 – “Unlimited Potential (Our Approach to a Ubiquitous Society),” ICT4 Development, SMSI, Genève, 11 décembre 2003
26 – African Media Village, ICT4 Development, SMSI, Genève, 11 décembre 2003
– “Infowar : reports from the Front” with Sasha Costanza – Chock (FTAA IMC), Rene Baralt, Jesus Rodriguez (Venezuelan Community Media), Jaquie Sohen (Big Noise Tactical Media). The conference begins “with an edited 20-minute showing of the documentary ‘The Revolution will not be televised,’ which offers a fascinating inside perspective on President Chavez’s popularity and the way that media can bastardize the truth for political gain,” L’Usine, Genève, 11 décembre 2003
– “Polymedia Lab: an intervention into the reorganisation of power, communication and information.” The polymedia lab is a media and communication laboratory during the WSIS, collectif Geneva03, Palladium, Genève, 11 décembre 2003
27 – “L’information ne se vend pas, elle se partage !”,
146–6 ▲ Polymedia Lab, Palladium, Genève, 11 décembre 2003
– Conférence de presse : “Les peuples autochtones et les Technologies de l’information et de la communication” avec Ole-Henrik Magga, président de l’Instance permanente sur les questions autochtones à l’ONU, Sumiland ; Mililani Trafk, membre permanente pour la région Pacifique, Hawaii, salle de conférence de presse, Media Center, SMSI, Genève, 11 décembre 2003
25 – “Open Source Software : Pros and Cons From a Development Perspective”, avec : Tengku Mohd Azzman Shariffadeen, président et CEO, MIMOS Berhad, Malaisie ; Edgard David Villanueva Nunez, sénateur, Pérou ; Vincent Landon (modérateur), journaliste scientifique, Swissinfo/Swiss Radio International ; Robert Kramer, vice-président, Global Public Policy, Computing Technology Industry Association (CompTIA) ; Bildad Kagai, coordinateur, Free Software and Open Source Foundation for Africa (FOSSFA), Kenya ; Pedro Urra, directeur, Infomed, Cuba, salle de conférence 1, ICT4 Development, SMSI, Genève, 12 décembre 2003
– Manifestation organisée par le collectif Geneva03 contre le Sommet mondial sur la Société de l’information, zone piétonne du Mont-Blanc, Genève, 12 décembre 2003-I
29 – Manifestation organisée par le collectif Geneva03
149–9 ▲ contre le Sommet mondial sur la Société de l’information, zone piétonne du Mont-Blanc, Genève, 12 décembre 2003-II
– Lancement du Fonds de solidarité numérique avec Christian Ferrazino, maire de Genève, le conseiller du Président du Sénégal M. Abdoulaye Wade, Gérard Collomb, maire de Lyon, salle de conférence de presse, Media Center, SMSI, Genève, 12 décembre 2003
– Conférence de presse de clôture du Sommet mondial sur la Société de l’information avec F. Lambert, porte-parole de l’ONU, Y. Utsumi, Secrétaire général du Sommet et Secrétaire général de l’Union internationale des télécommunications, P. Couchepin, président de la Confédération suisse, N. Desai, secrétaire du Secrétaire général de l’ONU, M. Leuenberger, Ministre suisse de la Communication, salle de conférence de presse, Media Center, SMSI, Genève, 12 décembre 2003

“Groupes de travail, Jinan” [Work Groups, Jinan], China, 2004

7 photographs; Ilfochrome prints mounted on aluminum, frame and glass, 40 × 51 cm each
Edition of 3 + 2 AP

– Group (Hillview Residential Quarter, Jinan, 8 août 2004)
– Group (Weidi Sculpture Limited Company, Jinan, 9 août 2004)
– Group (Jinan Beer Group Corporation, Jinan, 11 août 2004)
– Group (Cantonniers et villageois, 12 août 2004)
150–2 ● – Group (Jinan General Embroidery Factory, Jinan, 13 août 2004)
● – Group (CNHTC, Volvo Truck, Jinan, 13 août 2004)
150–3 – Group (Briqueterie, Jinan, 13 août 2004)

“World Social Forum, Mumbai,” 2004

17 photographs; Ilfochrome prints mounted on aluminum, frame and glass, 125 × 156 cm each
Edition of 3 + 2AP

31 – Welcome Delegates, Main Entrance of the 4th World Social Forum, Nesco Grounds, Goregaon, Mumbai, 15 janvier 2004
– Waiting for the Opening Ceremony of the 4th World Social Forum, Goregaon, Mumbai, 16 janvier 2004
– “Another World is Possible,” World Social Forum, Mumbai, 2004
38 – “Violence Against Women,” World Social Forum, Mumbai, 2004
32 – Opening Evening, speeches by : Ahmed Ben Bella (Algeria), Abdul Amir al Rekaby (Iraq), Arundati Roy (India), Chico Whitaker (Brazil), Jeremy Corbyn (UK), Shabana Azmi (India), Shirin Ebadi (Iran), Mustafa Barghouti (Palestine), World Social Forum, Mumbai, 16 janvier 2004
– Opening of Mumbai Resistance 2004 Forum, Veterinary College, Goregaon, Mumbai, 17janvier 2004
– “Rainbow Planet : A Dialogue between Various Movements on Sexuality Issues,” Hall 2, World Social Forum, Mumbai, 2004
33 ▲ – “Land First Mela,” Rural Festival on Land Rights,
151–7 Kandivali, World Social Forum, Mumbai, 2004
37 – World Social Forum, Mumbai, 2004
– “Help, Help, Help,” World Social Forum, Mumbai, 2004
34 – “Judge Not, Support Sexual Preference,” World Social Forum, Mumbai, 2004
– Workshop: “Let’s Create Solidarity of Workers confronting Multinationals,” World Social Forum, Mumbai, 19 janvier 2004
149–1 ▲ – Rally against US imperialism and Iraq Occupation
36 organised by Mumbai Resistance 2004, Kranti Maidan, Mumbai, 20 janvier 2004
– Delegates Of Mumbai Resistance at rally against US Imperialism, Kranti Maidan, Mumbai 2004
35 ▲ – “Condemn World Bank,” World Social Forum, Mumbai, 2004
146–7 ▲ – “Union Flags, Mobilising Solidarity,” Hall 5, World Social Forum, Mumbai, 2004
39 – During the Closing Ceremony of the 4th World Social Forum, Azad Maidan, Mumbai, 21 janvier 2004

Luna Park, Bilbao, 2005

8 photographs; Ilfochrome prints mounted on aluminum, frame and glass, 40 × 51 cm each
Edition of 3 + 2 AP

– Recherche d’une personne ensevelie
– Recherche d’explosifs
41 – Groupe (Brigade cynophile de la police basque)
– Parcours d’entraînement
– Attaque
43 – Contrôle d’identités
– Recherche de drogues
42 – Exercice d’obéissance

"Sommet mondial sur la Société de l'information, Tunis" [World Summit on the Information Society, Tunis], 2005

13 photographs; Ilfochrome prints mounted on aluminum, frame and glass, 125 × 156 cm or 40 × 51 cm each
Edition of 3 + 2AP

152–4 – Un peu avant la cérémonie d'ouverture de la phase 2 du Sommet mondial sur la Société de l'information, salle des Plénières, Kram Palexpo, Tunis, 16 novembre 2005
47 – Conférence de presse de Kofi Annan, Secrétaire Général de l'ONU, Media Center, Kram Palexpo, Tunis, 16 novembre 2005
46 – Discours du Secrétaire général de l'Union internationale des télécommunications, Yoshio Utsumi, lors de la cérémonie d'ouverture de la phase 2 du Sommet mondial sur la Société de l'information, salle des Plénières, Kram Palexpo, Tunis, 16 novembre 2005
147–5 – Professeur Nicholas Negroponte pendant la présentation du nouveau rapport de l'Union Internationale des Télécommunications, "The Internet of Things", salle de conférence de presse, Media Center, Kram Palexpo, Tunis, 17 novembre 2005
150–5 ■ – M. Joe Shirley Jr, président de la nation Navajo, salle de conférence de presse, Media Center, Kram Palexpo, Tunis, 18 novembre 2005
49 – "Connecting People", ICT for All, Business Sector, Kram Palexpo, Tunis
48 – Salle de réunion, Kram Palexpo, Tunis
50 152–5 – "What's Behind the Information Society?", ICT for All, Business Sector, Kram Palexpo, Tunis
– "UNESCO/Egypt", ICT for All, Business Sector, Kram Palexpo, Tunis
51 146–5 ● – Avenue Mohammed V pendant le Sommet mondial sur la Société de l'information, Tunis, 16–18 novembre 2005
– Vers le secteur privé, Kram Palexpo, Tunis
45 – Zone sécurisée pendant le Sommet mondial sur la Société de l'information, Kram Palexpo, Tunis, 16–18 novembre 2005
147–2 – Les peuples autochtones revendiquent leur droit à intégrer la Société de l'Information, salle de conférence de presse, Media Center, Kram Palexpo, Tunis, 18 novembre 2005

Calais, 2006–2008 ★

23 photographs; Ilfochrome prints mounted on aluminum, Plexiglas frame, 125 × 158 cm or 50 × 62.5 cm each
Edition of 5 + 2AP

66 – Abri #1, Calais, juillet 2006
81 ■ – Algeco, quai de la Moselle, Calais, juillet 2006
80 ■ – Chemin à l'aube 1, Calais, juillet 2006
– Chemin à l'aube 2, Calais, juillet 2006
78 ■ – Abri #2, Calais, décembre 2006
79 – Abri #3, Calais, décembre 2006
65 – En attendant la distribution des repas, quai de la Moselle, Calais, décembre 2006
76 – Abri #4, Calais, avril 2007
■ – Abri #5, Calais, avril 2007
77 ■ – Abri #6, Calais, avril 2007
■ – Destige (après destruction), zone industrielle des Dunes, Calais, avril 2007 (50 × 62.5 cm)
73 ■ – Passer en Angleterre, accès terminal transmanche, Calais, juillet 2007
150–7 ■ – Deux hommes, zone des dunes, Calais, juillet 2007
■ – Vestige (bois pour chauffage), zone industrielle des Dunes, Calais, juillet 2007 (50 × 62.5 cm)
75 ■ – Vestige (sac de couchage), Calais, juillet 2007 (50 × 62.5 cm)
– Abri #7, Calais, juillet 2007
72 ■ – Au bord de l'autoroute A16, Calais, juillet 2007
– Terrain vague, Calais, décembre 2008
69 – A proximité de la Mairie, Calais, janvier 2008
70 – Passage, zone industrielle des Dunes, Calais, janvier 2008
71 – Groupe d'hommes I, Calais, décembre 2008
67 – Groupe d'hommes II, Calais, décembre 2008
145–2 ▲ – Feu de camp, Calais, décembre 2008 (50 × 62.5 cm)

Risky Lines, 2006

Digital slideshow, 81 photographs, and credits
Edition of 3 + 2AP

La Otra, 2006

15 photographs; Ilfochrome prints mounted on aluminum, frame and glass, 125 × 156 cm each
Edition of 3 + 2EA

54 – Dimanche 23 avril 2006. État de Mexico. Réunion avec des adhérents de la Otra Campaña, Xalatlaco
57 ■ – Lundi 24 avril 2006. État de Mexico. Meeting du "Delegado Zero" au Colegio de Ciencias y Humanidades de Naucalpan
53 – Mardi 25 avril 2006. État de Mexico. Discours du "Delegado Zero" sur la place principale de San Cristobal, Ecatepec
– Mardi 25 avril 2006. État de Mexico. Rassemblement des adhérents et sympathisants de la Otra Campaña sur la place principale de San Cristobal, Ecatepec
62 146–1 – Mercredi 26 avril 2006. État de Mexico. Rassemblement des adhérents et sympathisants de la Otra Campaña devant la mairie de Netzahualcoyotl
– Vendredi 28 avril 2006. Région Est de la ville de Mexico (Iztapalapa, Iztacalco et Tlahuac). Discours du "Delegado Zero" au Colegio de Ciencias y Humanidades de la région Oriente
63 152–6 – Vendredi 28 avril 2006. Région Est de la ville de Mexico (Iztapalapa, Iztacalco et Tlahuac). Bienvenue au "Delegado Zero". Lienzo Charro Los Reyes FPFVI-UNOPII, Iztapalapa
– Vendredi 28 avril 2006. La garde du "Delegado Zero". Lienzo Charro Los Reyes FPFVI-UNOPII, Iztapalapa
61 151–4 – Samedi 29 avril 2006. Ville de Mexico. Ouverture du premier Rassemblement National Ouvrier, Colonia Huichapan, Delegación Miguel Hidalgo
149–3 ▲ – El Otro Primero de Mayo. Ville de Mexico. Manifestation de l'ambassade des États-Unis jusqu'au Zócalo
58 – El Otro Primeo de Mayo. Ville de Mexico. Discours du "Delegado Zero" sur le Zócalo
– El Otro Primero de Mayo. Ville de Mexico
59 – Mardi 2 mai 2006. Ville de Mexico. Rassemblement et discours du "Delegado Zero" à l'Universidad Nacional Autónoma de México, Forum de la Cité Universitaire
55 – Mercredi 3 mai 2006. Ville de Mexico. Rencontre du "Delegado Zero" avec des commerçants adhérents de la Otra Campaña, marché de la Merced
60 – Mercredi 3 mai 2006. Ville de Mexico. Rassemblement et discours du "Delegado Zero", Plaza de las Tres Culturas, Tlateloco

Rise Up, Resist, Return (New Delhi and Dharamsala), 2008 ★

12 photographs; Ilfochrome prints mounted on aluminum, frame and glass, 125 × 156 cm or 40 × 51 cm each
Edition of 5 + 2AP

149–5 ▲ – Manifestation des Tibétains à Jantar Mantar, New Delhi, à l'occasion du passage de la torche olympique, 16 avril 2008
84 – "Run For Peace", départ du relais de la torche tibétaine, Samta Sthal, New Delhi, 17 avril 2008
149–7 – Le relais de la torche tibétaine de Samta Sthal à Jantar Mantar, New Delhi, 17 avril 2008
– La torche tibétaine arrive à Jantar Mantar, New Delhi, 17 avril 2008
85 – "March to Tibet", Jantar Mantar, New Delhi, 17 avril 2008
86 147–7 – Conférence de presse des organisateurs de la Marche du retour vers le Tibet : au micro, Tsewang Rigzin, président du Tibetan Youth Congress, accompagné de Choeying, président de Students for Free Tibet, Rajgarh, Gandhi Samadi, New Delhi, 18 avril 2008
87 – Les moines participant à la Marche de retour vers le Tibet se rassemblent au Mausolée de Gandhi, Gandhi Samadi, New Delhi, 18 avril 2008
83 – Départ de marcheurs de New Delhi pour la frontière indochinoise, 19 avril 2008
89 – Département d'histoire orale, Library of Tibetan Works and Archives, complexe gouvernemental tibétain en exil, Gangchen Kyishong, 21 avril 2008-I
– Département d'histoire orale, Library of Tibetan Works and Archives, complexe gouvernemental tibétain en exil, Gangchen Kyishong, 21 avril 2008-II
90 151–1 – Prière quotidienne à la mémoire des victimes des manifestants de Lhassa en mars 2008 tuées par l'armée chinoise, face au temple de Tsuglagkang, McLeod Ganj, 23 avril 2008
91 146–2 – "Two Worlds", McLeod Ganj, 23 avril 2008

Tibet in Exile (Dharamsala), 2008 ■

12 photographs; Ilfochrome prints mounted on aluminum, frame and glass, 125 × 156 cm or 40 × 51 cm each
Edition of 5 + 2AP

99 147–1 ● – Ouverture de la 6ᵉ session de la 14ᵉ Assemblée des députés tibétains en exil, Gangchen Kyishong, lundi 8 septembre 2008
98 – Discours d'un député, 8 septembre 2008
97 – Bâtiment du Parlement tibétain en exil, Gangchen Kyishong, 9 septembre 2008
101 – L'exilé, McLeod Ganj, 9 septembre 2008
– Centre d'accueil des réfugiés tibétains (1987), McLeod Ganj, 9 septembre 2008
95 – Archives du Centre de recherche sur le Tibet (Research Center for Tibet Affairs), 10 septembre 2008
96 – Salle de lecture du Centre de recherche sur le Tibet (Research Center for Tibet Affairs), 10 septembre 2008
93 – Salle des archives de la Bibliothèque des œuvres et archives tibétaines (Library of Tibetan Works and Archives), complexe gouvernemental tibétain en exil, Gangchen Kyishong, 11 septembre 2008
94 – Livre sur l'éducation des moines, XVIIᵉ siècle, Salle des archives de la Bibliothèque des œuvres et archives tibétaines (Library of Tibetan Works and Archives), complexe gouvernemental tibétain en exil, Gangchen Kyishong, 11 septembre 2008
100 – "Adding value to your souvenir. Buying as a social service," Tibetan Handicraft Production Society Ltd, McLoed Ganj, 12 septembre 2008
– La pause, Tibetan Handicraft Production Society Ltd, McLeod Ganj, 12 septembre 2008
– Les tisseuses, Tibetan Handicraft Production Society Ltd, McLeod Ganj, 12 septembre 2008

Kosovo, 2009

Series in progress; 13 photographs; Ilfochrome prints mounted on aluminum, frame and glass, 125 × 156 cm or 40 × 51 cm each
Edition of 5 + 2AP

115 148–2 ▲ – Newborn, Pristina, mardi 17 février 2009
116 ▲ – Célébration du premier anniversaire de l'indépendance du Kosovo, Pristina, mardi 17 février 2009
103 ▲ – Ibrahim Rugova (1944–2006), Zahir Q. Pazajiti (1942–1997), avenue Mère Teresa, Pristina, mardi 17 février 2006
147–4 ▲ – Sur l'avenue Mère Teresa, Pristina, mardi 17 février 2009
117 ▲ – "Indépendance 2009". Tournoi international de boxe (Albanie, Bosnie-Herzégovine, Kosovo, Macédoine, Monténégro), Pristina, mardi 17 février 2009
104 – Une rue de Pristina dans le quartier des ministères le jour de la célébration du premier anniversaire de l'indépendance du Kosovo, mardi 17 février 2009
113 ▲ – Fondations, Pristina, septembre 2009
107 146–9 ▲ – "10 ans de stabilité", Pristina, septembre 2009
▲ – "Déesse sur un trône. Symbole de l'identité culturelle du Kosovo", musée du Kosovo, Pristina, septembre 2009
111 ▲ – 1998–1999, musée du Kosovo, Pristina, septembre 2009
110 ▲ – Bibliothèque nationale du Kosovo, Pristina, septembre 2009
112 ▲ – Livre de condoléances et livre de l'Indépendance, Bibliothèque Nationale du Kosovo, Pristina, septembre 2009
105 ▲ – Rue principale de Pec, Kosovo, septembre 2009
109 ▲ – En allant vers Mitrovica, Kosovo, septembre 2009
106 – Boulevard Bill Clinton, Pristina, Kosovo, septembre 2009
108 – "May this Bridge be a link between People", Mitrovica, Kosovo, septembre 2009

La Route de l'aéroport, Pristina, février 2009, 2009 ●

Slideshow, 126 slides, 24 × 36 cm
Edition of 3 + 2AP

New Fabris, Châtellerault, 2009

9 photographs; Ilfochrome prints mounted on aluminum, frame and glass, 125 × 156 cm or 40 × 51 cm each
Edition of 5 + 2AP

121 151–6 ● – Assemblée générale des salariés en grève, New Fabris, Châtellerault, jeudi 23 juillet 2009
119 – Occupation de l'usine New Fabris, Châtellerault, jeudi 23 juillet 2009
125 145–1 ● – Feu de machines, New Fabris, Châtellerault, jeudi 30 juillet 2009
128 146–10 ● – Fax de soutien aux salariés de New Fabris en lutte, Châtellerault, jeudi 30 juillet 2009
126 – Manifestation des salariés de New Fabris,

Châtellerault, jeudi 30 juillet 2009

122 – Stock de pièces détachées, usine New Fabris, Châtellerault, juillet 2009

127 ● – Guy Eyermann, représentant CGT, annonce aux
147–6 salariés les conditions de départ obtenues après un mois de lutte, New Fabris, Châtellerault, vendredi 31 juillet 2009

120 – Machine à vendre (À vendre. Pas vendu), New Fabris, Châtellerault, juillet 2009

123 – “Oui ou non l’usine New Fabris doit-elle être détruite par ses salariés ?”, Châtellerault, vendredi 31 juillet 2009

Biography

Born in 1968 in Châtellerault (France), Bruno Serralongue lives and works in Paris. He is represented by the galleries Air de Paris (Paris), Baronian_Francey (Brussels), and Francesca Pia (Zurich).

www.brunoserralongue.com

Selected Solo Exhibitions

2010
Feux de camp, Jeu de Paume, Paris*
Focs de camp, La Virreina, Barcelona*

2009
Wiels, Brussels*

2008
A World of Difference, Francesca Pia Gallery, Zürich

2007
Calais, Air de Paris, Paris
Risky Lines, Le Bleu du Ciel Gallery, Lyon*
Backdraft, Centre de la Photographie, Geneva*

2006
Caravane, Baronian_Francey Gallery, Bruxelles
Société de l'information, Centre photographique d'Ile-de-France, Pontault-Combault
Circulations, with Philippe Durand, galerie Arena, École nationale supérieure de la photographie, Arles*
La Salle de Bains, Lyon*

2005
Rapports de forces, Le Triangle, Rennes

2004
Groupes de travail, Air de Paris, Paris
Association Entre-Deux, Nantes

2003
Institute of Contemporary Art, Overgarden, Copenhagen

2002
Centre national de la photographie, Paris*

2001
Derniers Souvenirs, Centre de Création Contemporaine, Tours*

2000
Jornal do Brasil, Air de Paris, Paris
Jornal do Brasil, Le Hall, École nationale des Beaux-Arts, Lyon
I Love Dijon, L'Usine, Dijon*

1999
Villa Arson, Nice
l'elac, Lausanne

1998
Concernant quelques événements de ces dernières années, FRAC Corse, Corte*

1997
Tomorrow will be better, Air de Paris, Paris
On ne rencontre guère de gens ordinaires, par ici, Espace Images, Médiathèque, Beauvais

*Catalogue

Selected Group Exhibitions

2010
Project Europa—Imagining the (Im)possible, Harn Museum of Art, Gainesville*
Dans la forêt, FRAC Aquitaine, Bordeaux
Uneven Geographies, Nottingham Contemporary, Nottingham

2009
Libertad, Igualidad, Fraternidad, La Lonja, Saragossa; Sala de exposiciones Alcalà, Madrid; Centro de Arte Contemporaneo Huarte, Huarte-Navarra; La Regenta, Las Palmas de Gran Canaria*
Great Expectations, Casino Luxembourg, Luxembourg
Nothing is Permanent: Albert Baronian, profession galeriste, La Centrale électrique, Brussels*

2008
Dreamland, Domaine départemental de Chamarande, Chamarande
Esto no es una exposición, Centro de Arte Contemporaneo Huarte, Huarte-Navarra
Street & Studio. An Urban History of Photographic Portraiture, Tate Modern, London; Museum Folkwang, Essen*
Servitude et Simulacre en temps réel et flux constant, espace agnès b., Paris

2007
Airs de Paris, Centre Pompidou, Paris*
Nice to meet you, MAMAC-Musée d'art moderne et contemporain, Nice*
Otra de Vaqueros, Laboratorio Arte Alameda, Mexico*

2006
The Last Chapter. Trace Route: Remapping Global Cities, 6e Biennale de Gwangju, Gwangju*
"Super Défense" in La Force de l'art, Grand Palais, Paris*
Stories, histories, Fotomuseum, Winterthur
Notre histoire, Palais de Tokyo-Site de création contemporaine, Paris*
Old News, Cneai, Chatou*

2005
BMW, 9th Baltic Triennial, Concemporary Art Center, Vilnius*
Parallel Life, Frankfurter Kunstverein, Francfort*
Covering the Real, Kunstmuseum, Bâle*
Universal Experience: Art, Life and the Tourist's Eye, Museum of Contemporary Art, Chicago; Hayward Gallery, London*

2004
Primavera Fotografica, MACBA-Museu d'art contemporani, Barcelona
Éblouissement, Jeu de Paume, Paris*
De leur temps, Musée des Beaux-Arts, Tourcoing*
Paysages invisibles, Musée d'Art contemporain de Rochechouart, Rochechouart

2003
Strangers, International Center of Photography, New York*
Représentation du travail/travail de représentation, Centre de la photographie, Geneva
Coollustre, Collection Lambert, Avignon*
Propaganda, Fondation d'entreprise Ricard, Paris*
Prix Altadis, Anne de Villepoix Gallery, Paris & Soledad Lorenzo Gallery, Madrid*

2002
Less Ordinary, ARTSONJE-Contemporary Art Center, Seoul*
Manifesta 4, Frankfurt*
Actualités, Le Rectangle-Centre d'art contemporain, Lyon*

2001
Traversées, ARC-musée d'Art moderne de la Ville de Paris, Paris*
Contre-informations, Centre atlantique de la photographie, Brest

2000
Vivre sa vie, Tramway, Glasgow*
Form follows function, Foto Biennale, Rotterdam*
Cette culture qui vient de la rue, Galerie municipale, Vitry-sur-Seine*

1998
La Photographie en France, Kunstverein, Berlin*
Bruits secrets, CCC, Tours

1996
Starter, La Station, Nice

1995
Banal, trop banal, Mai de la Photographie, Péniche le Diable Bleu, Reims*

Public Collections

Musée national d'Art moderne/Centre Pompidou, Paris
Musée d'Art moderne de la Ville de Paris, Paris
Fonds national d'art contemporain, Puteaux
Cité nationale de l'histoire de l'immigration, Paris
The Kadist Foundation, Paris
FRAC Ile-de-France, Paris
Fonds municipal d'art contemporain, Paris
FRAC Corse, Corte
FRAC Poitou-Charentes, Angoulême
FRAC Basse-Normandie, Caen
FRAC Nord-Pas de Calais, Dunkerque
FRAC Franche-Comté, Dôle
Tate Modern, London
Fotomuseum Winterthur, Winterthur
Fonds cantonal d'art contemporain, Geneva
ARTSONJE, Seoul

Selected Bibliography

Monographs & Artist's Books

- La Otra, texts by Jordi Vidal and Joerg Bader, "La Salle de Bains" series, Les presses du réel/Centre de la Photographie, Dijon/Geneva 2007
- Risky Lines, texts by François Bon and Gilles Verneret, "Le Traitement" series, no. 5, Le Bleu du Ciel, Lyon 2007
- Ode à Sylvain Schiltz, text by François Bon, poster, La Salle de Bains, Lyon 2007
- Rapport de forces, artist's book, Onestar Press, Paris 2004
- Spillovers, artist's book, Cneai/Air de Paris, Chatou/Paris 2004
- Bruno Serralongue, text by Nicolas Bourriaud, Actes Sud/Altadis, Arles 2003
- Bruno Serralongue, texts by Pascal Beausse, Eric Troncy, and Alexis Vaillant, Janvier/Les presses du réel, Dijon 2002
- Concernant quelques événements de ces dernières années, exh. cat., text by Pascal Beausse, FRAC Corse, Corte 1998

Photographic Inserts

Pacemaker, nos. 1–11, ed. Toastink Press, 2003–2006
Version Magazine, no. 0.5, 2005
Frog, no. 1, Spring/Summer 2005: "Gianni Motti/Christophe Buchel, CCS, Paris, 2004"
Frog, no. 3, Spring/Summer 2006: "Le Voyage intérieur, Espace EDF Electra, Paris, 2006"
Multitudes, no. 23, Winter 2006
Frog, no. 5, Spring/Summer 2007: "Guy de Cointet, CRAC, Sète, 2007"
Pazmaker, no. 0 & 2–3, ed. Perros Negros, Mexico City 2006
Multitudes, special edition, no. 1, Spring 2007: "Risky Lines"
Old News, no. 3, Pork Salad Press, 2007/2008
Amokkoma, vol. 2, no. 2, April 2009
Checkpoint, no. 2, Fall/Winter 2009: "Rise Up, Resist, Return (New Delhi and Dharamsala)"
May, no. 2, October 2009: "Calais"

Exhibition

This book is published on the occasion of the exhibitions:

Bruno Serralongue. Feu de camp, Jeu de Paume, Paris, June 29–September 5, 2010

Bruno Serralongue. Focs de camp, La Virreina Centre de la Imatge, Barcelona, November 2010–January 2011

Bruno Serralongue, Wiels, Brussels, March 21–May 30, 2009

The exhibition Bruno Serralongue. Feu de camp, has been organized by the Jeu de Paume and coproduced with La Virreina Centre de la Imatge.

Exhibition Curators, Jeu de Paume/La Virreina
Bruno Serralongue, Marta Gili, and Carles Guerra

Exhibition Curators, Wiels
Bruno Serralongue, Dirk Snauwaert

Jeu de Paume

Director
Marta Gili

Coordination
Élisabeth Galloy

Registrar
Maddy Cougouluègnes

Technician
Olivier Filippi

Head of Communication, Fundraising, Audience Development
Anne Racine

Head of Publications
Françoise Bonnefoy

The Jeu de Paume is supported by the Ministry of Culture and Communication.
It is also supported by Neuflize Vie, its major patron.

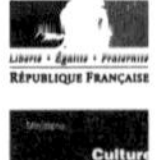

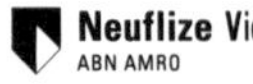

La Virreina Centre de la Imatge

Director
Carles Guerra

Coordination
Eva Carbó Estrada and Montserrat Casanovas Boyano

Wiels

Director
Dirk Snauwaert

Coordination
Charles Gohy

Installation
Fredji Hayebin, Kwinten Lavigne, Olivier Ernould, Romain Poussin

Education and Audience
Frédérique Versaen

Press and Communication
Angie Vandycke

Bruno Serralongue's exhibition at Wiels was supported by Culturesfrance.
Wiels is supported by Vlaamse Gemeenschap, Communauté française de Belgique, Région de Bruxelles-Capitale – Brussels Hoofdstedelijke Gewest Vlaamse Gemeenschapscommissie, Loterie National – Nationale Loterij, Duvel Moortgat, Maroquinerie Delvaux, Puilaetco Dewaay Private Bankers, Leon Eeckman, Levis, Fondation Bernheim Stichting

Publication

Editorial Coordination
Clément Diré

Introductory Texts
Bruno Serralongue

Translation from the Spanish
(essay by Carles Guerra): Jeffrey Swartz
Translation from the French
(conversation, introductory texts): Susan Pickford

Translations from the French
Susan Pickford

Design
Gavillet & Rust, Geneva

Assistance
Vincent Devaud

Typeface
Antique (François Rappo)

Cover Photographs
- Abri #7, Calais, juillet 2007
- New Fabris, juillet 2009

Color Separation and Print
Musumeci S.p.A., Quart (Aosta)

Artist's Acknowledgments
I would like to thank all the lenders, because before lending the works they chose them.
Thank you to Dirk Snauwaert, Marta Gili, and Carles Guerra for their trust.
Thank you to the whole team at Air de Paris: Florence Bonnefous and Édouard Merino, for their presence at my side since 1996, as well as Jérémie Bonnefous, Lorraine Féline, Hélène Retailleau, and Vincent Romagny, who have been there for a long time.
Thank you to Albert & Françoise Baronian, Edmond Francey, and Francesca Pia.
Thank you to Choi N'Guyen, Stéphane Fusil, and Franck Bordas for the prints.
Finally, thank you to everyone who has contributed to these three exhibitions and this publication.

Printed in Europe

Published by
JRP|Ringier
Letzigraben 134
CH-8047 Zurich
T +41 (0) 43 311 27 50
F +41 (0) 43 311 27 51
www.jrp-ringier.com
info@jrp-ringier.com

ISBN 978-3-03764-141-5

(French edition available from Les Presses du réel:
ISBN 978-2-84066-407-9)

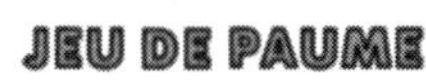

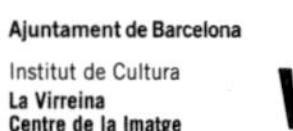

WIELS